Managing the World Economy

John Mills

First published in hardcover 2000

First published in paperback 2003 by
PALGRAVE MACMILLAN
Houndmills, Basingstoke, Hampshire RG21 6XS and
175 Fifth Avenue, New York, N. Y. 10010
Companies and representatives throughout the world

PALGRAVE MACMILLAN is the global academic imprint of the Palgrave Macmillan division of St. Martin's Press, LLC and of Palgrave Macmillan Ltd. Macmillan® is a registered trademark in the United States, United Kingdom and other countries. Palgrave is a registered trademark in the European Union and other countries.

ISBN 0–333–77134–6 hardback (outside North America)
ISBN 0–312–23579–8 hardback (in North America)
ISBN 1–4039-1208–4 paperback (worldwide)

This book is printed on paper suitable for recycling and made from fully managed and sustained forest sources.

A catalogue record for this book is available from the British Library.

Library of Congress Catalog Card Number: 00-042239

10	9	8	7	6	5	4	3	2	1
12	11	10	09	08	07	06	05	04	03

Printed and bound in Great Britain by
Antony Rowe Ltd, Chippenham and Eastbourne

Contents

or whether it is the result of policy decisions which could have been different. Part of the reason why these questions remain unanswered is, of course, that in absolute terms Europe, North America and Japan are still doing very well. All have far higher living standards than the world average. This applies particularly to those who are most well off in each country, who, generally speaking, are the people who make the running in establishing opinions. Across the board, there is therefore a fair degree of complacency. This in turn is reflected in a lack of any great general concern that economics, as taught in schools and universities, and used as the intellectual background to formulating policies, cannot convincingly explain what has gone wrong. Most people then assume that nothing can be done which will make any real difference, and that the reason why slow growth and other manifestations of poor economic performance have to be tolerated is that there is no practical alternative to accepting them as an inexorable fact of life. It then becomes easy to draw the conclusion that higher living standards are bound to lead to a fall-off in the growth rate, and that if the consequence is less and less efficient use of the labour force, and more and more expensive tax outlays on the resultant dependency, nothing can be done about it.

The thesis in this book is that this view of the world is wholly unjustified. Far from there being no way of explaining the deficiencies in performance of the West's economies, it argues that there are clear reasons why they have occurred. Furthermore, there are immediate practical steps which could be taken to improve matters. There is no persuasive case for believing that mature economies must necessarily grow more slowly than those which are less developed, although there are identifiable and important reasons why this frequently happens. The root cause for the poor results, at least in relation to their potential, achieved by most of the advanced industrialised economies lies, as much as anywhere else, in the failure of conventional economic theory to explain satisfactorily and sufficiently cogently how economic growth happens, and its relationship to full employment and acceptable levels of inflation. As a result, those in powerful positions lack a sufficiently coherent and persuasive set of prescriptions about how to make the changes needed, some of them not obvious, to make performance improve. The objective of this book is to put forward proposals to remedy some of these major defects.

This is evidently a formidable task, though one which I believe is achievable. While, in the end, I obviously have to take responsibility for the ideas which this book puts forward, I could and would not have embarked on it without being able to draw on the help of many other people. Some are close associates. I have been very fortunate in having a circle of friends and acquaintances who have shared my interest in economic affairs for a long period, many of whom have made distinguished contributions to economics and politics in their own right. Douglas Jay, Peter Shore and Bryan Gould were major political figures in Britain. The economist who most influenced the ideas in this book – and I hope he would have been pleased by it – was Shaun Stewart, who sadly died in 1997. Not only was he exceptionally well informed, he also set me standards of thoroughness in research – and scepticism of received wisdom – with which I have had to struggle to keep up. Other people with whom I have worked closely, and whose ideas are reflected in this book, include Austin Mitchell, Brian Burkitt, Geoffrey Gardiner and Chris Meakin. In addition, there are many people whose books and articles I have read, but whom I do not know personally. Where I have used information taken directly from them, I have included acknowledgements in the endnotes. There is also a bibliography, listing the main publications and articles which I have read in preparation for writing this book. Inevitably it is incomplete, and I need to thank not only the authors cited but all the others not mentioned whose writings have influenced my views on the way history and economic ideas have developed.

However important the books listed may be in shaping my approach, I have relied on them only to a limited extent for factual and statistical information. It is not that I necessarily distrust second-hand figures, although it is surprising how often they are wrong. I believe you are always more likely to get the fullest and most accurate picture from primary sources. Fortunately, an enormous range of publications is available to provide the quantitative as well as qualitative backing that the kinds of arguments found in this book require. The major sources I have used are the wide range of publications available from the International Monetary Fund, the World Trade Organisation, the United Nations Organisation, the European Commission and the Organisation for Economic Co-operation and Development. For information on the American economy, I have relied particularly on various editions of the *Economic Report of the President*, the *Statistical Abstract of the United States*, and the *National Income and Product Accounts of the United States* for earlier years. I also need to acknowledge how much I have drawn on the work of Angus Maddison, not only in his invaluable OECD publication *Monitoring the World Economy 1820–1992*, but also other books by him which are cited in the bibliography. I have, in addition, relied heavily on figures in a publication by Thelma Liesner for *The Economist* called *Economic Statistics 1900–1983*, which provides long and revealing runs of statistics for a number of the world's major economies, going back to the beginning of the twentieth century. Whenever any particular statistics are quoted in the text, their source is detailed in the endnotes.

There are other people too who need to be thanked, especially among my extended family. My wife Barbara has not only tolerated all the time I have spent reading and writing while preparing this book, but has also checked and corrected successive drafts. We share the view that books should read well, whatever their contents. Above all, the meaning should be clear. Sentences should be short. Adverbs should be used sparingly. The text should be succinct and concise. These worthy objectives are easy to list, but more difficult to achieve consistently, and her help, and that of Charles Starkey, have been invaluable. Neither of them are economists. The test applied was that anything either of them could not understand the first time they read it had to be rewritten. I have to say that this is a process which I think might be used with advantage on a fair proportion of other writings on economic issues. You do not, in my opinion, need to be a trained economist to follow the basic arguments with which economics is concerned.

For this book, as with previous ones, my sister Eleanor and her husband Stephen have allowed me and my wife to use their house near Avignon in France as a retreat from distractions, to allow drafting to be done. My mother has provided another exceptionally pleasant environment for redrafting and revisions at her house near London. My office, and especially my secretary Jan and her colleague Janet, have been very tolerant of my use of all the facilities there, and have been exceptionally helpful.

I am also very grateful to Macmillan, and especially to Tim Farmiloe, their recently retired Publishing Director, for allowing me to write yet another book for them. With their international connections, the quality of their production, and the care which they take over every book they produce, no one could ask for a better publisher, or a more professional organisation with which to work.

This preface needs to end, however, on a note of some anxiety. I am well aware of the scale of the task which this book tackles, and the size of canvas which it covers. I am familiar enough with the literature on economics in Europe and in North America, both in its academic and more popular form, to know that many of the ideas this book sets out are not ones which are common currency. The proposals this book sets out for dealing with some of the more important problems which the West faces are therefore ones which the average reader may not have seen put forward before. I know they go against the grain. I am well aware of the fact that they do not conform with established views. I ask you, therefore, perhaps more than most authors would, to look at them with an open mind. Please do not pre-judge the issues which are tackled. Let the argument unfold, and see whether, at the end, you find it convincing.

The West had a long start on the rest of the world, but its pre-eminence is being eroded. There must be some reason why the USA has peculiarly serious problems with its balance of payments, why many Americans still earn the same amount now in real terms as they did twenty-five years ago, why the USA swung round in much less than a decade, in the 1980s, from being the world's biggest creditor to being its largest debtor, and why almost every toy bought in America nowadays is made in China. Equally, there must be an explanation why some 10% of the European Union labour force is out of work, why the growth rate in the EU has dropped since the early 1970s to only about 40% of what it was previously, and why Britain, with the highest living standards in the world a hundred years ago, has now been overtaken by some twenty other countries. Let this book see whether it can provide you with convincing explanations for these developments, and persuade you that there are solutions to the problems which they present.

1
Introduction

'The decisive problem of economics is not how the price of goods is established. Nor is it how the resulting income is distributed. The important question is how the level of output and employment is determined.'

John Kenneth Galbraith

This book sets out to provide convincing responses to a number of questions to which generally accepted answers do not exist. The key ones are about issues central to economics. What causes economies to grow? Why has the record of success among economies which have industrialised been so patchy? Why, having established themselves with a reasonable growth rate, have so many permitted it to slow down, allowing others to overtake them? Why do so many economies suffer from such high rates of unemployment? Are the numbers out of work in some way inevitable and unavoidable, or is lack of jobs the product of policy choices which could realistically have been different? What is the trade-off between inflation and other major economic policy goals? Is it true that the only way to sustainable and reasonably high rates of economic growth is to establish a régime of subdued price increases and low interest rates?

Perhaps the first observation to be made, in tackling these questions, is to ask why they remain unanswered to the extent which clearly is the case. It is not as though the issues they raise are unimportant. Indeed, much of this book is devoted, among other things, to showing just how comprehensively significant they have been in the past, and will be in

1

the future, to the whole human enterprise. Somehow or other, however, as knowledge and hence control over events has expanded in most other fields of experience, this has not happened to the same degree in economics.

Why has economics, which has certainly not been neglected judging by the vast number of people who study it, and the calibre of many who have been involved in its development, not come up with answers to the central questions with which the subject ought to be concerned? Evidently it has not done so. Even so eminent a practitioner as Professor Paul Krugman of the Massachusetts Institute of Technology has the candour to state in as many words in one of his highly readable books about the state of the American economy that '... apathy among the experts becomes a little more comprehensible if we ask how economists answer two central questions about America's productivity slump: Why did it happen? And what can be done about it? The answer to both is the same: We don't know.'[1] There appear to be complex reasons why this should be the case, and this book will try to answer this question, too.

A brief *tour d'horizon*, illustrates how critically important it is to find the answers to these major economic questions. A central theme in the chapters that follow is that the failure of economics to come up with an adequate description and explanation as to how modern industrialised economies work has cost humanity a massive price, not only in lost output, but in many other ways as well. Once the processes central to the Industrial Revolution had been discovered, should it have been possible for the world economy to grow at a faster rate than it actually has done? If so, the consequence would have been much higher standards of living, but also many other benefits too. Almost certainly, the world population would have been considerably smaller. The pressures on the world's ecology, given reasonably competent management of the resources available, could have been greatly reduced. More speculatively, the amount of conflict and the number of destructive wars, particularly World War II, which stemmed largely from the gross economic mismanagement of the inter-war period, might have been avoided. If economics had advanced as a branch of knowledge as effectively as many others, thus providing the intellectual framework to enable the world's economy to have been much better managed over the last two hundred years, the pay-off would have been huge.

Just how big the difference might have been can be readily demonstrated by some broad estimates. World gross domestic product (GDP) per head rose from about $650 in 1820 to $5,145 in 1992, a rise of 690%

over the period, entailing an average cumulative increase of 1.2% per annum.[2] Had the increase in GDP per head been 1.5% per annum instead of 1.2%, the average standard of living would now be over 60% higher than it actually is, excluding any impact that better economic performance might have had on world population. If the cumulative increase had been 2.0% per annum over the whole period, the impact would have been much greater, producing levels of GDP per head at the end of the twentieth century almost four times as high on average as they are at the moment. Of course there are important qualifications to be applied to calculations of this sort, but even after all of these have been made, they do not detract significantly from the enormous impact which relatively small differences in cumulative change make over a long period of time.

The importance to be attached to providing better economic prescriptions is therefore clear. Can they be found? This book sets out to persuade you that they can be, and this has determined the structure of the material which follows. The rest of Chapter 1 amplifies the territory which needs to be covered, and puts forward some explanations as to why solutions to the outstanding problems in economics may have been slow to be forthcoming, and how wide the ramifications of this deficiency have been. Chapter 2 sets out an explanation for the process of economic growth. It discusses the sources of productivity increases and the circumstances in which they can be generated. It reviews the policy requirements necessary to create an environment in which cumulative economic growth can be achieved, and highlights the reasons why it can also sink down, or go into reverse, or be maintained and enhanced.

The following four chapters turn to history. Economics is not a field of inquiry like many scientific subjects where experiments can be conducted to prove or disprove theories, thus providing a relatively simple method of demonstrating conclusively that one or another proposition is correct. Among the social sciences, where economics is to be found, the tests have to be different. Those applied here are to see whether the ideas about growth in output set out in Chapter 2 can explain systematically and convincingly the way economic history has actually evolved over the last two centuries. The first part of Chapter 3 looks at the world before the Industrial Revolution began, to see why cumulative growth did not occur to any significant degree throughout many centuries despite most of the necessary ingredients appearing to be present at least in some parts of the world. The second half covers the period from the late eighteenth to the early twentieth century when the Industrial Revolution spread from Britain across the European world, including North America, leading to the dominance of European powers for all of this period. Chapter 4 is concerned with the disruption and disorganisation of the world economy during the first half of the twentieth century, during the decades from the start of World War I to the end of World War II. This is an exceptionally revealing period, with highly contrasting policies being pursued in otherwise relatively similar countries especially during the inter-war period. The 1930s are generally regarded as being years of almost unredeemed failure. A closer look, however, shows that this is far from being the case. The 1930s also produced some remarkable successes.

Chapter 5 covers the period from 1945 through to the early 1970s, when a sea change overtook the world economy. The quarter of a century after World War II saw an unprecedented increase in prosperity throughout the western world, accompanied by low inflation and full employment. It also saw the start of significant rises in living standards in other parts of the world, particularly Japan, and the first major economic challenges to the prevailing western lead. All these largely benign trends looked set fair to continue, but the subsequent decades to the end of the twentieth century, which are the subject of Chapter 6, show that such optimism was unwarranted. The period from the 1970s to the 1990s generally exhibited, at least in the West, lower growth rates than had been apparent during the previous twenty-five years. It also manifested much greater problems with inflation, and an increase in both unemployment combined with low productivity and real income growth among large numbers of those who remained in work. Mirroring the change in world economic fortunes came a major shift in intellectual fashion, as monetarist ideas largely supplanted the Keynesian approach which had underpinned the policies pursued with near universal success during the 1950s and 1960s, until their apparent inadequacies were exposed in the early 1970s.

Chapter 7 turns to the labour force, and reviews the extent to which using those available for work to the full is a key component of fast economic growth as well as being a critically important social requirement. It looks at the remarkable degree of both unemployment – mainly in Europe – and underemployment, reflected in low productivity growth – mainly in North America – as symptoms of severe deficiencies in modern economic policy formulation, and proposes remedies to deal with them.

The major appeal of monetarist thinking lay in its claim that there were comparatively simple policy rules to be followed in controlling the money supply, which would contain inflation and thus provide a stable economic environment for other objectives. Chapter 8 reviews whether the causes of inflation are anything like as simple as monetarists say they are, whether price rises are either as damaging or as unavoidable as they claim, and whether, therefore, it makes sense to have the battle against inflation as the centrepiece of economic policy, as, in a significant proportion of modern economies, it has tended to become. It argues, on the contrary, that not just currently, but over the last two centuries, periods of severe inflation have been the exception rather than the rule, and that, given reasonably competent management, inflation at damagingly high levels is not a major threat.

Chapter 9 provides both a summary and a platform for considering the future. It looks again at the costs humanity has borne as a result of the world's economies, especially those which have been industrialised for longest, being run so much less effectively than they might have been. It summarises the changes in policy which need to be made to remedy this state of affairs, and considers their practicality. It considers once more the intellectual climate which apparently has made it so difficult for viable solutions to slow growth and unemployment to become generally accepted. It concludes by looking ahead to the twenty-first century, when it is going to be at least as important as it has been in the twentieth to make sure that economic opportunities are not wasted.

The case for economic growth

The case put forward in this book depends heavily on there being substantial positive net advantages to a higher rate of economic growth, and the fuller use of all the available resources thus entailed. This is not to deny that rapidly increasing output can bring disadvantages in train. It is to argue that, on balance, more problems are solved than created by faster growth, and that, therefore, if there is a price to be paid, it is one worth paying.

This is not, however, an argument which is universally accepted. There is a vocal, if not numerically large, coalition of people who are opposed to higher rates of growth, even if they could be achieved. Some point to the problems of sustaining high and rising levels of industrial output, reflecting the concerns expressed by the Club of Rome in the early 1970s.[3] Others express doubt whether higher living standards make everyone happier, arguing that a less complicated and stressful life would be better than the pressures of consumer-driven societies. Another form of scepticism challenges whether economic growth statistics really measure anything meaningful at all, because of the difficulties of comparing one year with another at a time of rapid technological and cultural change.

There has always been an anti-growth tradition, harking back to Rousseau's simple savage. The Romantic Movement never liked factory regimentation, and the break with established and hallowed practices which the Industrial Revolution entailed. More recently, particularly from the left of the political spectrum, scepticism about the benefits of economic growth have materialised in a steady undertow of criticism of the same ilk. Targets have been the impersonality of modern production relationships, the alienation and loneliness of current lifestyles, the vapidness of much contemporary culture, and the unfairness in the distribution of the wealth and incomes which economic growth is alleged to produce.

No one can deny that there are valid concerns about the impact of industrialisation and increasing output. This is a different matter, however, from there being a compelling case that humanity as a whole would have been better off, or would have preferred, given the choice, not to have had the benefits which the economic changes in the developed countries have produced. There is no evidence at all that most people would prefer a lower rather than a higher standard of living, as conventionally measured. On the contrary, it is overwhelmingly clear that being better off in material terms is a high priority for almost everyone. Elections are won or lost on economic issues. The world abounds with pressure for migration from poor countries to those which are richer. Almost everyone wants to earn a higher wage or salary.

A reasonably high rate of economic growth is therefore clearly what most people would select, given the choice. Nor are the benefits to be secured, of course, private only to individuals. There is a large public dimension as well. Increased output generates the tax base to pay for a wide range of goods and services which are more sensibly and practically provided collectively than individually. It makes it possible to run the kind of social security programmes which are the hallmark of cohesive communities. It provides the wherewithal for the construction and operation of public facilities, from schools to libraries, roads to parks, airports to museums, which are necessary and widely appreciated components of modern societies.

Contrary to the apparent position at first sight, economic growth also provides the only realistic way to pay the costs of avoiding the degradation of the environment that a rising population and increased output would otherwise entail. The most pressing ecological issues across the world are supplies of clean drinking water, the provision of adequate sewage facilities, and the removal and processing of rubbish and waste. Protecting water supplies and the water table, in both the Third World and the developed countries, is expensive. So are all the steps which need to be taken to stop waste building up and the environment being polluted.

In fact, as living standards rise and economies become more advanced, there is a tendency for the raw material content of finished output to fall. This happens as products become more sophisticated and services become a larger component of final output. The result is that, with reasonably competent management, the average economy's capacity to cope with environmental problems can be made to rise faster than its inclination to cause ecological damage. Rising living standards also tend to entail lower population growth, again improving the trade-off between expansion and ecological pressures. There is therefore no convincing case against growth on environmental grounds.

On the other hand, leaving aside the clear preference which almost everyone has for higher living standards, both in terms of private consumption and public provision, there are other reasons for believing that a reasonably high rate of economic growth is overwhelmingly important as a political and social objective. These overlapping considerations concern unemployment, social strains, fiscal imbalance and every country's ability to relate to the rest of the world.

The unemployment issue is simple and straightforward. There is a marked tendency for the average level of productivity of everyone in employment to rise. This stems from a variety of causes, all of which are likely to continue. They include increased use of computers, better management techniques, competitive pressures on manning levels, better and more focused training and education, and technological advances. The impact of these changes is to increase output per person employed in large swathes of the more sophisticated parts of the economy by around 2% per annum on average, even if investment levels are quite low, and total output is growing slowly or not at all. The result, however, is a mixed blessing. It means that a rate of economic growth of about 2% per head per annum is required in any developed country just to keep all the existing workforce in employment, with living standards rising in line with the expansion of the economy. If the growth rate falls below about this level, one of two outcomes is certain. Either unemployment will increase, or the output per head of those competing especially at the bottom end of the labour market will be forced down, as labour is shaken out of higher productivity occupations. If the potential workforce is growing, as it is in most countries, sometimes very fast, an increase in effective demand of considerably more than 2% is required to stop either unemployment rising or a marked increase in productivity dispersion occurring.

The situation in most of Europe illustrates one variation on this theme. For many years, the European Union (EU) economies have not been growing at 2.4% per annum, the rate needed to stop unemployment rising then 2.4% is made up of around 2% per annum, to allow for rises in productivity, plus another 0.4% per year to allow for the increasing size of the labour force. Instead, over the long period between 1979 and 1998, the average growth rate has been 2.1%,[4] which is about 0.3% less than a reasonable estimate of the increase in output per head. With substantial social security structures in place, greatly reducing the pressure on the population to accept low paid jobs, the effect has been to increase unemployment by something like 0.3% per annum. This has generated a cumulative increase for the whole of the period of about 6% in the numbers out of work, as rises in productivity have exceeded growth in demand. This is the reason why in the EU both the claimant count registered unemployment figure – currently about 10% – is so high, and why so many other people have dropped out of the labour force. In total, some 17% – more than one in six – of all those potentially capable of working in the EU are not doing so at present.[5]

In the USA, where unemployment benefits are far scarcer, the impact on the labour market of fast expansion of the potential labour force combined with relatively slow growth in the economy as a whole has not been on unemployment but on productivity. The number of people available to work in the USA has risen dramatically – from 83m in 1970 to 138m in 1998 – and the number of people in employment has gone up from 79m to 131m.[6] America created a staggering 52m new jobs in twenty-eight years, an increase of 67%. Over the same period, however, the US GDP per head has risen by only 49%.[7] The result has been a huge proliferation of poorly paid, low productivity jobs. In 1970, the aggregate income of the poorest 40% of families in the USA was 17.6% of the total. In 1996 it was 14.2%.[8] Meanwhile the proportion going to the top 20% rose from 40.9% to 48.1%. It is not unemployment which has caused this huge increase in the dispersion of incomes. 4.9% of the labour force was out of work in 1970 and 4.5% in 1998.[9] The culprits are low productivity and poor pay.

The social impact of low wage, insecure employment, or no work at all, caused by slow growth, has been enormously damaging. In all countries suffering from these blights, it has produced ghettos, especially in inner-city areas, where almost no one has a regular job which pays a reasonable wage. It is hardly surprising that in this environment crime rates rise, educational standards fall, social cohesion evaporates, anti-social behaviour such as drug abuse proliferates, and high levels of deprivation are passed down the generations. It has also produced regional imbalances, where the less favoured areas have been unable to attract sufficient economic activity to keep the indigenous population in work. When the pressure of demand is high enough, employers have little alternative to siting their operations in less favoured areas, because the workforces they need are unlikely to be obtainable elsewhere. If there is a surplus labour force almost everywhere, no such incentives exist.

Together with low pay and unemployment goes resentment, particularly towards foreigners. If almost everyone has a good job, it is hard to blame inadequate incomes on those from outside. If many people do not have regular jobs paying a decent wage, it is much easier to attribute lack of employment opportunities to strangers, particularly if they are willing to work for wages, and in conditions, which the resident labour force regards as unacceptable. It is a relatively short step for this kind of resentment to be channelled by political movements into policies with a heavy xenophobic and racial dimension. There have always been politicians in all countries who are ready to exploit tensions of this kind, capitalising on the bitterness and frustration which lack of economic opportunities so easily generates.

There are also vital issues concerning every country's place in the world which are intimately bound up with the country's economic performance. In the last analysis, political influence is almost entirely a function of economic power. European countries were pre-eminent in the world in the nineteenth century because they were much more economically developed than those anywhere else, apart from the United States, which at that time was little interested in world power. Britain's exceptionally strong position during this period resulted almost entirely from its lead in industrialisation. The outcome of the two world wars had little to do with the merits of the war aims of the participants, or the nature of the régimes involved, and everything to do with industrial and economic capabilities ranged on either side. The hegemony of the United States in the post-World War II period was again almost entirely a function of its economic capability.

Power relationships generally change relatively slowly. A difference in growth rate over a year or two of 2% or 3% is barely perceptible. Multiplied over a decade, let alone quarter or half a century, however, the position changes radically. A differential growth rate of 4% will cause one economy to double in size relative to another in about seventeen years. This kind of change in economic weight makes a massive difference to any country's or region's industrial, financial, military and diplomatic power, to its self-respect, and to its ability to look after its interests *vis à vis* other parts of the world. Much of the history of the last two hundred years, since industrialisation began, has been a function of differential growth rates.

What will happen to the United States, for example, if its growth rate remains at an average of about 2.4% per annum in the foreseeable future, while the average for the rest of the world continues to be perhaps as much as 4%, and the Pacific Rim countries, having largely overcome their recent problems, go back to achieving anything between 6% and 10%? The outcome is bound to be a major additional attenuation in the relative status of the USA compared to other parts of the world. The USA is still an overwhelmingly powerful nation, but it could be overtaken, as in past centuries were Spain, the Netherlands and Britain in turn, each of which looked impregnable before the change occurred. Some people argue that the very high growth rates in the Pacific Rim countries cannot last, and that their rate of progress will inevitably slow down. For reasons to be discussed later in this book, such an assumption may not be well founded. Even if there is some slowing down, however, the difference in growth performance could be so large that within a few decades the gap will be closed. The sheer size of the population of China makes it feasible for the total Chinese GDP to exceed that of the USA before long, while if Japan could recover even a proportion of its growth record of previous decades, it might overtake the USA in GDP per head of the population in a decade or two.

There are thus strong arguments on both environmental, social and external grounds for all countries to maintain high growth rates if they can. Achieving faster growth on a consistent basis, with all that this entails for the standard of living, is also clearly in line with the wishes of a vast majority of the population. For the past decades most, indeed nearly all, of the world's developed economies have not performed as well as they might have done, generally by a wide margin. The issue is whether there are underlying reasons which explain why this has happened, enabling more effective policies to be implemented in future.

Lost opportunities

Anyone alive two hundred years ago would be astounded if he or she could see the world as it is now. The changes in living standards, technology and lifestyles have been immense. For many people, although not all, not only have there been vast increases in disposable incomes, there have also been huge improvements in educational standards, health care, life expectancy and life chances. No one can deny that humanity has achieved wonders since the Industrial Revolution began to show the way to sustained output increases. Complaints that more could and should have been done therefore need to be seen in perspective. Nevertheless, a critical look at the way economic events have unfolded shows that however much may have been accomplished, there is still a great deal that could have been done more effectively, and many opportunities to achieve better performance which are clearly not being realised at present.

Looking back over the history of the last two centuries, perhaps the strangest phenomenon to observe is how extremely uneven economic progress has been not only between different parts of the world, which is relatively understandable, but within the same economies, which seems, at first sight, much more difficult to explain. The Industrial Revolution began in earnest in Britain during the last quarter of the eighteenth century, and gathered pace relative to the rest of the world until about 1850, leaving most other countries even in Europe, let alone elsewhere, far behind. By 1850, GDP per head in Britain was 42% higher than in France and 60% higher than in Germany, and 30% higher than in the USA. By 1880, the British lead over the French and Germans was close to 70% in both cases, the gap having widened even further, although the USA had caught up strongly, and was by then only 10% behind. By 1913, however, the British lead over the Germans had shrunk to 27%, over the French it was 41%, while the Americans had pulled 7% ahead.[10] Why did the British, who were in an apparently invincible military and financial position while this relative deterioration took place, allow this to happen?

After the upheavals of the two world wars and the tumultuous period in between them, in 1950 the living standards in Europe had widened again. Britain, which had been on the winning side in both wars, then had GDP per head 31% higher than France and 60% more than Germany, although the USA by this time was 40% ahead of Britain. Yet only twenty years later, the position had radically changed. By then French living standards were 13%, and those in Germany 23%, higher than those in Britain, while the US lead over Britain remained the same as it had been twenty years previously. The huge relative change in economic performance between Britain and its continental neighbours is, of course, explained by the difference in growth rates. Between 1950 and 1970, the French economy grew at a cumulative rate of 5.1% per annum, while

Germany did even better at 6.3%. The British economy, meanwhile, grew at only 2.8% a year.[11]

The trends in Europe, however, were not to continue. After the seminal events of the early 1970s – the breakdown of the Bretton Woods system, the first oil crisis, the surge in inflation, and the change in intellectual fashion towards monetarism – the growth rates in all West European countries converged towards the relatively poor level of achievement in Britain. Why did this happen? If those governing the countries which had so successfully pursued high growth, full employment policies, combined with generally low levels of inflation for twenty years had known the answer to this question, it seems extremely unlikely that they would have allowed the much poorer levels of performance of the subsequent decades to occur. The thesis in this book is not that it was ineluctable changes in circumstances which caused this sea change to take place. On the contrary, it was the lack of clear economic prescription which led to entirely avoidable policy errors, resulting in an enormous shortfall in performance compared to the potential which might have been achieved.

Even more remarkable was the relative rise of Japan during the post-World War II years. In 1950, Japanese GDP per head was 20% of the level in the USA. By 1990, it was 85%.[12] Again, it was hugely different levels of economic growth which were responsible. Between 1950 and 1990, the cumulative rate of growth in the Japanese economy was 6.9%, while in the USA it was 3.4%. Once more, however, there has been a massive reversal. During the 1990s, while the US economy has surged ahead, the Japanese economy has barely grown at all, and living standards have been static. Was this dismal outcome really unavoidable?

Another contrast has been the performance of several of the economies in the Far East. If the disruption to the world economy in the 1970s is portrayed as a convincing reason for the subsequent poor achievements of the economies in Western Europe, it is hard to see how this can be correct if the same decades saw the rise of the Tiger economies. Between 1970 and 1990, the Taiwanese economy grew cumulatively by 8.7% per annum, and South Korea by 8.8%.[13] Over recent years, the vast Chinese economy is claimed to have grown at a similar rate, or even faster, although there is some doubt about the reliability of the statistics. If some countries can grow as fast as this, why is it that others have to live with a much slower increase in GDP?

Nor are world economic problems confined to hugely varying rates of growth, suggesting that some areas could do much better than they have done in the past, or are achieving at present. Performance also varies widely in other respects. The development of chronic unemployment or underemployment in the western world has already been mentioned. Allied to large numbers of people either out of work altogether, as in Europe, or forced by lack of social security and unemployment benefit into low productivity jobs, as in the USA, has been gross under-use of the labour force in the economies where these conditions prevail. With poor job prospects go lack of training, which soon washes over into lack of motivation among those still in the education system, who see little likelihood of a high value demanding job when they start looking for employment. Slow rates of economic growth and poor job prospects at the bottom end of the job market also lead to an increasingly skewed distribution of income and life chances. One of the striking contrasts between the Tiger economies and the western world is the extent to which the disparities of opportunity in the most successful East Asian economies have been diminishing at exactly the same time as they have been widening in Europe and the USA.[14] Although on the surface other factors may seem significant, and explanations are often based on them, the fundamental reason for these divergent developments is to be found in the full use of labour resources in the fast growing Tiger economies, and its under-utilisation in the more sluggish West.

There are also vastly varying savings rates in different parts of the world, generally reflected in widely differing proportions of the national income being devoted to capital expenditure. Some countries have a much higher proportion of their economies devoted to manufacturing than others, and generally those with high savings ratios tend to have greater growth rates, and more manageable balance of payments positions although, especially recently, this has not been a universal rule. It is important to understand how cause and effect interlink in these respects. There is a wide dispersion in balance of payments performance across the world, with much of the current demand for most countries' exports being underpinned by a massive US trade deficit, which looks increasingly unsustainable. This pattern is necessarily reflected in capital movements, which always, as an accounting identity, mirror current account deficits or surpluses, but whose rationality can often be called into question, and whose stability is therefore unreliable. In these circumstances, it is not surprising that the case for free trade and liberalised capital movements is often challenged. The danger is then that policies swing too far away from the optimum balance between freedom and control, because of pressures which could have been avoided if the world economy had been better managed. There are respectable cases both for free trade and for allowing capital to move to where it can be used most productively, but only if a number of ancillary conditions are fulfilled. Establishing a policy framework which gets the best out of market forces, without letting them romp damagingly out of control, is another crucial piece of the jigsaw.

As well as those parts of the world which are relatively prosperous, there are vast numbers of people who are still steeped in poverty scarcely different from that experienced by their ancestors centuries ago. A recent survey showed that over one-fifth of the world's population lived in extreme poverty, of whom about 70% are women. Over 13m children under five die each year from poverty-related afflictions such as measles, diarrhoea, malaria, pneumonia and malnutrition. Nor is the situation, in many areas, improving. During the 1980s, the world's poorest 20% of the people saw their share of global income reduced from 1.7% to 1.4%. In 1994, at least 1.1bn people were subsisting on cash incomes of less than $1 a day. Their total assets came to no more than $400bn, compared with the $200bn worth of property reported not long ago to be owned by the world's 160 billionaires.[15] Recent data suggest that one of them alone may have been worth $100bn.[16]

Much of the reason that so many people are in deep poverty, concentrated largely in poorly performing economies, has to do with the actions, or lack of them, in the richer parts of the world. Lack of opportunities to trade is largely responsible, and although successive tariff reducing rounds have helped in recent years, there are still many restrictions on the goods which rich countries could import from poor ones, such as a wide range of foodstuffs, woven fabrics (covered by the Multi-Fibre Agreement), and simple products such as shoes. If unemployment levels are in double figures, the reasons why well off countries are reluctant to open their doors to cheap imports are not hard to detect. The results in poorer countries, however, are to make it difficult to achieve rates of growth which keep up with the high population increases which almost invariably go with very low incomes.

These developments will be responsible for the major problems with which the world is going to be confronted in the foreseeable future. Leaving aside cataclysms such as the use of mass destruction weapons, the most significant threats to humanity are likely to be the consequences of a rising population combined with inadequate resources to avoid the damage that more and more people are capable of doing to the world's ecology. Furthermore, the lower the standard of living in the poorer countries, the more rapid the rise in population is likely to be. The key issues are then going to be the provision of adequate water supplies as the water table sinks, the disposal of increasing amounts of sewage and rubbish, and the control of greenhouse gas emissions, leading to global warming, climate change and the rising of the sea level. All of these problems are, in principle at least, soluble if the resources are available, but are also likely to become increasingly hazardous if they are not.

Although, therefore, some of the world has done well over the last two centuries, large tracts of it, and many people, have not fared nearly as satisfactorily as they might have done. There is still a huge agenda to be tackled. Dealing with it nowadays, more than ever, requires better management of the world's economy as a whole, as trade and capital movements continue to expand more rapidly than total output, and economies everywhere therefore become more closely interlinked. The solutions are to get the world growth rate up and to bring the labour force into the most productive use to which it can be put, while containing the disruption which unmanageable levels of inflation will cause, but which moderate price increases do not create. Explaining how to achieve all these objectives should define the central core of economic theory and prescription, providing much more clarity than is available at present on how to find practical ways of resolving pressing problems.

Economics and ideology

The development of human institutions and practices over the last ten or twelve thousand years, since civilisation began, has been wholly dependent on the inventions and ideas which have been discovered and formulated, and handed down the generations. The essence of the best of them is that they appear so obvious when they become well known, that it seems almost inconceivable that no one could have thought of them before, or that anyone could really have believed something different. How could it be that among all the millions of people living in North America in 1492, when Columbus and his associates arrived, none of them nor any of their ancestors had thought of practical uses for wheels? Why did thousands of years elapse after horses were domesticated, before anyone invented the stirrup, in the seventh or eighth century AD[17] – a development which revolutionised warfare, making possible, in particular, the medieval attacks on Europe, India and China from the steppes of Asia, creating the vast empire presided over by Genghis Khan?

The essence of the best ideas is a combination of their simplicity and their ability to be both true but not obvious. The underlying framework for the development of civilisation has been the accretion of such ideas, each of them making it easier and more practical to understand, and hence to control, events and processes. Countless thousands of people have contributed to this cause in smaller or greater ways, and many of the inventions and ideas which have radically changed history have involved the combined efforts of more than one person. Furthermore, each new development has always rested on the accumulation of existing knowledge. It is not difficult, however, to pick out some of the key innovations which have shaped human history. The domestication of animals and the development of agriculture, and then of towns and cities; the invention of trade and credit and, much later as we shall see, of money; the development of writing, mathematics and astronomy; the series of innovations which led, especially during the Middle Ages, to vastly improved ships and navigation, and the discovery of America; the printing press; the escapement mechanism which made reliable clocks possible; eyeglasses, which doubled the working life of everyone whose occupation depended on good eyesight; gun-powder, and a host of other military inventions which transformed warfare.[18]

More recently, the rate at which inventions, ideas and knowledge have accumulated has vastly increased. In many fields, particularly those associated with scientific inquiry, procedures leading to innovations have been systematised, generating an enormous effusion of new products and processes. Part of the reason is the dominance of the scientific method, pioneered by Francis Bacon (1561–1626) at the beginning of the seventeenth century in a series of highly influential works, written mostly during his long retirement from active involvement in government. In non-scientific areas, progress has tended to be slower, no doubt because ways of testing new ideas are necessarily more diffuse, therefore making it harder to prove them correct and to get them accepted. It is a commonplace that social science subjects lack the rigour of true science, and economics is no exception.

Even after making all such allowances, however, it is extraordinary that the study of economics has made such odd and patchy progress over the last two centuries. Clearly, there are issues of central importance which remain unresolved, especially those to do with the causes of economic growth, unemployment and inflation, where there is simply no agreed unified explanatory theory. The huge strides forward made in technical subjects are perhaps best mirrored in economics by the many thousands of articles published in learned magazines, nearly all dealing with some small part of the puzzle, but not the big picture. The twentieth century, in particular, has produced few thinkers in economics remotely comparable in breadth of intellectual invention to those who achieved the major breakthroughs in science and mathematics. John Maynard

Keynes (1883–1946) surely ranks in the first order, and perhaps Milton Friedman does too in a different context. Unquestionably important work was done by people like Simon Kuznets (1901–1985) in inventing national statistics. A series of economists from Austria, particularly Joseph Schumpeter (1883–1950) and Friedrich Auguste von Hayek (1899–1992), wrote seminal and influential books. Undoubtedly, there have been a succession of high profile and accomplished expositors of the prevailing wisdom, some of whom have also made important original contributions to economic theory. Mostly, these have been professors of economics, from Alfred Marshall (1842–1924) of Cambridge University at the end of the nineteenth century in Britain to Paul Krugman of the Massachusetts Institute of Technology in the USA at the end of the twentieth. In a different mould, there have been prolific and pointed critics of conventional views, such as Professor Kenneth Galbraith. However much one may admire the work of these people, it is, nevertheless, difficult to credit any of them with having a comprehensive view about how to solve the central issues with which this book argues that economics ought to be concerned.

Interestingly, the eighteenth and nineteenth centuries, in some important respects, rank higher. *The Wealth of Nations*, written by Adam Smith (1723–1790) and published in 1776, the same year as the American Declaration of Independence, moved the nascent subject of economics a huge distance from the mercantilism which preceded it. Thomas Malthus (1766–1834), whose most influential work, *Essay on the Principle of Population*, was published in 1798, had a marked and depressing effect on subsequent thinking about the prospects for improving the lot of ordinary people, heavily influencing the work of Karl Marx (1818–1883). David Ricardo (1772–1823), whose contributions included the theories of comparative advantage and diminishing returns, published his major work, *Principles of Political Economy* in 1817. Building on these foundations, and the ideas of others such as Richard Cobden (1804–1865) and John Bright (1811–1889) on free trade and the 'philosophic principle' of the greatest good for the greater number, John Stuart Mill (1806–1873) codified and structured the classic economic theories which underpinned policy in the nineteenth century. His *Principles of Political Economy* was published in 1848. With its emphasis on *laissez-faire*, and its confidence that minimum government interference was appropriate, this was a doctrine which endorsed the status quo, and which had little to say about promoting activist policies to change the course of economic development. With the exception of the Marxist tradition, therefore, the nineteenth century saw little development of a substantial positive role for government in economic affairs. Towards the end of the century Alfred Marshall formalised the importance of demand and supply, and introduced the concept of marginal utility, his major work being *Principles of Economics*, which was published in 1890.

All these writers were based in Britain. It is not surprising that much of the early work in economics took place there in view of the pre-eminence of the British industrial achievements at the time, but economists in other countries made important contributions too. Of particular note were the Physiocrats in France at the end of the eighteenth century, and also Jean Baptiste Say (1767–1832), whose most significant work was *Traité d'Economie Politique*. The major contribution of the Physiocrats was the development of the *laissez-faire* principle, which was to have a long and influential subsequent history, as was their concept of the fundamental role of land in economics. This was to have an important renaissance in the USA a hundred years later in the work of Henry George (1839–1897), whose Single Tax proposals were most widely publicised in his *Progress and Poverty*, which, in various editions and reprintings, had a circulation in the millions.[19]

The works of Karl Marx have probably had more influence on the twentieth century than those of any writer on economics, though his influence was much more substantial on the political world than on economic theory. Perhaps this provides some guidance towards determining the root cause of the malaise from which economics suffers. Marx had a plethora of ideas to expound, many of which have stood the test of time well. His view on the impact of economic interests on politics, for example, very much an original concept at the time when he propagated it, is now the common currency among historians and sociologists. Marx's influence on mainstream economics, however, has been almost insignificant. His analysis of the way capitalist society was developing at the time, and his projections for the future, based, as they were, on the labour theory of value, which failed to stand the test of time, had a profound impact on political thinking. They did not, however, have great influence on economic theory. It is difficult to avoid the conclusion that this happened partly because Marx wanted to come to the cataclysmic conclusions contained in *Das Kapital*, and that he therefore developed his economic theories to help to buttress a case he wanted to develop and propound for other reasons.

This is a pattern which has been inclined to repeat itself subsequently, though with most more recent influential economists being broadly in favour of liberal capitalism rather than wanting to overthrow it. With the exception of a few major thinkers, such as Keynes, the impact of economic theory has therefore tended to reinforce the prevailing ethos, and to explain and justify current events in familiar idiom, rather than to challenge the prevailing orthodoxy in radical terms. Even when apparently significant changes have been proposed, as happened with the advent of the monetarist ideas particularly associated with Milton Friedman, they have tended to be ones with which the politically powerful felt exceptionally content. The result has been that economics, lacking many effective impulses pushing it in any other direction, has tended to develop an orthodoxy of its own which has mirrored the political views, interests and prejudices of those in a position to call the shots. The outcome is that the true but not obvious insights which might have lifted economics to a considerably greater coherence and prescriptive value than it is at present have failed to materialise.

It is hardly surprising that in these circumstances, economic theory has not been a great deal of assistance to those faced with taking many practical decisions. When, towards the end of the nineteenth century, people in Britain began to realise that, although the country was still in a powerful position, it was losing ground to its competitors, there was no clear explanation as to why this was happening. If the Japanese had fully understood the reason for the immense strides forward that their economy had made between 1950 and 1990, it seems hard to believe that they would have let their country stagnate for years on end thereafter. It seems unlikely, too, that European leaders would have allowed the growth rate in West Europe to decline in the last quarter of the twentieth century to less than half its previous level if they had known how to stop this happening. Nor have newer ideas, such as monetarism, helped policy makers to any significant extent. When inflation engulfed much of the world in the 1970s, and monetarism became fashionable, those countries which then pursued overtly monetarist policies did not in fact subdue price rises faster than others which adopted less ideologically driven prescriptions. Indeed, the evidence suggests, allowing for the necessity for competent day-to-day running of all economies, that inflation largely cured itself. Draconian policies for restricting the money supply may have made problems with the rising price level worse rather than better in the countries which tried them.

Why has economic theory remained so undeveloped? This is a puzzling question, to which it would be very helpful to find a convincing answer. Policies capable of generating economic growth, which keep the labour force fully employed, and which keep inflation at tolerable levels, are obviously of such critical importance that it seems strange that so comparatively little effective effort has been directed at establishing how they might be successfully formulated. Some of the answers are there, but evidently not sufficient of them. The result is that those in charge of economic policy have to operate to a significant extent in a vacuum of well thought-through and coherent theory about the most pressing problems with which they have to contend.

In a field as politicised as economic policy, the remaining vacuum – even a partial one – has not stayed empty. Because there has been no clear explanation of events, and because there was no agreed conceptual framework to define what needs to be done, there has been endless scope for the promotion of special interests, and the manipulation of ideas, mostly designed to suit the rich and powerful, who have always been generally content with the status quo. In the nineteenth century, when the concepts comprising classical economics were established in Britain, perhaps inevitably they reflected the way that the powerful financial interests in the country wanted to see ideas about the management of the economy developing. Whatever its merits classical economics is primarily a defence of the status quo rather than a recipe for change. Whenever there have been any challenges to its tenets, whether by major figures such as Karl Marx and John Maynard Keynes, or by more minor ones, hardly surprisingly, therefore, they have tended to be resisted by those in control. As a result of these successful rearguard actions, there has been a constant tendency for economic ideas to regress back to the non-interventionist norm. The popularity of monetarism – essentially an updated version of nineteenth-century classical economics – is thus all too easy to explain. The problem with too many of the proposals which have been put forward for making the world's economies perform better is that they have been insufficiently convincing to stand up to sectional pressures. As a result, they have been consistently pushed aside by less radical and more conventional views with which those in control of events have tended to feel more comfortable.

A major problem with economics is that so much which seems at first sight to be obvious turns out not to be so on closer inspection. This is why no subject more urgently needs new ideas which are simple and clearly true when explained, but which, like so many important concepts, remain obscure and unaccepted until this occurs. Finding these ideas is indeed the only way of overcoming special interests, and the huge advantage in manipulating events and ways of looking at them which the already rich and powerful possess. They have to be convinced that an alternative view of the world is more to their advantage. Unless they realise that they have a common interest with everyone else in seeing the world's economy run a different way, nothing will change. The growth of democracy shows how this has happened in politics. The strong have accepted that it is in their interest, as well as that of everyone else, for their power and control over events to be shared. Their security, life chances and wealth are enhanced – not diminished – by their willingness to merge their interests with those of other people less fortunate than themselves. A similar accommodation needs to be found in the world of economic policy. The major objective of this book is to help to provide some building blocks necessary to enable this to be done.

Economics and politics

Changing economic perceptions also have a substantial bearing on the world of politics. In particular, the inability of the leaders of the industrialised countries to get their economies to grow fast enough to keep their labour forces in employment, and the lack of credible policies to ensure that this happens, have had a profound impact on the way political thinking has developed over the last quarter of a century.

In nearly all of the developed world in the 1950s and 1960s, the dividing lines between the left and right of the political spectrum were reasonably clear, as was the location of the consensus centre-ground. The left believed in expanding both the executive and regulatory roles of the state, and in using taxation and public expenditure to even out incomes and life opportunities. The right was inclined to resist encroachments of this kind, but by and large accepted the case for large-scale state involvement in the economy. Taking the rough edge off the capitalist system had its costs, but high rates of growth meant that the expense was relatively easy to bear. In particular, the fact that there were jobs available for almost everyone who wanted to work meant that dependency was relatively low, and the strain on the fiscal system correspondingly bearable.

When growth and full employment slipped away from the developed countries, the basis for the consensus found in most of them went with it. As Keynesian policies for maintaining full employment conditions apparently lost their effectiveness, politicians everywhere began to realise that they were now facing much more difficult choices, with harsher consequences for those who were more vulnerable. A new, globalised economy hove into view, where nobody seemed to be in control. No country, it was claimed, could now pursue an independent economic policy, since all attempts to buck the market would lead to certain and painful reversals as currency traders showed their disapproval. Any country which tried to protect its citizens from the full rigours of free enterprise capitalism was in danger of plunging deeper into unemployment and slow growth. No country could afford to increase the progressiveness of its tax system, for fear of losing essential high earning people and investment to others with more accommodating stances. High interest rates were required to drive down the level of economic activity to a point where price rises were quiescent, especially if they might add to the strains on a relatively weak balance of payments position. It was then hoped – against all the evidence – that low levels of inflation would encourage productive investment. Fiscal deficits were in danger of generating inflationary pressures, which could not be afforded, and which needed to be avoided, even at heavy deflationary cost.

The result of the implementation of these kinds of policies led inevitably to widening income and wealth differentials – a hallmark of almost all developed countries over the last quarter of a century.[20] Aided by the collapse of the erstwhile Soviet Union, and the further discrediting of collectivist policies which followed, the left began to see less and less future in its previous adherence to the goals of equality, universal benefits and collective provision. Armed with the intellectual protection of monetarist doctrines, and the supposed inevitability of market forces, the right led the charge for privatisation, deregulation and self-help. For a while, as a result, right-of-centre governments were the norm throughout the developed world. When, in the 1990s, electorates tired of them, the parties of the left which replaced them, having taken on board large sections of the right's agenda, were almost unrecognisable as the successors to the organisations which had borne the same names twenty-five years previously. Gone, perhaps understandably in the light of the Soviet débâcle and the generally successful results achieved in the West through the sale by the state of former nationalised industries, was nearly all the former enthusiasm for public ownership and state control. Much more fundamentally, however, gone too was any serious commitment to full employment, a universalist welfare state, redistribution of income, and protection for employees from whatever the consequences of largely unbridled competition might bring. Especially in the United States and Britain, 'Third Way' policies along these lines replaced the traditional approaches, with every sign that the rest of Europe and Japan were likely, with varying degrees of reluctance, to fall in line behind the same banner.

Indeed, Third Way parties, such as the British Labour Party, often went further than their right-wing predecessors had done, passing control over interest rates to the Bank of England, and then restraining public expenditure almost certainly more tightly than the Conservative Party would have done. Throughout the European Union, nominally left-of-centre governments have handed over large elements of economic control to the unelected European Central Bank, whose *raison d'être*, set out in the 1992 Maastricht Treaty, is to keep inflation low as a priority over all other policy objectives. In the USA, the stock exchange boom has continued to make the rich much richer, while Middle American incomes have barely risen in real terms, and the poor are still much poorer than they were twenty-five years ago. With monetary policy in the West now largely out of direct political control, Finance Ministers have far less power than they used to have, particularly because of the ineffectiveness of fiscal policy – changes in taxation and expenditure – in isolation from other instruments, particularly interest rate and monetary policy.[21] A further major theme running through this book is that these political changes which have taken place over the last quarter of a century are not only a direct result of the failure of economic theory to explain how to overcome the manifest problems of the developed world's economies. They are also damaging and limiting in ways which ought to be unwelcome to people on both the left and the right of the political spectrum. If the industrialised countries ran their economies better, they would also be in better shape politically.

From the left's perspective, most of the reason why efforts to make society fairer and life chances more equal have been put on one side is not because of loss of interest in traditional objectives. It is because, against the background of slow growth and high unemployment, they appear to have become increasingly unattainable and unrealistic. If the economy grew faster, and everyone who wanted a job had one, however, the prospects for producing a more genuinely egalitarian society would be much more favourable, like they were in the 1950s and 1960s. As the left has found throughout the developed world, nothing is more corrosive to its aims than economic failure, and nothing more conducive to their achievement than prosperity.

From a right-of-centre perspective, faster growth and full employment also bring major advantages. No one likes to see his or her country slipping back in the relative prosperity league, with all that this entails for loss of prestige, power and influence in the world. Property is likely to be more secure, and crime lower, in a society whose economy is doing well, and which is therefore reasonably content with itself. Society is likely to be more cohesive, with fewer alienated groups to cause disruption. Lower levels of dependency may mean lower overall levels of taxation.

Perhaps more important than any of these traditional issues, however, are new ones which are looming up, which are going to put new and

2
Economic Growth

'It is in the interests of the commercial world that wealth should be found everywhere.'

Edmund Burke

As we have seen, the economic history of the developing world since the start of industrialisation has been remarkably uneven. Britain experienced a long period of rapid growth in the first half of the nineteenth century, but then slowed down between 1850 and 1900. The USA grew rapidly during the whole of the nineteenth century and, more intermittently, through to 1945, but then slowed relative to new challengers. Germany and the Netherlands did much better during the second half of the nineteenth century than the first, and better still during the early years of the twentieth century, leading up to World War I. The 1930s were a particularly interesting and important period, with the USA and France languishing, Britain doing far better than previously, and Germany surging ahead at an astonishing pace. There have been decades when most of the most prosperous economies of the time were expanding very quickly, as they did in the 1950s and 1960s, although the USA did not grow as fast as others during these decades. After the post-war boom, in the 1970s, increases in output slowed in the developed countries. The world's growth rate of 4.9% per annum cumulatively between 1950 to 1973 slowed to 3.0% per annum from 1973 to 1992.[1] Crucially for the arguments in this book, however, the lower growth rates in the later period were far more marked among those economies where relatively high standards of living already prevailed, most markedly in Western

Europe and Japan. It was poor performance by the already industrialised countries which pulled down the world average.

Table 2.1: Comparison between the Growth Rate of the Industrialised Countries and the Rest of the World between 1950 and 1992

		Increase in GDP 1950–73	Increase in GDP 1973–92	Ratio Fall between % Increases
Western Europe	Total Ratio Increase:	2.86	1.50	
	Average per Annum:	4.7%	2.2%	53%
Western Offshoots USA and Canada	Total Ratio Increase:	2.47	1.58	
Australia and New Zealand	Average per Annum:	4.0%	2.4%	40%
Japan	Total Ratio Increase:	7.65	2.02	
	Average per Annum:	9.2%	3.8%	59%
Whole World	Total Ratio Increase:	2.99	1.74	
	Average per Annum:	4.9%	3.0%	39%
Whole World less Western Europe,	Total Ratio Increase:	3.11	1.90	
Offshoots and Japan	Average per Annum:	5.1%	3.4%	33%

Source: *Monitoring the World Economy 1820–1992* by Angus Maddison. Paris: OECD, 1995, Tables G-2 and C-16a.

Why did these changes in relative performance occur? Why was growth so much faster in some periods than others, and what can policy makers do to create the conditions where growth takes place? How can they avoid it slowing down? The objective of this chapter is to set out an explanation for the causes of economic growth, and the processes by which it takes place. If we can understand why some economies grow fast and others slowly, and why some succeed in employing their resources of labour and other factors of production more fully than others, much will be revealed. It then becomes possible to see not only the reasons for past history, but what might be done to alter the course of events in the future.

The starting point is to understand the circumstances which allow and encourage economic expansion to take place. Growth is achieved by creating conditions where the output of goods and services rises. Essentially, this can be done in two ways. One is to increase inputs – to employ more labour, to educate and train it better, and to use more capital equipment, land and buildings. The second is to achieve more output in relation to inputs than was attained before – increasing total factor productivity. This is done by improved management, better design, and enhanced production efficiency. Any convincing explanation of the way output can be increased needs to take account of both these components of the growth process.

High growth rates are achieved by keeping all the factors of production, particularly labour and capital, in use as intensively as possible. The expansion of the economy thus achieved will be reflected in increased output per head, which is how productivity is raised. At the level of the individual enterprise, this is accomplished in three principal ways. The first is by investing in machinery and equipment which makes it possible for the existing labour force to achieve increased production. The second is by better management and training of the workforce, and enhancing its skills and experience. The third is by increasing sales, so that all the available resources of labour and capital are used to maximum capacity.

The potential for improved production as a result of capital investment is a familiar concept. The power, dexterity and speed with which machinery operates made the Industrial Revolution possible. During the past two centuries, the development of a huge range of machines has been matched by many other inventions and technological developments which can be used to increase output, from internal combustion engines to electronics, from steamships to airliners, from new building techniques to plastics. All these developments make it possible to produce goods and services of greater value per labour hour. We shall see, however, that there is a huge variation in the return on different types of investment. Some are very much more productive, and therefore conducive to expanding output than others. One of the ways of increasing economic growth, and making it much easier to achieve, is to create conditions in which the economy is biased towards the most highly productive use of investment. It is also the case that productivity increases are much easier to secure in some types of economic activity compared to others. This, too, is a factor of major policy significance.

The quality of management is extremely important. Many improvements in working practices which lead to more production, or changes in output designed to make it more attractive to consumers, involve little capital outlay but a great deal of human skill. Some of this comes from good education and training. An even more important factor is ensuring that the best available managerial talent is concentrated in those areas of the economy where it can be used most effectively to improve economic achievement. Where talent is actually employed depends critically on economic rewards, and the social status which follows behind them. The second element in improving economic achievement is to shift both rewards and social status towards those involved in running the parts of the economy where good management has the best chance of increasing performance.

The third vital component is to create enough pressure of demand on the economy to ensure that all the available resources of capital and labour are, as far as possible, fully utilised. To achieve most from capital equipment, it needs to be used as intensively as possible. To get the best out of the labour force, it needs to be fully employed. When there is a shortage of jobs, it may make sense to increase output by using relatively low productivity machinery and more employees. As supplies of labour run short, this no longer becomes a viable option. There is then no alternative to labour-saving equipment. At the level of the enterprise, a full order book at profitable prices is needed, with highly efficient machinery used to capacity to produce goods which the market is hungry to buy, operated by a well trained and motivated labour force, led by able managers. Despite recent setbacks, these are the conditions which still widely prevail in Korea, Taiwan and the fast developing parts of China, which is why these economies are expanding so rapidly. They were also replicated in Germany, France and Italy – indeed, over most of Western Europe in the 1950s and 1960s – when all these countries were growing much faster than they are now.

There is nothing mysterious about the conditions needed to make any country's economy expand fast. The problem lies in persuading those in control to allow the appropriate environment to be created.

Competitiveness

What are the conditions which enable economies to prosper? How is an environment created which encourages expansion to take place? What can those responsible for the performance of any economy do to ensure that its performance is as good as that achieved by the best performers in the growth league. It is often claimed that the solution is to concentrate on the supply side of the problem. The way to higher growth, it is said, is to improve efficiency by better education and training, by higher levels of investment, and by improving productivity. This will make domestic output more competitive, allowing more growth to take place. The problem with this approach, however, is that improving efficiency will not necessarily result in lower prices and greater competitiveness. It depends on the price charged to the rest of the world for the economy's output. Nor does increasing productivity necessarily result in rising total output.

A variation on the supply side theme is to blame poor growth performance on production techniques and design sophistication which are not as advanced as those available elsewhere in the world, perhaps compounded by ineffective salesmanship, late deliveries and inadequate after-sales service. This has certainly been a well recognised problem in the past, especially in countries with a high output per head, but where growth has slowed down relative to new challengers. The car industry is a particularly obvious example, where all western economies experienced severe difficulties in competing with the Japanese, but there are many others to which the same strictures could have been, and were, applied. Nowadays, in the West, there is much greater awareness of the need to set high standards to compete internationally. The problem is that at present there is still too little that many western countries, but particularly the USA, are capable of producing which the rest of the world wants to buy at the prices at which it is on offer.

Of course, productive efficiency has some bearing on competitiveness, but actually surprisingly little. The higher the level of productivity, the more efficiently goods and services will be produced, but it does not necessarily follow that they will then be internationally competitive. As we shall see, high output per head is closely associated with high standards of living, but has no meaningful relationship with competitiveness. This is why there is no observable correlation between the growth rates of rich and poor countries. It is, nevertheless, true that in any economy which is expanding, productivity will be increasing. This leads many people to conclude that concentrating efforts on raising output per head will push up the growth rate.

Unfortunately, this conclusion is not correct. There are many examples of countries round the world where output per head is increasing relatively rapidly, but overall growth in the economy is slow. The result is the rising unemployment and unused resources which are such conspicuous features in the European Union. In the USA, on the other hand, unemployment is low, and rapid increases in productivity in some parts of the economy produce a different problem. With insufficient effective demand to generate enough high quality jobs for everyone, rising productivity among some sections of the labour force is inevitably reflected in low or negative rises in output per head among large sections of the remaining working population.

Striking confirmation of these propositions is provided by comparing the position of the USA and the Tiger economies of the Far East during the period since World War II. After 1945, the US labour force was vastly more productive than the largely peasant workforces of Taiwan and Korea. The levels of training and education in the USA were far superior to those in most other countries in the world, while high proportions of the Taiwanese and Korean labour forces were unskilled. The value of capital per head in the USA was many multiples of the almost non-existent industrial capacity in Taiwan and Korea. Despite all these huge advantages, the USA has been completely outpaced in the growth race since World War II by these economies.

It is not, therefore, productivity which is the key to making economies potentially capable of growing fast. It is competitiveness. It is the prices charged for the economy's output to buyers both in the home and export markets, compared to foreign suppliers, which count. This is partly a function of how productive the domestic economy is, but it is also a question of how much its exporters charge the rest of the world for their output, whatever the level of productivity. This is determined by the exchange rate. Even if productivity is very low, and everything is wrong with the output of the economy, if it is cheap enough, a fair proportion of it will sell. However high the quality of the output, if it is too expensive, market share will be lost. In the end, it is price which balances out all the other quality factors. This is why the exchange rate is so critically important.

Other things being equal, the lower the exchange rate, the less the domestic economy charges the rest of the world for its labour, land and capital, and the more competitive, compared with the rest of the world, the domestic economy will be. This condition bears directly on the three requirements identified earlier for increasing both productivity and output. First, for all those economic activities which require capital investment to secure increase in output, the lower the associated labour and interest costs, measured in international terms, the higher the profitability of the capital investment, and the more of it will be undertaken. Second, the more competitive the output produced, the easier it will be to sell larger quantities at a profit, and the greater the capacity utilisation. Third, the higher profits thus generated, the more those sectors of the economy which are engaged in producing internationally tradable goods and services will be able to attract the most talented people into management positions. Exceptional profitability will also enable them to employ and make best use of the most competent people available to staff at every level.

Just as a company's competitive position is heavily disadvantaged if its costs are significantly out of line with the rest of the market, the same is true for the whole economy. There is, however, one further important difference between companies and economies. If the exchange rate is too high, bringing it down is an even more potent way of cutting costs across the board than anything an individual company can do. All companies have fixed costs which are difficult, and sometimes impossible, to reduce significantly. This is not true of the economy as a whole. Changing the exchange rate carries with it the costs of every factor of production. No wonder countries with overvalued exchange rates suffer so grievously, and those with undervalued exchange rates do so well.

The relationship between productivity and competitiveness is therefore the reverse of what is often supposed. It is not increasing productivity which produces greater competitiveness. It is greater competitiveness which generates the conditions where increased productivity is most easily achieved, and with the greatest advantage. This is not a trite conclusion. It has profound implications for determining the conditions which will make economies grow, and the policies which need to be pursued to make this happen.

The competitiveness, or lack of it, in any economy's export sector is thus crucial to its capacity to grow, and to keep its labour force fully employed. The huge growth rates achieved by many of the economies on the Pacific Rim stem from the fact that they managed to maintain this condition for decades. Economies which, for whatever reason, have allowed this *sine qua non* to slip away have paid a heavy penalty in slower growth and sub-optimal use of the available labour force. The USA is a pre-eminent example of an economy in the second category. For the whole of the period since shortly after the end of World War II, the output of the goods and services produced by US companies has not, on average, been sufficiently competitively priced in world terms. As a result, the share of the US home market taken by imports, particularly manu-factures, has risen dramatically, while simultaneously the share of world trade achieved by US exporters has fallen heavily. As late as 1963, the USA imported 8.6% of the world's manufactures and exported 17.4% of them. By 1994, imports were 17.5% of the world total, and exports 13.1%.[2] In 1950, manufactured goods represented only 7.5% of all US merchandise imports. By 1960, the ratio was 20%, by 1983 it was 50% and in 1996 it was 56%.[3]

As a result of these persistent trends, the USA has forgone the direct benefit which would have been secured by having a larger proportion of its GDP devoted to manufacturing and related sectors of the economy, where, in the right conditions, increases in output and rising productivity are relatively easy to achieve. The US economy has also been exposed to persistent balance of payments problems, which have constrained the capacity of successive administrations to expand the economy as fast as they might otherwise have chosen. It has therefore been impossible for buoyant consumer demand and high rates of investment to fill the gap left by sluggish foreign trade performance. The combined impact of these major influences provides the fundamental explanation for the relatively slow growth the US economy has achieved since the war. The reverse conditions, applying at the other end of the spectrum to the Tiger economies, explains how they have managed to surge ahead.

Protectionism and free trade

It is often proposed, particularly by those suffering from price competition which they find hard to combat, that the way to create favourable conditions for growth is through measures designed to shield domestic producers from world competition. All countries tend to have vocal minorities demanding protection from the rigours of world trade. Agriculture, where arguably special circumstances apply, is heavily protected almost everywhere. So, also, in most other economies are many other sectors. Some of the protection is secured overtly with tariffs and quotas, but informal methods can often be just as effective, as is often claimed to be the position in Japan. If the result is a severe trade imbalance, as has been the case, for example in trade between the USA and Japan, this condition can easily lead to pressure on export surplus countries to restrict their exports in sensitive areas such as cars and electronic components. 'Orderly marketing arrangements' and 'voluntary export restraints' are then put in place, and protectionism in a different guise becomes apparent.

Buttressing these arguments are others which have been the common coin of economic debate for centuries. By imposing a tariff, the domestic economy can tax the foreigner to its advantage. Because those selling to the domestic economy will have to lower their prices to compete in its protected market, the terms of trade will improve. The domestic economy will then obtain more imports per unit of exports than it did before the tariff was imposed, thus making itself better off. Furthermore, if the effect of putting on import duties is similar to reducing the exchange rate, having higher tariffs on some commodities than others may give the domestic economy advantages that would not be obtained by a devaluation. For example, if import duties are imposed on finished goods but not on raw materials, the domestic economy may be able to protect its manufacturers without raising their costs.

The arguments in favour of free trade, provided certain essential conditions are fulfilled, are nevertheless extremely strong. In modern conditions, there is an impressive and persuasive case against reverting back to a protectionist approach, and indeed for moving further towards opening up world markets to foreign competition wherever possible. The arguments for free trade and keeping all the world's economies open to foreign competition are as important now as they ever were, provided they are not undermined by inappropriate exchange rate policies, which can all too easily generate protectionism which politicians find difficult to resist.

First, there are the traditional comparative cost arguments for foreign trade. The relative costs of producing a wide range of goods and services varies from country to country. It pays countries to trade with each other if they swap those products where their relative costs are low for others produced elsewhere which could only be made at a relatively high cost domestically. It is important to note that the case for international trade for comparative cost reasons is independent of absolute levels of productivity. Countries with such low productivity that they produce everything relatively inefficiently can still trade with advantage with countries which produce everything more efficiently. It is the variances round the norm which make this trade worth while.

Second, there is the spur to efficiency produced by competition from abroad. Most people prefer a quiet life, and do not relish the prospect of having to adapt constantly to changing tastes and fashions, to new technology and methods of distribution. Provided it is not overwhelming, foreign competition keeps them on their toes. A copying process results as those who are behind the times replicate the trends set by the market leaders. They buy in or duplicate foreign technology and equipment, management techniques and sales methods. It is possible to achieve high rates of growth behind tariff barriers, as, for example, Spain did for a long period during the Franco régime, and Japan has done in different ways for decades. The output produced in these circumstances, however, tends to lack the quality of the goods and services available in countries which are more exposed to the world economy. Japanese manufactured goods may be superb, but much of the domestic economy in

Japan, particularly in services, is a byword for inefficiency and wasteful use of people in low productivity jobs. The informal protectionism which is Japan's speciality has been, in some obvious ways, extremely expensive for its citizens.

Third, there are great advantages in producing competitive exports if all the raw materials, intermediate goods and other inputs which have to be bought in from abroad can be obtained at the lowest possible price. One of the problems with either import tariffs or quotas is that they generally increase the costs of domestic production. It is now more difficult than it was to draw a clear distinction between raw materials and finished goods, with tariffs imposed on the latter but not the former. If the key to long-term improved economic performance is to increase the competitiveness of domestic producers of goods and services at home and abroad, it does not help to increase their costs more than can be avoided, or to restrict access to raw materials and components at the best available prices.

Fourth, tariffs or quotas have a fundamental flaw if they are employed to deal with an underlying lack of competitiveness. The problem is that while it is conceivable that there should be relatively low import duties, or a limited number of products subject to quotas, as soon as the height of the tariffs gets beyond a fairly low level – about 20% – the distortions they entail become more and more difficult to justify. Administrative problems also mount rapidly when import restraints increase in complexity. It is not possible to keep on raising tariffs or tightening quotas indefinitely without dramatically diminishing returns setting in. Economic distortions get worse, evasion becomes an increasing problem, and complicated appeals procedures are difficult to avoid.

If the root problem, however, is lack of competitiveness on the export market, as much as too much import penetration – and of course the two go together – then either the tariffs will have to be increased, or quotas tightened beyond any realistic point. Alternatively, the real remedy needed, which is changing the exchange rate, will have to be adopted. This is because tariff protection will not increase exports, but a growing economy will need more imports. There is no way out of this problem short of eventual autarchy, which forces the protected economy to produce more and more of its needs in the home market, even though it would be much cheaper to buy them from abroad.

There are, therefore, strong arguments for maintaining economies in the developed world as open as is politically feasible, although there may be a practical case for some measure of protection because of the difficulties of ensuring that exchange rates are always correctly aligned. This is the justification for the North American Free Trade Area, for the European Union's Common External Tariff, and for similar arrangements in South America, the Pacific area and elsewhere. Achieving equality in competitiveness between economies within a customs union area, which is a vital component of good economic management, may in practice, therefore, be easier to achieve behind a common external tariff high enough to contain an unmanageable volume of foreign competition. It has to be said, however, that even this conclusion is disputed, and in an ideal world, regional customs areas would be unlikely to exist.

Nevertheless, in the real world there are arguments for a degree of protection which are difficult to resist. They are weaker for quotas than for tariffs, and there is a stronger case for low tariffs than for high ones. When there is unmanageable competition, there is always pressure for protection. The case to be made in these circumstances, however, almost invariably depends on exchange rates being in the wrong position in the first place. Protectionist policies are then all too readily inclined to become the justification for failing to correct the exchange rate fundamentals. There is therefore no valid argument for a retreat into further protectionism as a major plank of economic policy. There is a much more effective way of dealing with the problems of major trade imbalance, for which tariffs and quotas are not the solution. This is to make greater efforts to position exchange rates at the right level, and to allow them to keep adjusting themselves as circumstances change and relative competitive advantage alters, so that the need for protectionist measures falls away.

Facing international competition

So far we have looked at the conditions favourable to economic growth in a static context, but the process we are considering is far from stationary. It is one where movement and change are essential elements. There are two particular features which need to be highlighted. The first is that rapid economic growth, once established, has a strong capacity to reinforce itself. On the whole, therefore, fast expanding economies tend to stay growing rapidly. The second is that this virtuous circle of fast growth cannot be taken for granted. It can slow down or even stop for a time altogether, as has been the experience across much of Europe since the mid 1970s, and particularly strikingly in the case of Japan since 1991. It is important to be able to explain both what causes growth to accelerate to a fast pace, and why it can slow down, stop, or even go into reverse. This means pinpointing the mechanisms involved in both the virtuous circle of import saving and export led growth, and the vicious circle of import led stagnation.

One of the keys to understanding this issue is to appreciate a particularly important characteristic of a large proportion of the investment taking place in all countries in those parts of the economy which produce internationally tradable goods and services. This is the large increases in output which investment of this sort is capable of producing at relatively low run-on costs, as fixed expenses become spread over greater volumes of output. Indeed, this characteristic provides the main explanation for the enormous growth in international trade which has occurred over recent decades. The result is a special feature of the production costs of internationally traded goods and services. They almost all involve steeply falling cost curves. This means that the expense involved in producing the first batch of any new good or service may be high, but all subsequent output is much cheaper. The average cost of production therefore falls quickly as the volume of output builds up.

This characteristic of internationally traded goods and services is highly significant. Any country with macro-economic conditions making it relatively easy to sell the output from this kind of investment – in particular low interest rates, a plentiful supply of credit and a competitive exchange rate – will achieve rapid growth. Once the initial investment is on stream, low marginal costs of production lead to high sales and profits, which are then available to finance the risks involved in subsequent waves of investment. High profitability also enables these enterprises to attract and hold the most able people in management positions, making it more likely that the next round of investment decisions will be shrewdly judged, and efficiently carried out. The low cost of production makes it relatively easy to keep plants fully occupied as higher output leads to even lower production expenses, and the capacity for yet more competitive pricing.

This virtuous circle thus tends strongly to fortify itself. Higher sales and greater profitability make it easier to finance research and development, and to keep ahead. They also provide the cash flow needed to sustain high selling costs, so that new markets can be penetrated. The competitive position of successful enterprises is strengthened by better design, advertising and selling efforts, and after-sales service, all of which are expensive. On the back of a large volume of profitable sales, however, they can be relatively easily afforded. Profits remain high, making expenditure to produce increased output easy to finance. Both the savings ratio and the rate of investment as a proportion of national income tend to be high and rising in economies with strong export sectors. With substantial rewards in successful enterprises go social status and political power, thus attracting and retaining more and more of the best talent. It cannot be stressed too strongly how important a contribution to achieving sustained growth is accomplished by having a high proportion of the country's most able people involved in making and selling goods and services, especially those involved in foreign trade. Creating the right economic conditions for the virtuous spiral of import saving and export led growth may be the precursor to economic success, but there is no substitute for the highest possible standard of efficiency at the level of the firm. This is where management quality is as critical as any other factor, perhaps the most significant of all. Sustained high growth rates can be achieved only by the difficult processes of making good judgements about increasingly complicated problems, managing more and more complex organisations, dealing with rapid and frequently technically intricate change, and assessing and sometimes anticipating accurately market trends, often covering the whole world.

The crucial question then is what makes it possible to break into the virtuous circle of import saving and export led growth? What are the conditions which cause import led stagnation? The exchange rate is the most critical determinant, for reasons which Table 2.2 makes clear. The table shows in schematic, but not unrealistic form, the costs and pricing options available to companies competing in international trade in three different economies; one with a parity in line with the world average, one with an exchange rate undervalued by 20%, and one with an exchange rate which is overvalued by the same percentage. The example shown here involves manufacturing, where the impact of high or low exchange rates is particularly pronounced, but similar results are obtained when considering internationally traded services.

The costs of manufacturing companies are made up of a number of components, some of which are determined by world prices, and some locally. In the table, raw materials are shown as 20% of international prices for the firm's output in the averagely competitive economy. There is a world market for nearly all commodities, but favourable selling conditions for exporters tend to go with efficient and low cost raw material suppliers in economies whose manufacturing base is expanding rapidly. There is also an understandable tendency for economies with strong export sectors to lack significant tariffs or other restrictions on raw material imports, whereas economies with weak balance of payments positions are more prone to try to protect their remaining industries with import constraints. Raw material costs are therefore likely to be lower in highly competitive economies than in those which are uncompetitive. The figures in the table show a 5% spread round the average.

Table 2.2: Options Available to Companies Producing Internationally Tradable Goods in Economies with Parities at Varying Levels

	Countries with Average Parities	*Countries Undervalued by 20%*	*Countries Overvalued by 20%*
Costs fixed in World Prices			
Raw Materials	20	19	21
Capital Depreciation	<u>10</u>	<u>8</u>	<u>12</u>
Total Internationally			
determined Costs	30	27	33
Costs fixed in Domestic Prices			
Labour Costs)			
Local Supplies)			
Land & Premises)			
Interest Charges)	<u>60</u>	<u>48</u>	<u>72</u>
Total Costs	90	75	105
World Prices for the			
Company's Output	<u>100</u>	<u>100</u>	<u>100</u>
Trading Profit or Loss			
at World Prices	10	25	−5

Source: Derived from OECD National Accounts.

Second, there are capital costs, which, when depreciated over output achieved in the average economy, are shown as 10% of selling prices. These costs, however, are even more likely to be lower than raw materials in highly competitive economies, and greater in those which are uncompetitive. Not only do fast growing economies tend to have cheaper and more efficient suppliers for capital equipment than elsewhere, but they also benefit from potentially much higher levels of capacity utilisation. The result is that the cost of capital depreciation per unit of output tends to be much lower in companies in competitive economies than in those which have high domestic costs, a factor further reflected in the figures in the table.

Third, there are all the costs which are incurred locally. An overvalued currency implies that the average wage costs per hour, adjusted for local productivity, are necessarily above the world mean level by a similar proportion to the overvaluation. Indeed, it is the costs which the domestic economy charges the rest of the world for its labour, adjusted for productivity, which substantially determine whether the currency is over- or undervalued in the first place. Since employee costs make up some 60% of total charges incurred in developed economies, this factor makes a large difference to the prospects for the average company. Higher wage levels, adjusted for productivity, affect not only the employee costs the firm directly incurs, but also the labour component in all the goods and services it buys in from local suppliers. Moreover, in an economy with an overvalued currency, interest charges will also almost certainly be higher than average, and high interest rates tend to push up the cost to the firm of land and premises, as well as borrowing for all other forms of capital expenditure. Taking all these locally determined costs together, they are shown as accounting for 60% of the selling prices for manufacturing companies in averagely competitive countries. These costs, however, measured against world prices for the firm's output, will be proportionately 20% higher in economies with overvalued currencies, and 20% lower for those whose currencies are undervalued. Finally, the table shows the firm in the averagely competitive economy making a 10% net profit on sales.

Now consider the options available to companies operating in the economy with the undervalued currency. If these companies sell at world prices, even with normal capacity utilisation, they make huge profits. This happens because their locally determined costs are 60% times 20% less than the world average, giving them a 12% cost advantage, in addition to the 10% net profit for which allowance has already been made. An alternative strategy, which would still give them a 10% net profit on turnover, would be for them to sell at prices some 15% lower than the world average, providing them with an enormously competitive price advantage. They could then use their capital equipment much more intensively, reducing its depreciation charges as a percentage of selling costs by perhaps a fifth, the ratio used in the table. They could do this by relying on the large volume of orders which can be obtained at lower prices to achieve very high capacity working. In practice, the evidence from all the rapidly growing economies is that once reasonable profits on turnover are being made, companies which are already highly competitive tend to go for lower prices and higher volumes of sales, rather than trying to keep prices up. This leads to even more rapid export led growth than would otherwise occur.

The companies in the overvalued economy, on the other hand, face very different prospects. Their higher domestic costs amount to 12% of the world selling prices for their output. These excess charges are more than the 10% net profit made by their competitors in the averagely competitive economies. Their higher locally incurred costs therefore wipe out all profitability for firms in countries with heavily overvalued currencies, if they sell at normal world prices, leaving them trading at a loss. They then have two choices. They can cut their current expenses by paying lower wages and salaries, worsening employment conditions, cancelling investment projects and abandoning research and development programmes. Steps such as these may help in the short term, but are fatally weakening for the future. Alternatively, they can try to sell at higher prices. If they do this, however, unless they are in niche businesses which are not subject to normal competitive pressures, orders are bound to fall away, leading to lower capacity working, and higher depreciation costs per unit of output. To make a 10% net profit on turnover, allowing for lower capacity working, the firms shown with the cost structure in the table in the overvalued country would have to charge nearly 20% above the world average. It is clearly impossible to compete at such high prices, especially against aggressive companies in the undervalued economies. All they can do, therefore, is either to withdraw from the market altogether, or to persevere with prices which are the best compromise they can find between total lack of profitability and holding on to some market share.

It is all too clear which of these three examples is closest to the recent cost-base experience of many of the producers in the more mature economies of the world, particularly in those sectors confronted with competition on consumer goods from newly industrialising countries, many of them in the Far East. Faced with the familiar problem of being uncompetitive, however, why cannot companies facing such conditions increase their productivity to whatever level is required to be competitive with the world average, as all those who advocate industrial strategies and wage restraint are essentially trying to achieve?

Some companies can and will succeed in doing so. These are the ones which will survive even in the harsh conditions portrayed in Table 2.2 for companies in uncompetitive countries. Critical, however, to economies as a whole is not the performance of exceptional companies. It is the average achievement which counts. The required change might be made if it were possible to engineer a sudden huge increase in productivity across the board which competitors could not emulate, without any of the rise in output being absorbed in extra wages and salaries. One has only to look at these conditions, however, to see how completely unrealistic they are. It is far more difficult to increase productivity in slowly growing economies, with depressed levels of investment, low capacity utilisation, and relatively poorly paid staff, than in economies which are already growing fast, and where productivity will inevitably already be increasing rapidly. It is impossible not to share rises in output with the labour force to a substantial degree. What may be possible in isolated companies cannot be done across the board in all companies.

In economies with overvalued exchange rates, the more perspicacious managers of manufacturing companies do not persevere with attempts to improve productivity when they realise that they will never achieve sufficient increases in performance to be able to compete. They conclude that the safest, most profitable and rational strategy is to abandon man-ufacturing in the domestic economy. Some of them decide to buy from abroad whatever their sales forces can sell, perhaps reinvesting the proceeds from selling off factory sites and installations into manufac-turing facilities in other parts of the world. Others sell out to multinational companies, who then use ready-made channels to distribute their output. The less perspicacious plough on until their companies go out of business. One of the paradoxical reasons why industrial strategies will always fail in economies with overvalued currencies is that the better the management in industry at seizing profitable opportunities, the faster the process of de-industrialisation is likely to be. This is why many companies with the best performance records in slow growing economies are those which have closed down their manufacturing operations fastest, and moved them to other countries where costs at the prevailing exchange rates are much lower.

Investment and productivity

A characteristic of much of the investment which tends to occur in rapidly expanding economies strongly reinforces the virtuous growth spiral. This investment is found mainly in manufacturing, especially in light industry, and also some parts of the service sector, where the returns are not only high but also tend to be very rapid. This is an extremely important component of the success of fast growing economies, not least because it explains clearly why some countries have been able to continue expanding exponentially as their standards of living rise. Once the right conditions for growth are established, economies everywhere respond remarkably quickly and consistently, whatever their level of income per head.

It is sometimes assumed that because capital investment is subject to competition, it will therefore always earn about the same overall rate of return. As a corollary, it is often generally supposed that productivity

Table 2.3: Changes in Output per Head of the Working Population between 1977 and 1997 in the United States

	Output Value in constant 1992 $bn	Labour Force 000s	Output per Head $
1977			
Manufacturing	796.5	19,682	40,468
Construction	213.8	3,851	55,518
Mining	82.4	813	101,353
Sub total	1,092.7	24,346	44,882
Agriculture, Forestry & Fishing	61.1	4,143	14,748
Transport & Utilites	346.8	4,713	73,584
Wholesale Trade	201.0	4,723	42,558
Retail Trade	364.5	13,792	26,428
Finance, Insurance & Real Estate	742.7	4,467	166,264
Services	712.5	15,302	46,563
Statistical Discrepancy	37.3		
Not Allocated	–2.4		
Government	717.4	15,127	47,425
1977 GDP	4,273.6	86,613	49,341

increases, as they occur, are roughly evenly spread over the whole of any economy. Neither of these suppositions is remotely true. Taking the productivity issue first, Table 2.3 shows the experience of the USA, far the largest and one of the most diversified economies in the world, over the twenty-year period between 1977 and 1997. Far from productivity increases being evenly spread, they could hardly be more varied.[4] Output per head in agriculture increased at 5.7% per annum over this period. Manufacturing, mining and wholesale trade all increased at around 3% per annum. All the rest of the economy did much worse, with both construction, government and services, in particular, showing significant falls in productivity over the period. The much vaunted financial services sector achieved a cumulative annual increase in output per head over the whole of the two decades of only 0.4% – a dismal result by any standards, although the high absolute output per head of those involved, reflected in correspondingly generous remuneration, should be noted. There are some special reasons for the heavy fall in output per head in services in the US economy which will be discussed later, but these do not change the general pattern, which is replicated in the statistics covering economies across the whole of the developed world.

It is also highly significant that the sectors of the US economy showing the fastest productivity growth were those mostly involved in international markets. This, again, is a characteristic which manifests itself across the whole of the developed and developing world. This strongly suggests that any economy which wants to grow quickly would be wise to try to concentrate as much of its activity as it can in those sectors where large productivity increases are relatively easy to achieve. This can only be done by having the economy's cost base at a competitive international level, which the USA has failed to achieve over a long period. The resulting major reason for the very low increase in output per head in the USA between 1977 and 1997 – only 0.8% per annum on average – is that so much of US economic activity is concentrated in sectors where productivity increases are hardest to achieve.[5] Only 15% of the US labour force is employed in manufacturing and 8% in other high growth areas. All the remaining 77% is employed in areas of the economy where output per head is either close to static, or actually falling.

One of the major reasons why the increase in output resulting from investment is so variable is that the return to the economy as a whole is much greater than the proportion which comes back either as dividends or interest to the people who put up the money to pay for it. The 'private' current return on investment, which investors typically receive, net of inflation, is seldom above about 10%, even in those economies which are doing very well. However, it is by no means only investors who benefit directly from the projects for which they put up their money. Many others do as well.

The management and the employees in the enterprises where the investment has been made, whose productivity rises in consequence, almost invariably share in the benefits by obtaining salary or wage rises. The state also obtains a return through increased tax receipts. In addition, the consumer, who is provided with a better product or service, or a lower price, or both, is also a gainer. If the aggregate rather than just the private rate of return is considered, then across a wide swathe of much of the investment in fast growing economies, the total return to the economy is much higher than 10%. This is not a particularly difficult ratio to calculate from national accounts. For those familiar with the concept, it is the reciprocal of the incremental capital to output ratio. It is often 40% or 50% per annum, and sometimes higher still.

From the point of view of the investor, the build-up period for an investment is not normally particularly important. This is the time between when the investor starts to forgo the alternative uses to which his or her financial resources could be put, and when the investment comes on stream, starting to produce output and income. It is the time taken to build or construct the project into which the money is being put. The investor's concern is that, once the project is in operation, it should be able to provide a sufficient return to cover the interest charges during the build-up period as well as producing a reasonable private return subsequently. For everyone else in the economy, however, and indeed for the economy as a whole, the build-up period provides no return at all because the outlay for the investment is not yet producing anything. There is no additional output to defray the private rates of return, or to contribute to the total rate of return, until the project on which the money has been spent is physically in use.

It is therefore extremely significant that investment projects typically found in rapidly growing economies combine the following characteristics. First, they have a high total rate of return. Second, they have a short build-up period, often of the order of six months, or even less. Third, they tend to be used fully once they are in place, because of the high level of demand which fast growth entails. When these three factors are put together, a truly astonishing cumulative rate of return on investment projects of this type becomes relatively easy to achieve. Those which produce a total rate of return of 50% or more in six months or less, if the return on all the new output thus created is saved and reinvested, can produce a cumulative rate of return in excess of 100%

per annum. This makes it possible for the whole of that part of the economy where this type of investment is taking place not only to double its output every year, but to generate all the savings required for this to happen. This kind of increase can still be seen, despite the recent turmoil, in some parts of the economies of countries such as Korea, Taiwan, and Malaysia and, until recently, Japan, and now in the fast developing parts of China. The huge returns on investment in the production of internationally traded goods and services, and the tendency for them to be reinvested, explain why rapidly growing economies have such high savings ratios, and why their industries, if competently run, have relatively few financing problems.

These large rates of return cannot, however, be attained across the board. It is impossible to obtain 100% returns on outlays in the social infrastructure, housing, public works and the like, except in rare and unusual circumstances. Many private sector investment projects do not fulfil these qualifications either. Anything which takes a long time to build, whether large-scale infrastructure projects, or complex products requiring years of development, will inevitably have a low cumulative total annual rate of return. These are not the projects which produce fast economic growth. Those that do, however, are exactly those with which the most profitable and rapidly growing international trade is concerned.

This is so because they have the same characteristic significant initial costs, with falling cost curves as production builds up and rising output per head comes through. Here, then, is another essential element in the strategy for achieving rapid economic growth. It is to pitch the exchange rate at a parity which enables fast export expansion and import saving to be achieved. This policy is needed not only because it creates and expands sectors of the economy where productivity growth will be very high. In addition, the total rate of return it can achieve is so large that it is capable of generating the whole of the saving required to finance its own expansion, even if this entails doubling its output every year.

Two extremely important conclusions flow from these considerations. The first is that the lower the parity, the more chance there is of achieving not only self-sustaining but self-financing growth at a high rate. The rise in exports which is thus likely to be achieved is more than sufficient to take care of any increased import requirements there may be. Since any import restraints will make the exchange rate higher than it otherwise would be, the case for as few and as low tariffs as possible is reinforced. The second is that the large increase in productivity and output makes it much easier than might be supposed to deal with the inflationary pressures caused by rapid growth. We return to this important point in Chapter 8.

The hugely varying rates of return to the whole economy achieved by different classes of investment project may also throw light on an important and puzzling economic growth paradox. Compared to the international average, the USA achieves a relatively high return on the comparatively low level of investment it undertakes. This is why the growth rate of the American economy averaged a little over 3% per annum over recent decades despite its low reinvestment rate.[6] By contrast, many of the fast growing economies in the Pacific Rim score very poorly in this respect. Most of their high growth can be accounted for by large amounts of increased inputs – labour, education, and particularly high levels of capital investment. The explanation for the poor returns, particularly to investment, in many Pacific Rim countries, surely lies with the mixture of investment projects which are undertaken. Countries like Korea, which have spent, at government instigation, large sums of money on grandiose industrial schemes to produce ships, chemicals, cement, and so on, have a large proportion of their total investment producing low cumulative returns. This balances off the very high compound returns produced in the large Korean light industrial sector to produce an unimpressive average. The USA, with proportionately far smaller involvement by the government in industry, has avoided these pitfalls. What could the US economy achieve if its internationally tradable sectors had the competitive advantages which Korean light industry has had, unaccompanied by the cronyism, corruption and waste which the Korean *chaebol* system brought in train?

Altering the exchange rate

Is it possible for the exchange rate to be influenced by policy changes? Or is the parity entirely determined, as monetarists claim, by market forces over which governments have little or no control? If it is really the market which controls exchange rates, and governments are powerless bystanders, then attempts by monetary authorities to position the foreign exchange value of the currency where they want it to be are bound to fail, unless they simply ape the market's wishes. If, on the other hand, government policy can have a powerful impact on the parity of the currency, then the scope for using exchange rate policy to shape the performance of the economy generally is much enhanced.

One of the most important tenets of the monetarist school is that the exchange rate for all economies is very largely, if not entirely, fixed by market forces, so that no action taken by the government to change it will make any significant difference. Monetarists have built up an elaborate theory which is intended to prove that there is an equilibrium exchange rate towards which every parity has a strong tendency to return. The traditional form of this theory was known as the Law of One Price, and the modern form is sometimes referred to as International Monetarism. It states that if attempts are made by the authorities to move to a parity away from the one established as the equilibrium point by the markets, then differential rates of inflation will soon pull it back to where it should be.

In particular, it is argued that any attempts to make the economy more competitive by devaluing will automatically cause a rise in inflation which will rapidly erode any increased competitiveness temporarily secured. This will leave the economy not only as uncompetitive as it was before, but with an extra-inflationary problem to add to its other difficulties. It is also contended that if, as a result of a temporary disequilibrium, the currency is overvalued this will exercise a strong downward pressure on the price level, thus reducing the rate of inflation without sacrificing competitiveness, except perhaps in the short term. There is little doubt that many people believe this theory to a greater or lesser degree. What is there to confirm that this proposition is correct?

The reasons why devaluations do not always produce a corresponding increase in inflation will be reviewed in detail in Chapter 8. Suffice to say for the moment that the empirical evidence for the monetarists' contentions is extremely weak, and that there are good reasons, both theoretical and practical, for believing that on this issue they are wholly wrong. A review of the amply available statistics on the impact across the world of exchange rate changes on the price level, is all that is required to establish whether there is an iron law which determines that parities cannot be altered without differential inflation rates at once starting to bring them back to equilibrium again.

All the evidence shows beyond any reasonable doubt that monetarist contentions that exchange rates are entirely a function of market forces over which governments have no control cannot be correct. Without question, governments can, and frequently have, changed both the nominal and the real exchange rates of the economies for which they were responsible by very large amounts. A conspicuous case was the huge rise in the rate for sterling which took place at the end of the 1970s and the early part of the 1980s. This was a direct result of the tightening of the money supply and the increase in interest rates which began under the Labour government of the time, and which was continued and reinforced by the incoming Conservative administration after 1979. As a result, the nominal value of the pound – excluding allowance for any differences in the inflation rate between sterling and other currencies – rose on the foreign exchanges from $1.74 in 1977 to $2.32 in 1980, an increase of 33%, and against the Deutsche Mark from DM3.85 in 1978 to DM4.54 in 1981, an increase of 18%.[7] This happened despite far above average inflation in Britain over this period, thus enormously decreasing the country's competitiveness. In consequence the real exchange rate – allowing for varying inflation rates in different countries – rose by 25%, with calamitous results for British industry.

Another telling example comes from the early part of the Reagan presidency when the USA drove up the nominal value of the dollar by no less than 60% against the Deutsche Mark (from DM1.83 to DM2.94) between 1979 and 1985,[8] although the inflation rates in the two countries were similar. A current example of a currency being held at a rate which is far from a market clearing rate is the *franc fort* policy pursued by the French, though now subsumed into the euro. The cost to the French economy in holding the rate for the franc against the Deutsche Mark has been enormous. Growth languished, investment slumped, and unemployment has risen to nearly 12%[9] of the labour force, while the economy has had to be forced by deflation to run a balance of payments surplus without which the *franc fort* policy would have collapsed.

Governments can also bring down the external value of their currencies if they want to do so. Between 1982 and 1989 the nominal rate for the US dollar against the yen fell by an astonishing 45% (from ¥249 to ¥138), while the rate for the dollar against the Deutsche Mark went down by 38% (from DM2.84 to DM1.76) in just four years, between 1984 and 1988.[10] Of course, there is a limit to the extent to which governments can resist market pressures, as the USA discovered when the dollar was devalued at the beginning of the 1970s. There is still, however, considerable scope for monetary authorities in any country to choose whether they want to be at the high or the low end of the range of possibilities which the market will accept.

Nor does a longer perspective do anything to improve monetarist theory's credibility. One of the most striking cases of a successful devaluation was that of France at the end of the 1950s. The government of Charles de Gaulle, faced with increasing competition from Germany as the Common Market became established, devalued the French franc twice, by a total of 29%.[11] Inflation in France rose sharply for a few months, but by nothing like as much as the devaluation. Within a year or so it dropped back to where it had been before. French competitiveness *vis à vis* the German economy was established. The result was a long boom which took the French average growth rate to 5.5% per annum for a decade and a half, more than doubling the national income in fifteen years.[12]

The evidence clearly shows that it is well within the power of any government to choose from a spectrum of possibilities where it wants the real exchange rate to be, and over the long term to hold it there within reasonably narrow margins. Of course there will be short-term fluctuations, but these are not important. It is the medium-term trend which counts. There is without doubt a range of policies which any government can pursue to change the exchange rate, and then hold it at or near the preferred level, all of which need to be used in a co-ordinated fashion.

First, and underlying all else, is the monetary stance adopted by the government. There is overwhelming evidence that tight money policies, and the high interest rates which go with them, pull the exchange rate up, and that more accommodating monetary policies and lower interest rates bring it down. Study after study has shown that interest rates have a powerful effect on the exchange rate, significantly greater than other changes, for example alterations in the availability or cost of raw materials such as oil.

Second, the actions and stance of both the government and the central bank in dealing with the foreign exchange market have a major influence where expectations and opinion are almost as important as the underlying realities. If the government has a clearly expressed view that the exchange rate is too high or too low, the market will respond, as it did for example in the United States during the 1980s. The operations of central banks in buying or selling foreign currencies can and must be made consistent with other government policies.

Third, the government should have a clear strategy as regards foreign trade balances. In the short term, fluctuations are unavoidable, but in the longer term these can to a large extent be ironed out. If balance of payments surpluses are allowed to accumulate, as has happened in Japan, there will be strong upward pressure on the exchange rate. The converse is clearly the case, reinforcing the arguments for taking a liberal view on protection, and in general avoiding impediments to imports. The balance of payments is also a function of the level of domestic activity. Deflation produces a larger surplus or smaller deficit, and upwards pressure on the parity, and reflation the opposite. The strength of domestic demand is therefore a further important determinant of the exchange rate.

Fourth, the government has a considerable degree of control over capital movements, with or without formal exchange controls. Any policy which encourages repatriation of capital and discourages capital outflows – particularly high domestic interest rates – will push up the exchange rate, and vice versa. One of the problems which may occur if a policy of growth based on increased competitiveness is successfully pursued is that capital may be attracted in undesirably large quantities as a result of exceptional investment opportunities. This may make it more difficult to keep the exchange rate down. The answer to this problem is likely to be lower interest rates, if these are feasible, or deliberately deciding not to fund the whole of the borrowing requirement to discourage an inward flow of money. Domestic sources of capital funds can also be encouraged by concentrating economic activity as far as possible in those parts of the economy which can generate their own savings and investment at a high rate. If there are enough domestic savings to finance all the economy's capital needs, there is no merit in stopping any surplus being invested abroad. Still less is it sensible to insist on capital being repatriated which is not required, unless circumstances are such that it is necessary to get the exchange rate up. If the exchange rate needs to be kept down, there are, on the contrary, positive advantages to capital exports.

Finally, allowance needs to be made for the well known 'J' curve effect. If the value of the currency falls, there is a tendency for imports to stay at more or less their previous volume while the domestic revenue from exports decreases because the exchange rate has gone down. This produces a worsening in the balance of payments position until the volume of exports increases in response to lower prices. If the value of the currency falls slowly, a succession of 'J' curve effects flows from each move downwards in the exchange rate, giving the impression that no improvement is in sight. The United States had something of this experience in the mid 1980s. The reverse tendencies are to be found if the exchange rate appreciates, giving the false impression for a few months, until market forces work their way through, that making exports less competitive does not make the balance of payments position worse. Part of the reason for the 'J' curve, however, is the belief by importers that any reduction in the profitability of their activities may shortly be reversed by an appreciation of the exchange rate, caused by the authorities trying to reverse an unwanted change from the previous parity. If it is clear, however, that a radical change in policy on the exchange rate has taken place, which is unlikely to be reversed, it is possible to alter the behaviour of importers much more quickly.

With the battery of policy instruments available, governments can therefore determine the level of the exchange rate within wide limits. There is ample empirical evidence of government instigated parity movements which have been successfully accomplished. Obviously it is impossible for all countries to move towards being competitive with each other simultaneously, although it would be possible for the world economy as a whole to adopt more expansionist policies. The evidence shows that it is practical for any individual country to decide where, within wide bounds, on the spectrum of international competitiveness, it wants to be, and, having chosen that position, to stay fairly close to its preferred location.

Is it true, therefore, that the markets can be bucked? They do not need to be. There are internally consistent policies which any government can adopt to hold the exchange rate down at least to a level which allows the current account to be balanced with full employment and a sustainable rate of growth. These include low interest rates, an accommodating monetary strategy, keeping the economy open to imports which are competitive with domestic supplies, and encouraging capital exports. There are also other policies, adopted for years by the French, for example, but also, perhaps less obviously, by the USA, which will hold the parity at a higher level than it really should be. Provided the markets are satisfied that the government has adopted a policy stance with which it is determined to continue, stability can be achieved over a wide band of different degrees of exchange rate competitiveness. It is not then necessary to buck the market. This is why, by choosing the right policy mix, it is always possible to choose a macro-economic stance which will ensure that external balance is combined with full employment and rapid growth.

Economics and history

We have seen that rapid growth takes place in economies which are competitive in world markets and which start with the advantage of costs at least as low as their competitors. This enables them to expand their exports, without suffering from excessive import penetration, thus providing them with opportunities to grow without the constraint of balance of payments problems. Internal demand can then be kept at a high and rising level, without undue inflationary pressures developing. These conditions were established and maintained for the USA during the nineteenth, and some of the first half of the twentieth century, albeit behind high tariff barriers which had other disadvantages. They applied to most of the rest of Western Europe – excluding Britain, which grew much more slowly – during the quarter of a century after the end of World War II. At least until the recent instability, the same conditions were to be found in the fast growing economies in the Far East. The reason why such sustained growth was achieved, why living standards much more than doubled in the course of less than two decades, why unemployment barely existed, and inflation was in nearly all cases relatively low and stable, was that the macro-economic conditions were right.

To achieve high exports, any economy has to sell at home and abroad both the output of its labour and of its other factors of production, taken together, at competitive prices. If it does so, it will be able to achieve import saving and export led growth. If it fails to do so, especially by a wide margin, it will plunge into import led stagnation. The only practical way of making any economy competitive is to position the exchange rate correctly. This is why the parity of the currency is so critically important. There is no other feasible way in which any country can change the price it charges for the whole of its output sufficiently to make the necessary difference.

The higher the proportion of any country's GDP involved in world trade, the more obvious it is that its exchange rate needs to be correctly aligned *vis à vis* its competitors. Perhaps one of the illusions under which the USA has suffered is that, because its foreign trade exposure is comparatively small, the impact on the economy of unmanageable competition from abroad may therefore have appeared to be relatively slight. Whether the parity of the dollar on the foreign exchanges was appropriate for the interests of the domestic economy may therefore have been given less attention than it should have been. In fact, the exchange rate of the dollar against all other world currencies has been as critically important in determining the US growth rate as it has been to all economies exposed to any significant degree of international competition, as the account of US economic history in subsequent chapters clearly shows.

In sum, the case set out in this chapter is a simple one. For any economy, pricing its output at a competitive level by maximising appropriate macro-economic policies is the key to expansion. The policy instrument available to any sovereign government to provide growth conditions is to position the exchange rate at a level which will enable its country's goods and services to compete successfully both at home and in world markets. The acid test for any theoretical framework such as this is not, however, that it should be able to produce explanations for particular events. The criterion to be applied is a much harsher one than this. To be worth while, and sufficiently convincing to form a basis for policy making in the future, it should be able to provide a general explanation for all the major historical developments which fall within its ambit. The next four chapters set out to show that this can be done. The test to be applied is whether a convincing account can be given not only of events where the outcome is reasonably clear and agreed, but also ones which have puzzled generations of historians and economists. Why did economic growth not take off before the eighteenth century, and what are all the components which needed to be in place before it could occur? Why, once the Industrial Revolution got under way, mainly in Britain, did the British allow their lead to be whittled away, and could this development have been avoided? To ask the same question another way, why did the USA and many of the economies on the continent of Europe grow much more quickly than the British economy during the half-century leading up to World War I? Why did the US economy perform so well in the 1920s, and so poorly in the 1930s? Why did the French and many other countries in Europe achieve mediocre results for the whole of the inter-war period, while Britain and Germany, after doing poorly in the 1920s, both achieved much better economic results in the 1930s, in Germany's case astoundingly so?

Turning to the post-World War II period, why did the USA, in a dominant position when the hostilities ended, gradually allow its lead to be whittled away, and could this have been avoided? Why did all the West European economies grow very rapidly during the 1950s and 1960s, but then move into a period of relative stagnation from the mid 1970s onwards? How do we account for the fact that Britain performed relatively poorly throughout this period? How do we explain the astonishing rise of the Japanese economy, but with over forty years of strong growth suddenly coming to a wrenching halt in the early 1990s? Why have the Tiger economies performed so well, and why have other countries, which might appear to have the some of the same characteristics, failed to emulate their achievements? What explains the recent turmoil among many of the Pacific Rim countries, including the Tigers, and what lessons should be drawn from this experience about globalisation, free trade and international capital movements?

The theme which runs through the next four chapters is that history has been shaped to a much greater degree than most people realise by the economic policies which the governments of all the world's economies have pursued, particularly those to do with the macro-economy. It is decisions taken on such matters as interest rates, the control of the money supply, the systems for regulating the creation and control of credit, and fixing the exchange rate which have been crucial. Vital though these decisions may have been, however, they were generally taken without any clear view of their likely impact. Governments had no robust and reliable theory to guide them. As a result, to a remarkable extent, those responsible for economic policy in all countries during the last two hundred years have been flying blind. They have had to rely on the conventional wisdom, much of which was inadequate, and some of which was simply wrong. Those political leaders who ran their economies more successfully than others did so mostly because they took the right decisions, often for the wrong reasons, rather than because they were working within a coherent framework of well conceived and articulated ideas about how the economies for which they were responsible really worked.

Into the vacuum left by lack of adequate economic theory marched an army of people with axes to grind. With no clearly defined reasons for choosing one policy rather than another, the scope for sectional interests abounded. This throws up another pattern which runs through all the next four chapters. As any of the world's economies began to prosper over the last two centuries, the centre of gravity of political influence shifted. In all of them, there has been a tendency for first generation entrepreneurs to metamorphose into second and third generation successors who wanted to hold on to their wealth. As societies became richer, financial institutions prospered, particularly banks, run generally by people with a marked tendency to caution, aversion to risk and demand for safe but relatively high returns. Political power then shifted from new money to old, from industry to finance and from risk taking entrepreneurs to the safe hands of company bureaucrats. With this shift of political power went changes in macro-economic policy which suited those with accumulated wealth. Unfortunately, and no doubt unwittingly, the financial circumstances which were wanted by the now established groups in power tended to be those which produced exactly the wrong conditions for fast growth. Stable currencies, as free as possible from exchange rate fluctuations, with low rates of inflation, coupled if possible with relatively high real interest rates, provide precisely the conditions in which growth slows, manufacturing goes into a relative decline, exports languish, and deflationary policies – seldom exceptionally painful for those in power – become the order of the day.

This is largely the explanation for another thread which runs through the history of the last two centuries. Major upheavals, whether caused by lost wars, internal revolutions or abrupt and drastic social and political changes, have tended to be the precursors of much better economic performance, as Mancur Olson pointed out.[13] This is the correlative of the tendency for the reverse to occur, as countries develop and maintain stable social fabrics which both stifle new, non-conforming energetic people, as well as producing a macro-economic environment in which it is relatively hard for them to prosper and break through.

A final and crucial point to be made about macro-economic policy – again contrary to much received wisdom – is that any sovereign country has a remarkably wide capacity to make decisions on the crucial variables with which it is concerned. As we have seen, it is not true that any individual country is hemmed in by the global economy into being unable to make any changes. Of course, they have to be made in a co-ordinated way, so that the total policy stance makes sense. Within this constraint, however, there is nothing to stop any country making radical alterations to its policy on interest rates, its money supply and its exchange rate, with all that flows from the impact such changes bring in train.

The implication is that history, especially during the two centuries since the beginning of the Industrial Revolution, need not necessarily have taken the form it did. Had different and perfectly feasible decisions been taken by those in power, Britain's lead need not have been whittled away in the nineteenth and again in the second half of the twentieth century, growth need not have slowed up from the 1970s onwards in what was then the European Economic Community. In addition, World War II might well have been avoided, Middle America need not have had stagnant real incomes for a generation, much Third World poverty could have been eradicated, and the world could have been a very much richer place than it is now. Humanity has paid a heavy price for the failure of economists to explain better how the world's economies work and grow.

3
The Industrial Revolution

'There be three things which make a nation great and prosperous: a fertile soil, busy workshops, easy conveyance for men and goods from place to place.'

Francis Bacon

Civilisation began some eleven thousand years ago, shortly after the end of the last Ice Age. Our ancestors, after hundreds of thousands of years of formative experience in foraging bands, began to form permanent settlements, as agriculture began and the very small number of types of animals and birds which are key to farming started to be domesticated. In about 8500 BC, in the Middle Eastern Fertile Crescent, wheat, peas and olives began to be harvested, followed by barley, lentils, chickpeas, flax and musk melons. Sheep and goats were evidently the first animals to be reared in captivity for food and milk, followed by cattle, and horses for riding and pulling. Similar developments began in China about a thousand years later.[1]

An interesting and important question is at what stage did anything resembling economic activity begin? It seems plausible, before there were any settlements, that there were few significant transactions with any economic content. It is hard to believe, however, that as soon as farming and villages of any size formed there was not a need for the division of labour, the exchange of goods and services, and the establishment of some kind of recording of obligations arising from transactions which could not be simultaneous. At a time when there was nothing resembling money – a much later invention – debts, the beginning of a credit system, were probably initially recorded in the memory of the head of the settlement. It is likely that this was an important constraint on the growth in size which the villages of the time were able to achieve, and may form an important part of the explanation for the long period from the dawn of civilisation to the emergence of towns and then cities.

The first recognisable states make their appearance, again in the Fertile Crescent, about 3700 BC. To enable them to function a fair degree of economic organisation must have been essential, as indeed the evidence shows was the case.[2] The form of government was very much from the top down, but could not operate without significant division of labour. An elaborate system for recording debts and obligations was required, and ample evidence shows that this took the form of baked clay tablets, organised largely by the priesthood who formed the backbone of the state administration. This system provided an important step towards the creation of money, since the obligations recorded by the clay tablets could be transferred or assigned. Systems for keeping track of debts, owing from some and due to others, were thus created which were not quite money, because both the debtors and creditors were specific individuals or groups of people. It nevertheless provided a relatively flexible system for recording and discharging obligations, needed in an economy which was too big for everyone to know everyone else, and where there were too many debts and credits for any one person to be able to keep track of them all.

The next stage was the invention of money proper. Barter tokens were minted by the Chinese in the second millennium BC, but true coinage was invented in the western world in Asia Minor about 700 BC, in the Kingdom of Lydia. Originally made of electrum, a local natural amalgam of gold and silver, the first coins were produced by the fabled Croesus of Lydia (died 546 BC) in the sixth century BC.[3] Their value, which became separated from their intrinsic worth, had the major advantage of not requiring the involvement of any personal debtor or creditor. Their merit depended solely in the trust of those who used them, backed by the state which issued them, that others would recognise and accept them. The invention of coinage greatly increased the scope for trade, and it is no coincidence that the explosion in exchange of goods, and the establishment of colonies within the Mediterranean basin which followed, occurred over the next century or two after coins first appeared on the scene.

The ancient world, therefore, succeeded in developing the credit systems necessary to enable an extensive trade and commercial network to exist, to make it possible to establish large-scale states, to operate complex tax systems, and to form, maintain and fund large-scale armies. At first sight, it might appear that the Roman Empire, in particular, had all the necessary requirements to enable a beginning to be made on applying technology to the perennial problems of economic shortage. For nearly four hundred years after the consolidation which took place under Caesar Augustus (63 BC – AD 14), it encompassed a large and varied area, where peace and order generally prevailed. There was a relatively efficient and impartial legal system. The Roman Empire was plagued intermittently by inflationary problems, but there were substantial accumulations of capital. Interestingly, the Roman period is the only one when until very recently most of Europe was covered by a single currency.

Some industrial processes, such as smelting, were well known. A considerable quantity of theory about scientific matters, mostly developed by the Greeks, was available. Indeed, a steam engine of sorts, used as a toy, had been developed by the Greek polymath Hero, in Alexandria, one of the centres of Greek learning. There was a substantial artisan class, capable of contributing practical knowledge and experience to new ideas about production methods. The standards of education, especially among the more prosperous classes, were reasonably high. And yet, despite all of these apparently potentially favourable circumstances, there was almost no technological development at all for hundreds of years. Why did nothing resembling the Industrial Revolution occur? There appear to be several reasons, some of the more significant of which form an interlocking pattern.

First, there was nothing equivalent to the body of scientific knowledge that had accumulated in Europe by the time the Industrial Revolution got under way there, which was a very different matter from the speculations of ancient Greek philosophers. It is true that many of the early inventions which got industrialisation started in Britain were developed by highly skilled journeyman engineers rather than intellectuals. Examples are John Kay's flying shuttle (1733), Richard Arkwright's water frame (1769), James Hargreave's spinning jenny (1770),[4] and the steam engines developed by Thomas Newcomen as early as 1712, but greatly improved by James Watt from 1769 onwards,[5] Nevertheless, the climate of opinion in which all these people worked had undoubtedly been heavily influenced by the writings of those who had discovered the scientific method, and who had established the system of experimentation and verification on which technical advance was to be built. This was a far cry from the methods employed by the most influential intellectual leaders in the ancient world, particularly the most important

Greek teachers such as Plato (427–347 BC) and Aristotle (384–322 BC), who relied much more on derivation of conclusions from first principles than on empirical experiments.

Second, the Industrial Revolution was not a complete break with the past, in the sense that new practical inventions suddenly started materialising in a way which had never happened before. On the contrary, it was an acceleration of a process which had been slowly gathering pace for hundreds of years, providing a much more formidable basis for advance than existed at any stage during the ancient world. As well as high profile inventions such as the printing press, clocks, eyeglasses, and lateen sails, all of which were of crucial significance, there had been many other improvements in technology which had slowly accumulated over the centuries, or been imported from other parts of the world. These included the manufacture and use of gunpowder and paper, techniques for smelting many metals, and processes for handling a wide variety of other materials from glass and porcelain to sugar and tobacco.

Third, as well as technical knowledge, the Romans and Greeks lacked what may have been an equally crucial intellectual component, which was an adequate mathematical system. The whole of the ancient world operated on systems of counting such as Roman numerals. There was no true concept of zero. No calculations were possible which were more complicated than could be handled on an abacus. The universal modern numbering system was invented in India in the fourth century AD, and took eight hundred years to reach Europe via the Islamic Arab states. It was first publicised in the West by Leonardo Fibonnacci (c.1170–c.1250), also known as Leonardo of Pisa, in his *Book of the Calculator*, which appeared in 1202, and which rapidly led to the adoption of the so called Arabic – though originally Indian – notation first in Italy and then throughout Europe.[6] Not only did the new numbering system make it much easier to carry out relatively complicated calculations, it also made it possible for mathematics to develop greatly more complex ways of solving problems than had been possible previously. It is no coincidence that the advance of mathematics in Europe began to accelerate rapidly once the new notation had been introduced.

Fourth, another major requirement for the development of as complex a division of labour, and hence as complicated an economy as the Industrial Revolution required, was a much more sophisticated credit system than the ancient world ever had. Until well into the Middle Ages, no true banks existed. Of course, before then, there were merchants who kept their stores of wealth in the form of gold coins, and who were willing to lend against their security, and there were plenty of loan sharks and money lenders and changers in the ancient world, many of them ex-slaves.[7] The inefficiency of the old mathematical systems, however, and the difficulties involved in maintaining records before printing and paper manufacture had been perfected, both militated against sophisticated banking operations. These problems were solved by the advent of the new mathematical notation, major improvements in paper production, the invention of double entry book keeping, and the subsequent rapid development of accountancy as a profession. All added to the ease with which complicated records could now be kept. The result was the development of true banks, first in Italy and then throughout Europe, as great banking dynasties established themselves – the Medici in Italy, the Fuggers in Germany – with many smaller-scale banking enterprises following in their wakes.

Fifth, even the development of banking proper left the economies of the time heavily dependent on adequate supplies of gold and silver to provide sufficient coinage to make the financial system operate. Some leverage could be provided by the use of financial instruments such as bills of exchange, but the scope was limited until the invention of the next major step forward, which was the development of paper currency. Although, again, there had been precedents in China, the issuing of notes began in the West at the end of the seventeenth century, led by the Bank of England, established in 1694 as a private corporation, the status it retained until it was nationalised in 1946.[8] Bank notes were not originally designed for general use, but were issued in large denominations, mostly for the financing of trade. Essentially, they were bearer cheques, drawn on the Bank of England. Their impact, however, was to make it possible to separate still further the limited availability of gold and silver and the increasing amount of credit which could be extended by the banking system as a whole.

Sixth, even apart from the shortage of technical opportunities, the unconducive intellectual climate, the lack of appropriate methods of calculation, and the undeveloped credit system, there may be another perhaps even more fundamental reason why the ancient world failed to industrialise. Its society was too regimented, too top-down, too stable and therefore, despite the wrenching changes which periodically took place at the top, too stagnant and lacking in vigour to embark on the kind of free thinking progress that the Industrial Revolution required. It is no coincidence that much of the early impetus in Britain and elsewhere came from dissident, independent people, who were excluded because of their religion or for other reasons from the established mainstream, but who were not precluded by convention or fear of retribution from trying new ways of doing things. It was the combination of their attitude of mind with the availability of all the other components which the ancient world lacked which triggered off the start of industrialisation on a scale which was never reversible, and which was to spread and transform the whole of the rest of the world.

Even if the ancient Mediterranean culture of the Greeks and Romans failed to give birth to industrialisation, it does not necessarily follow that it could not have begun somewhere else before it did in fact begin in eighteenth-century Britain. Some of the factors required were available elsewhere, and perhaps most of them in some cases. There were major unified states in China, India and in the Islamic countries, and, for a considerable period, in central Asia too, as well as many smaller, reasonably stable polities, most of them with access to more technology than the ancient world possessed. In varying degrees they were in touch with at least some of the cultural and intellectual developments taking place in Europe. The state which came closest to breaking through into industrialisation was China during the fifteenth century, but the progress made was snuffed out by the country's leaders, who turned back to traditional ways.[9] India, on the other hand, never showed any more signs of sustained industrial development than the Romans, despite the ability of the Mughal culture to build the Taj Mahal, its high point of excellence both in design and execution. Nor were smaller nations any better at producing sustained economic growth. On the contrary, it was in Europe, divided into a large number of relatively small states, that there began to be a cumulative increase in living standards, starting early in the second millennium, which eventually produced the Industrial Revolution, and the transformation in prospects for humanity which it brought in train.

Early industrialisation in Europe

The Industrial Revolution, which began in Europe in the eighteenth century, rested on a foundation built over hundreds of years. Since the Middle Ages, and at least since the fourteenth century, there had been a slow increase in output per head in Europe, set back from time to time by wars, pestilence and bad government. This growth had come about partly as a result of improved agriculture, partly as a result of increased trade, based on the availability of an adequate credit system, but mainly because of the application of new ideas, some based on novel technology, to a wide variety of production processes.

The advent of the printing press vastly reduced the cost of producing books, and thus of disseminating knowledge. The developments in ship design and navigation greatly decreased the costs of trading, while opening up large sections of the world which had previously been unknown to Europeans. The resulting exchange of products enabled gains from specialisation in the production of goods and agricultural products to be realised which had never been available before. There was a steady improvement in the working of metals, providing the basis for the production of machinery. The Renaissance and the Enlightenment provided a ferment of ideas, some of which fed through to industry to provide a much clearer explanation of how industrial processes worked. Not least of these were advances in mathematics, mentioned previously, which made it easier for calculations relating to production processes to be done quickly and accurately. At the same time, there was a steady accumulation of practical knowledge acquired by increasingly skilled labour forces, capable of putting new ideas into operation.

The Industrial Revolution quickened and began to gather pace faster in Britain during the eighteenth century than elsewhere, allowing the British to take over economic leadership from the Netherlands. During the previous two centuries, the Dutch had built up a formidable economy based on a combination of trade and commerce, which had provided a higher standard of living than had previously been achieved anywhere. As was to happen so frequently in the future, however, the accumulation of wealth and financial power, which appeared to make the state so strong, gradually became its undoing. The exchange rate rose, and the rising costs of doing business in the Netherlands, compared to elsewhere, caused economic activity to drift away, not least to Britain.[10] The Dutch economy stagnated, and its lead was lost, though the reasons why this occurred were not appreciated at the time, or for a long period to come.

In the meantime, Britain had moved further away from the feudal system of the Middle Ages than most other countries in Europe. There was a more highly developed system of contract law, and generally a less arbitrary system of government than on the continent. As a result of successfully developed trading patterns, there was a reasonably sophisticated banking system and accumulations of capital which could be mobilised for risk ventures. There was stable government. Above all, there was an entrepreneurial class, much of it, characteristically, excluded from mainstream political life in the form of the non-conformists, which was attracted to commerce and manufacturing. There were also major agricultural interests, with much of the land owned by forward looking landowners, involved in exploiting new ideas in agricultural husbandry.

The Industrial Revolution thus got under way in Britain in textiles, pottery, mining and metal working, aided by improvements in communications such as the development of canals. A combination of outworking and factories led to big increases in output when production processes were broken down into individual specialised functions, as Adam Smith (1723–1790) accurately noted in *The Wealth of Nations*. This extremely influential book, published in 1776 at a remarkably early stage of the Industrial Revolution, contained an exceptionally powerful set of ideas about the changes taking place in the industrial and commercial worlds, and how government policy should be organised to take advantage of them. If the early pace in the development of economics set by Adam Smith had been maintained, the subsequent history of the world might have been very different.

Not only did the early Industrial Revolution involve rising living standards on average for the British people compared to those elsewhere, it also greatly enhanced Britain's power in the world. This made it possible for the British to build and maintain a dominant navy and to deploy and finance the coalition of land forces which eventually won them victory in the Napoleonic Wars. Thereafter, it enabled the British to extend their control over ever increasing areas of the world until, by three-quarters of the way through the nineteenth century, Britain ruled directly or indirectly about a quarter of the land surface of the globe. The accumulation of an empire on this scale undoubtedly provided Britain with ready access to raw materials and sources of supply of cheap food, as well as a partially protected export market. The relative decline in the British economy as the territories the British controlled grew in number, however, calls into question whether this endeavour entailed a net benefit. Faster economic growth elsewhere strongly suggests that the effort and bias in policy involved in building up and running the British Empire, and the cost of maintaining it, were more trouble than they were worth.

While France had at least as high a standard of living as Britain in the early eighteenth century, and perhaps higher, many of the other circumstances needed to get industry moving were also in place. The French, however, were much slower to take advantage of the new opportunities available in manufacturing. Partly this was the result of the arbitrary characteristics of the *ancien régime*, which lacked the contract legal system introduced shortly after the 1789 French Revolution.[11] Partly it was a matter of social pressures, also related to the sense of values of the pre-revolutionary period, which held industry and commerce in relatively low esteem. The result was that French industry tended to concentrate on the manufacture of individually produced items, some of them widely recognised as being of exceptionally high quality, rather than moving to mass production methods. French furniture, tapestries, china and jewellery were internationally renowned, but the cottage industry techniques used for producing them are not the stuff of which industrial revolutions are made.

Germany also suffered from disadvantages, many of them similar to those in France, compounded by the patchwork of small states which made up the country, each with its own tariff and economic policies. The southern states of Europe, Spain, Portugal, Italy and Greece, were all much poorer, and in a weaker position to start industrialising, as indeed remained the case for a century or more. The Netherlands, which had grown richer during the eighteenth century than anywhere else, faltered as its trading and financial success undermined its domestic industry – a story to be repeated many times in the years to come. It was therefore Britain which made the running for a long time into the nineteenth century.

Nineteenth-century Europe

Controversy over the value of the currency has a long history in Britain. Before the Industrial Revolution had really begun, in the reign of William III, the silver coinage which was circulating in the country had been debased by clipping.[12] The effect was to devalue the clipped silver currency in relation to gold. As a result, by 1695, the gold guinea, which was originally worth twenty shillings had risen to being worth thirty. Much of the international trade of the time was conducted in silver shillings. What should be done? Should the value of the silver coinage be re-established at the prevailing value, or should it be restored to its previous parity? Leading contestants in the dispute which followed were the philosopher John Locke (1632–1704), who advocated the former view, and Sir Isaac Newton (1642–1727), who favoured the latter. The King accepted Locke's deflationary advice – a dismal portent for the future. The consequences, as Newton predicted, were falling prices and depressed business conditions. Sir Isaac Newton nevertheless became Master of the Mint, and in 1711 he fixed the price of the pound at £3 17s 9d per ounce of gold. Apart from suspensions during and following the Napoleonic Wars and World War I, and two short breaks during the nineteenth century, caused by temporary financial panics, this parity remained intact until 1931.

The next major controversy over macro-economic policy took place towards the end of the Napoleonic Wars. The strain imposed on the British economy during the long wartime period, stretching almost without a break from 1793 to 1815, had stimulated output. The economy was much larger and more productive at the end of the wars than it was at the beginning. The high level of demand had, however, led to substantial inflation, which had nearly doubled the price level. Britain had gone off the Gold Standard in 1797 because the country banks of the time could not meet the demand for cash caused by the threat of an invasion. Too many holders of their bank notes wished to change them into gold. The banks were therefore freed to increase the note issue without gold backing, both in response to the increase in government borrowing to finance the wars, as well as the additional demand for money resulting from expanding national output. By 1810, prices had risen an estimated 76%[13] compared to 1790, and this was of course reflected in the price of gold, which had risen proportionately.

Had prices risen because the money supply had been increased? Or was extra money required to accommodate the growing need for cash as both prices rose and the size of the economy became larger, with the fundamental causes of inflation lying elsewhere? This controversy – still central to economic policy formulation – was the key issue addressed by the *Report from the Select Committee on the High Price of Gold Bullion*, published in 1810, which set out the arguments between the 'Currency School' and the 'Banking School'. The Currency School maintained that under a 'purely metallic standard', any loss of gold to, or influx from, other countries would result immediately and automatically in a decrease or increase in the amount of money in circulation. The resulting rigid control of the money supply would provide the discipline to keep price rises at bay. With a mixed currency of metal and paper, however, this system could not operate satisfactorily, unless it was managed as precisely as if it depended on the amount of gold backing the currency. Any deviation from this principle would lead to inflation.

The Banking School, on the other hand, denied that a purely gold-based currency would operate in the manner claimed for it by the Currency School. Because of hoarding and other uses to which gold could be put, it was far from clear that the amount available to back the currency was as constant as the Currency School claimed it would be. Furthermore, it was contended that the Currency School greatly overestimated the risks involved in expanding paper money. The Banking School believed, on the contrary, that the need for prudence in the process of competitive banking would exercise a necessary restraint on the issue of paper money. This approach would have led to a much more accommodating monetary stance and a lower exchange rate for sterling, but it was not to be. The Committee came down in favour of the currency principle, by advocating a return to the Gold Standard at the 1797 parity, despite the increase in prices which had taken place. The majority concluded that the price rises during the wars had come about because monetary discipline had slipped, and that the only way to secure financial stability in the future was to get the pound back to where it had been previously in terms of its value in relation to gold. The views which prevailed in this report, setting as they did the tone of British financial policy for many years into the future, were to have a profound impact on Britain's economic history to the present day.

Despite the reservations of the minority of the Committee, which included David Ricardo (1772–1823), sterling was restored to its pre-war parity against gold during the years following the end of the Napoleonic Wars. This objective was achieved by methods which have an all too familiar ring to them. The money supply was reduced, interest rates were raised, and the pound strengthened against foreign currencies which had mostly left their parities against gold or silver where they were at the end of the Napoleonic Wars. It took six years, from 1815 to 1821, to force wages and prices down sufficiently to enable cash payments in gold at the pre-war parity to be resumed. In consequence, there was a sharp depression as the post-war boom broke, leading to business failures, falling living standards, rising unemployment and great hardship for working people. Trade unions were crushed by the repressive Six Acts, which made them illegal. Opposition culminated in a riot in Manchester in 1819 – Peterloo – which was broken up by the cavalry, reviving echoes of the battle which had ended the Napoleonic Wars so successfully for Britain only four years previously. The final victory of the Currency School, easily recognised as having views close to those of modern monetarists, was the 1844 Bank Charter Act, which irrevocably locked the pound until 1914, and beyond, into a high value measured in gold.

The resulting relatively high cost of producing goods and services in Britain compared with the rest of Europe did not, however, hold back the British economy for long. During the first half of the nineteenth century, Britain was the only country which was industrialising fast. In consequence, the cost of goods produced in Britain fell rapidly compared with output elsewhere in Europe, making them very competitive despite the high gold parity. The British economy expanded by 2.8% per annum on average for the whole of the period from 1820 to 1851, when the Great Exhibition was held in London, marking the high peak of British pre-eminence. From 1851 to 1871 the growth rate slowed to 2.3%.[14] Even so, the cumulative increase in wealth and the standard of living was without parallel with anything ever seen in the world before, except in Australia and New Zealand, and especially in the United States, far away the other side of the Atlantic and heavily protected by tariffs, where high rates of growth were also being achieved.

With increasing confidence in its industrial capacity, the case for trade liberalisation in Britain became stronger. The Industrial Revolution had started in Britain behind substantial tariff barriers, themselves a legacy of the mercantilist policies of self-sufficiency against which Adam Smith had preached in *The Wealth of Nations*. As the expanding population pressed on the domestically produced food supply, however, necessitating increased imports of corn and other foodstuffs, the case for keeping down the cost of living by removing import tariffs and quotas seemed to become stronger. Free trade arguments were also extended to manufactured goods, leading to the trade treaties negotiated in the 1840s and 1850s. By 1860 the total number of dutiable items coming in to Britain had been reduced to forty-eight. By 1882 only twelve imported articles were taxed, and these purely for revenue purposes.[15]

Unilateral free trade, however, acts like a revaluation of the currency. It makes imports relatively cheaper than exports. Adopting free trade policies therefore had the same effect as raising the sterling exchange rate, which was already very high. Free trade in consequence also contributed to Britain's undoing as the nineteenth century wore on. All over Europe, but particularly in France, Germany and the Benelux countries, British manufacturing techniques began to be copied. The initial impulse came primarily from the development of railways, as their construction got under way on a substantial scale all over Europe from the 1840s and 1850s onwards. This necessitated not only major developments in civil engineering, but also large investments in production facilities capable of turning out thousands of kilometres of rail, relatively sophisticated rolling stock, and complex signalling equipment. Characteristically, while in Britain all these developments had been financed entirely by the private sector, in France and Germany the state was heavily involved in railway construction from the beginning, underwriting a considerable proportion of the high risks involved. Differing perceptions about the role of the state *vis à vis* the private sector across Europe have a long history.

British production techniques were soon copied in railways, and in virtually all other fields. Other forms of communications, such as canals, were constructed. Mass production of textiles followed, particularly in

North East France to start with, but soon spreading throughout Europe. Iron and steel output, greatly stimulated by the development of railways, but also providing the basis for the production of metal goods for a wide range of purposes, began to grow rapidly, particularly in Germany. The output of steel trebled there between 1840 and 1860, and trebled again between 1860 and 1880.[16] The economies of Europe became better able to compete with Britain for other reasons too. Germany was united first loosely under the *Zollverein* of 1834, and later more tightly under Bismarck, once Prussia had secured its position of leadership. Everywhere, although much more rapidly in some places than others, there were improvements in education, the legal system, the organisation of the professions and the training of skilled workforces.

A major turning point came in the 1870s, as the worldwide consumer and investment boom caused by the American Civil War and the Franco-Prussian conflict collapsed when they finished, as a result of the fall in demand for armaments, and a slow down in railway building. For the first time, Britain felt the full blast of foreign competition, and the British lead in industrial output became reduced. British exports fell from £256m in 1872 to £192m in 1879. Much of this fall was compensated for in volume terms by lower prices, but not all. The 1872 export figure was not exceeded until 1890. In the case of manufactures the ground lost was not recovered in terms of value until 1903, over thirty years later.[17] The growth rate of the British economy stabilised at 2.0% per annum for the last quarter of the nineteenth century. From 1870 to 1900 the economy in Germany grew by 125%, the Netherlands by 96%, Britain by 85%, Belgium by 82% and France by 56%.[18]

The sources of increases in output differed between France and Britain, which were falling back, and countries such as Germany which were pulling ahead. In Britain, in particular, more and more investment went abroad. In the slower growing economies, a rising percentage of investment went into housing and infrastructure, and a relatively low proportion into industry. Total investment as a percentage of GDP in these countries fell or remained static. Where investments were made in industry, more went into widening rather than deepening the industrial structure. In Britain, in particular, there was a vast expansion of the cotton industry and coal mining, both of which were labour intensive, but where large productivity gains were difficult to achieve.

In Germany, and to a lesser extent elsewhere on the continent, these trends were reversed. A higher proportion of investment went into new industries, such as the production of dyes and chemicals, sophisticated metal products, and later motor vehicles and electrical goods. The significance of these industries was that the scope for increased output and improved productivity was much greater than in the kind of industries to which Britain was moving. The circumstances which had given Britain the advantage in the early part of the nineteenth century were reversed. It was Germany and the Netherlands which now had more competitive exports, and which were less prone to import penetration because of the strength of local manufactures. Influenced particularly by Friedrich List (1789–1846), whose *Das nationale System der politischen Oekonomie* was published in 1837, the continental economies were also much more willing than the British to use tariffs to protect their rising industries. This made sense partly because they were much more nearly self-sufficient in foodstuff production so that free trade had less general attractions. They could therefore concentrate production where the growth prospects were highest, and were in a position to reinvest productively a greater proportion of their national incomes in their own economies.

The result was that by the start of World War I, much of the gap between the income per head in Britain and the rest of North West Europe had closed. Whereas in 1850, the income per head had been twice as high in Britain as in the most advanced parts of the continent of Europe, by 1914 the difference was only about a quarter.[19] Furthermore, in industrial capacity in many respects Germany was well ahead of Britain. German steel output had overtaken Britain's in the 1890s. By 1910, Britain was producing 6.5m tons of steel per year, but Germany was producing 13m.[20] Just before the outbreak of World War I, Germany had twice as many kilometres of rail track as Britain and was generating six times as much electricity.[21]

Economic power was seeping away from Britain, and with it the capacity of the British to continue dominating the world as had been possible for a hundred years. Between 1870 and 1913 the population in Germany grew a third faster than it did in Britain,[22] further strengthening Germany's military position. Rivalry between the great powers increased, and world war, with all its disastrous consequences for the world economy, came closer.

US economic history to World War I

When the first settlers arrived in North America from Europe, they brought with them immeasurable advantages over the indigenous population. The early colonists were by all historical standards exceptionally well endowed with their European legacy when they reached their destination, as indeed were many of those who subsequently followed in their steps. Nevertheless, the life of early settlers in the USA, and for many years subsequently, was tough and arduous. The country was enormous, and communications extremely primitive. Internal transportation was difficult and expensive, and sea-borne traffic provided the only practical solution to the movement of goods and people, producing a strong incentive for the development of efficient sailing ships. The population was overwhelmingly rural. Even as late as 1790, when it was about 3.9m, of whom almost 700 000 were slaves, there were only seven places with a population of over 5,000 and twelve with over 2,500. In these circumstances, manufacturing on anything but the smallest of scales was impractical, because internal transport problems so severely limited the size of the potential market. Almost all US export trade was in raw materials, primarily cotton, tobacco and wheat flour.[23]

The Declaration of Independence in 1776, followed shortly by the Napoleonic Wars, in which the USA did not directly participate, and then the 1812 war with Britain, produced both opportunities and disadvantages. Trade was disrupted, but domestic manufacturing was encouraged, and exports grew dramatically, if erratically. Overall, the value of exports, which had been $20m in 1790 had grown to $52m by 1815, while imports rose from $24m to $85m.[24] Part of the growth in output in the USA was attributable to its rapidly rising population, which had reached 7.2m by 1810 and 9.6m by 1820. The really explosive growth in the number of US citizens did not start, however, until about 1830, when the population was almost 13m. By 1860 it was 31m. The peak for immigration during this period was 1854, when 428,000 people moved to the USA.[25]

As early as 1820, the USA was among the richest countries in the world, judged by GDP per capita. Estimates show the USA a little over 25% below the British living standard of the time, a little under 20% behind the Dutch and Australians, and about on a par with Austria, Belgium, Denmark, France and Sweden. By 1850, Britain was still well ahead, but the gap was closing.[26] The disruption of the American Civil War held back the USA for a few years, but by 1870, the US growth rate was poised for the rapid increase in output achieved over the period between 1870 and 1913. During the fifty years between 1820 and 1870, the US economy had grown much faster than those on the other side of the Atlantic. Between 1820 and 1850, it grew cumulatively by 4.2% per annum, although the increase in output per head was much lower at 1.3% per annum, close to the British figure for the period of 1.25%. This was now to change. During the forty-three years from 1870 to 1913, the US economy achieved a cumulative growth rate of 4.3% per annum.

Allowing for compound population growth of 2.1% per annum, US GDP per head rose by 2.2% per annum.[27]

A differential in growth rates either in GDP or GDP per head of 1% or 2% per annum has a huge cumulative effect over a period such as the forty-three years between 1870 and 1913. If two economies start at the same size at the beginning of a period this long, one which is growing 2% faster per annum than its rival will be 134% larger forty-three years later. Even if the differential is only 1%, it will be 53% bigger at the end of the period. The results of the differential growth rates which occurred between the USA and most of Europe in the late nineteenth and early twentieth centuries thus presaged a seismic shift in world power. By 1913, the USA had overtaken Britain in living standards, leaving all the rest of Europe well behind. Only Australia and New Zealand were still ahead, but with much smaller populations and GDPs. By this time, the USA not only had a high GDP per head, but also a large population to go with it. By 1890 the US population was 63m, and by 1913 it was 98m.[28] As a result, the US economy was by then well over twice the size of its nearest rival, Britain, and more than four times that of Germany. Japan, which had grown by a respectable 2.8% per annum during the previous three decades, had an economy only about 13% the size of that of the US in 1913.[29]

These figures set the achievements of the US economy in an important context. It is often assumed that the rapid growth rates in the USA were the results of exceptional natural endowments, a tough but on the whole beneficent environment for enterprise, thrift and accumulation, and an increasing population to provide an expanding market and rising demand. No doubt having an expanding market was an important factor, but a rapidly rising population is a mixed blessing. It inevitably means that the available capital infrastructure has to be shared among a larger number of people. Offset against this in America's case, however, is the fact that much of the increase in population during the period from the end of the Civil War to the outbreak of World War I came from immigration. 26m people migrated to the United States during these years, most of them educated, of working age, and with a well developed work ethic.[30] This was a bonus by any standards. Perhaps the disbenefits of capital dilution from immigration were roughly offset by the arrival of millions of mostly young, hard-working and reasonably well trained people. In any event, although the US economy might have reacted to huge population increase by allowing the capital equipment per head of the population to decline, this did not happen.

On the contrary, during the latter years of the nineteenth century and the early 1900s, gross domestic investment as a proportion of GDP was much higher in the USA than it was in other countries. It averaged nearly 20% of GDP for the whole period, compared with about 7% for Britain and 11% for France.[31] Achieving a high investment ratio was as important in the nineteenth century as it is now. All these factors helped, but the key figures then, as now, were not so much expansion of the total economy but output per head. As the figures above show, large increases in the population meant that American living standards grew much more slowly than the American economy as a whole during the decades running up to World War I. It is noteworthy that Sweden and Denmark increased their GDP per head faster than the USA over this period.[32]

The overall growth achieved by the USA in the nineteenth century was nevertheless unprecedented. By 1900 the American economy was about twenty-five times as large as it had been in 1820. By 1980, another eighty years later, by comparison, the increase was to a little over thirteen times the 1900 figure.[33] The key period for expansion of the US economy, however, started during the decade before the Civil War when mechanisation and industrialisation really got into their strides. Between 1830 and the beginning of the 1865, manufacturing output increased nearly tenfold, while the population rose to about three times its 1830 figure. In the final decade before the Civil War began, steam engines and machinery output increased by 66%, cotton textiles by 77%, railroad production by 100%, and hosiery goods by 608%. As Reconstruction got under way, and the opportunities for a wide range of new technologies were exploited, improving communications and the quality of manufactures, the economy took off. The US gross stock of machinery and equipment increased by almost 400% between 1870 and 1890, and by 1913 it had nearly trebled again.[34]

It is no coincidence that it was the advent of large-scale increases in industrial output which triggered the rise in the US growth rate. The proportion of US GDP deriving from industry was on a strong upward trend throughout the nineteenth century. It employed 15% of the labour force in 1820, 24% in 1870, and 30% by 1913.[35] The USA also used its investment more efficiently than the average, especially towards the end of the nineteenth and beginning of the twentieth centuries, thereby gaining an important additional advantage.[36] This is a characteristic which the US economy still maintains, although the proportion of the US economy's output derived from manufacturing is now much lower than it was, down about 10% from the 27% average achieved during the post-World War II period.[37]

It is often alleged that a stable financial environment is the key to economic growth, and that low interest rates and low inflation are required to ensure high levels of investment and increases in output. It is hard to square this view of the world with the experience of the US economy in the nineteenth century. For most of the century, the USA had no central bank at all. The charter of the first Bank of the United States expired in 1811, when it was not renewed by the Jeffersonians then in power. The Second Bank of the United States, established in 1816, was wound up shortly after the re-election in 1832 of President Andrew Jackson, who bitterly opposed its existence.[38] Thereafter, until the establishment of the Federal Reserve system in 1913, there was no central control of the US money supply. Credit creation was in the hands of thousands of banks, spread all over the country, many of them poorly run, undercapitalised, prone to speculation, and liable to fail.

It is hardly surprising that, in these circumstances, US interest rates, prices and credit availability gyrated from boom to bust repeatedly during the nineteenth century. The abolition of the Second Bank of the United States in 1833 was followed only four years later by the most serious depression the USA had experienced so far, in some ways a worse crash than in 1929. Prices fell 40% between 1838 and 1843, railroad construction declined by almost 70% and canal building by 90%. Large-scale unemployment developed, and serious food riots broke out in New York City. It was not until 1844 that the next upswing started, culminating in the next downturn in 1856, which lasted until 1862. This pattern was to be repeated throughout the nineteenth century, accompanied every time there was a fall in economic activity by bank closures, bankruptcies and widespread defaults.[39]

Nor was the price level at all stable during the nineteenth century. Between 1815 and 1850, the wholesale price level fell by 50%, with substantial fluctuations in intervening years. It rose by 50% during the 1860s, peaking in 1866 as a result of the Civil War, with the impact of the Californian gold rush on the money supply, causing much of the underlying inflation. Between 1848 and 1858 California produced $550m worth of gold – 45% of world output between 1851 and 1855.[40] After 1870 prices fell until, by the turn of the century, they were 40% lower than they had been in 1870. They then climbed again about 25% during the years to 1913, mainly because the development of the cyanide process for extracting gold in South Africa led to another major increase in the world's monetary base, inflating the money supply and allowing prices to rise.[41]

Since World War II, promoting freer trade has been a major plank of US policy, also in sharp contrast to the high tariff protection promoted by successive administrations during the nineteenth century. Some import duties were imposed partly for revenue raising purposes, as they were the major source of government income at the time, but industrial protection was also a factor from the beginning. The tariff of 1816 imposed duties of 20% to 25% on manufactured goods and 15% to 20% on raw materials.[42] Thereafter the tariff level fluctuated, with the trade cycle, as always, playing a major role. The depression of 1837, for example, stimulated a new wave of protectionism as American industrialists blamed high unemployment on cheap imported goods. The major shift to a much more protectionist policy came in 1861 with the Morrill Tariff, designed to make the importation of most mass produced goods into the USA completely uneconomic. Import duties were not to be lowered again until 1913, under Woodrow Wilson, although even then they still stood at about 25%. Wool, sugar, iron and steel, however, were added to the free list.[43]

A distinguishing feature of the US economy has always been the low proportion, by international standards, of US GDP involved in foreign trade. Exports averaged about 11.5% of GDP during the period running up to World War I – much the same as now. Imports ran then at under 8%,[44] compared with about 13% at present.[45] Part of the reason for these low ratios has always, of course, been the sheer size of the country, and its ability to supply a high proportion of its needs from domestic sources. There is little doubt, however, that in the circumstances of the years up to 1913, the high tariff barrier helped the USA develop its manufacturing industries, unhampered by competition from abroad. Goods which might have been purchased from Europe were produced in the USA. The high level of demand, albeit subject to severe fluctuations, which the unregulated credit and banking system generated, provided opportunities which US manufacturers were quick to seize. Under the Gold Standard régime, which the USA joined in 1879,[46] when bimetallism was abandoned, it would have been difficult for the USA to have lowered its prices internationally sufficiently to have held off growing import penetration. The competitiveness of European exports at the time is amply demonstrated by the high proportion of their output which the European economies were capable of selling overseas during the nineteenth and early twentieth century. In 1900, about 25% of all British GDP was exported, and about 16% of all of Germany's. Even in 1913, Britain was still exporting twice the value of goods and services compared to the USA, although its economy was almost 60% smaller.[47]

The lessons to be learnt from the USA's economic history up to 1913 are just as relevant now as they were then. If the economy is to grow fast, advantage needs to be taken of the ability of industry, and particularly manufacturing, to generate high rates of growth of output. By 1870, a quarter of the US GDP came from industry, and by 1913, almost 30%.[48] The increase in productivity in manufacturing – and agriculture – during this period was about 50% higher than it was in the service sector – a ratio which has widened since then.[49] As the proportion of the US economy devoted to manufacturing rose, so did growth increase in the place where it really counts, which is not the size of the national income, but in output per head of the population, determining, as it does, the standard of living.

Lessons from a golden age

Between 1820 and 1913, economic output is estimated to have risen in the fifty-six major economies of the world by just over 300%, or cumulatively by 1.5% per annum. The rise in output per head was 140%, or a little under 1% per year.[50] These were much greater increases than had ever been seen on a wide scale in world history, demonstrating conclusively the immense power of the Industrial Revolution to change the prospects for humanity.

Could these ratios have been larger? Could the techniques used to garner the increased output obtainable from industrialisation have been spread significantly more widely, more intensively, and more quickly than they were? In theory, no doubt they could have been, although there were many practical obstacles. In the first place, it took even the most perspicacious observers, such as Adam Smith, some time to realise what a momentous change in production methods was taking place. Second, the diffusion of knowledge about the Industrial Revolution did in fact spread rapidly, partly because of the popularity and success of *The Wealth of Nations*. Jean Baptiste Say (1767–1832) published his own major work *Traite d'Economie Politique*, refining and extending Smith's work, in France in 1803. Translations into languages other than French increased its influence. There was also a stream of visitors from both home and abroad to British factories, supplemented by the publication of learned and practical journals, and exchanges of personnel and opinions in the relatively liberal world of the time.

The major practical constraints on spreading the use of the new industrial processes, which were then mostly being discovered in Britain, were those which had impeded the Industrial Revolution starting in other countries in the first place. Widely prevailing disparaging attitudes to industry, the disruption caused by wars, particularly the Napoleonic Wars which lasted for nearly a quarter of a century, the lack of stable government and enforceable contract law in many countries, and inadequate capital and credit facilities were major obstacles. Inevitably, also, there was a lengthy catch-up process which had to take place, even when copying of British techniques on a substantial scale began to take place. It took time to formulate plans, to arrange finance, to find and train suitable staff and to make the necessary physical investments even when the will to do so had been established. Nor can an industrial base be created overnight. A process of accumulation has to take place, often with the ability to move ahead depending on previous steps being accomplished successfully. Expansion from a small or almost non-existent base, which cannot be achieved even in the most favoured circumstances at more than a manageable pace, necessarily constrains the size of the total output achievable for a long way ahead.

The more challenging question about the nineteenth century, and indeed the one to follow, was whether, despite all the delays inevitably surrounding the adoption of new ways of organising production, different institutional developments might have speeded the process of diffusion and development, particularly since the basic constraints inhibiting progress had already been overcome. Could countries such as Britain, which slowed down, have maintained momentum and grown faster? If different economic policies, particularly those concerned with macroeconomics, had been adopted, would it have made a major difference?

The ideas set out in Chapter 2 provide a framework for answering this question. This certainly suggests that a number of significant and clearly identifiable policy mistakes were made in Britain. The re-establishment of the pre-Napoleonic Wars parity between sterling and gold in the period following 1815 not only severely depressed output for five or six years, but also, much more seriously, locked Britain into having a relatively high cost base compared to that potentially available in other countries when they started to industrialise. As long as Britain had world markets substantially to itself this was not of crucial significance, but once foreign competition got into its stride, British vulnerability became all too evident. The adoption of free trade then made a bad situation worse, by effectively revaluing sterling still further as Britain lowered tariffs while competitors raised them.

While other countries were able to expand their economies largely unconstrained by foreign competition or balance of payments problems, Britain was unable to do so. The British economy was therefore the major loser from inappropriate macro-economic policies in the nineteenth century. Why did Britain allow this to happen? Partly, it was because the reasons for Britain's relative decline were not understood, so there was no clearly articulated policy available for reversing it. Economic policy followed the classical precepts laid down by John Stuart Mill. Building on the work of his predecessors in the same tradition, the emphasis was heavily orientated to a minimalist role for the state with low taxation and public expenditure, financial stability in so far as it could be secured by clearly defined central bank operations, free trade, and the maintenance of the Gold Standard as the underlying stabiliser. This was a mixture of policies which well suited the growing strength and preponderence of the financial interests in Britain, exemplified pre-eminently by the City of London.

In these circumstances there was no place for a determined and well formulated series of policies to keep the British economy on a high growth track, although there was mounting concern about the extent to which Britain was falling behind its competitors. *The Final Report of the Royal Commission on Depression of Trade and Industry*, published in 1887, is full of agonised concern about the state of the economy. In the end, however, there was little serious challenge to the conventional views of the time, and the result was that those with accumulated wealth dominated the way the economy was run, as against those striving to create new industries. Sterling was too strong, encouraging imports and discouraging domestic production. Too much investment went abroad. Too few talented people went into industry and commerce. Too many went into the professions, administering the empire acquired almost entirely as a result of Britain's earlier economic pre-eminence, and into academic life, the civil service, the church – anything, if they could avoid it, except industry and trade.

If an effective challenge to the policy status quo was to come from anywhere, it would have had to come from the intellectual world, but it was not to be. The mainstream thinkers and writers of the time, such as John Stuart Mill, amplified and endorsed the classical economic approach, building on a tradition with a heavy emphasis on markets being self-regulating, and the role of the state being as non-intrusive as possible. Say's Law, propounded by the same Jean Baptiste Say who had publicised *The Wealth of Nations*, held that a deficiency in demand was impossible since the income from the sales of all the goods and services which were produced necessarily generated exactly enough expenditure to purchase all of them. This view, which was not seriously challenged until the advent of John Maynard Keynes, ruled out the possibility of any kind of systematic demand management. The most significant challenge to orthodoxy which did materialise, from Karl Marx, was not designed to make the capitalist system work better, but to get rid of it altogether. The major innovations in economics which the nineteenth century produced, from writers such as Auguste Walras (1801–1866), William Stanley Jevons (1835–1882), Alfred Marshall (1842–1924) and others, were mainly in micro-economics. They were primarily concerned with the formation of prices and marginal utility, rather than macro-economic issues which generated little interest. Britain, and the world in general, paid a heavy price for this trend in intellectual fashion.

4
International Turmoil – 1914–45

'A disordered currency is one of the greatest political evils.'
Daniel Webster

World War I began as the result of a network of treaty obligations being called into operation following the assassination of Archduke Franz Ferdinand in Sarajevo on 28 June 1914.[1] Although few had anticipated the outbreak of war, its advent was greeted with a surprising amount of enthusiasm. Huge crowds turned out in Berlin, Paris, Petrograd (St Petersburg), London and Vienna, clamouring for military action.[2] By 1945, all such enthusiasm for war had been spent. Two ruinous conflicts had cost millions of lives, had caused untold damage, and had set back the advance of living standards by an incalculable amount. Not only, however, had immense human and physical damage been done during the periods of open warfare. In addition, the network of international trading and financial arrangements which had allowed the world economy to function reasonably smoothly during the nineteenth century, and the early years of the twentieth, was wrecked by the impact of World War I. The result was a period of great instability and lost opportunities between the wars, as fragile booms in the 1920s collapsed into the worldwide slump of the early 1930s. Thereafter there was a sharp divergence, as some economies continued to decline while others made remarkable recoveries.

Throughout the period, the record of most of those responsible for economic policy was confused and inadequate. The near universal consensus among political and intellectual leaders up to the outbreak of

World War I was that the state should see its role as holding the ring rather than being a major player. Clearly, however, this stance made no sense at all at a time of total war. Within a very short time, therefore, in all the belligerent economies, the proportion of output which went through the government's hands rose dramatically. In Britain it increased from 15% in 1913 to an astonishing 69% in 1917,[3] while similar rises were seen in France and Germany. In the USA the peak, at 36% in 1918, was considerably lower, but even so this represented a dramatic change from pre-war days.[4] The outcome was that governments in all the countries involved in fighting the war were presented with problems for which they were singularly ill-prepared. While mobilising to produce vast quantities of guns, ships, aircraft and munitions, and recruiting and training large numbers of people to be under arms, was found to be problematic but achievable, securing these objectives without over-stretching and destabilising the economy proved much more difficult. Even in the USA, prices rose by about 50% between 1915 and 1918, but inflation was much less there during the war period than it was in other countries. Britain's price level rose nearly 80%, France's doubled, and Germany's increased by 200%.[5]

More than anything else, it was the disruption to the rough balance of competitiveness between the pre-World War I economies which turned out to be the bane of the inter-war period, compounded by the impact of the insistence by the victorious powers of payment of reparations by Germany, the major belligerent on the losing side. World total demand was depressed by the policies pursued by countries such as Britain, which was determined to restore sterling's pre-war gold parity, and willing to go through a period of severe deflation to do so. In Germany, until the advent of the Nazi régime, with very different ideas about how the economy should be run, a similarly cautious attempt was made to follow classical economic remedies, culminating in the cuts to unemployment benefit which, as much as anything else, led to Adolf Hitler (1889–1945) becoming Chancellor in 1933. In the United States, during the 1920s the economy was unconstrained by the balance of payments problems and the apparent need for deflation which afflicted most of Europe. The result was a major boom, culminating in a bout of speculation which left the banking and financial system heavily exposed to a downturn. When this came, the authorities were completely unprepared to deal with it. As elsewhere, vain attempts to balance a rapidly deteriorating fiscal position simply made an already catastrophic situation worse.

While the world's economies were languishing, work was being done by Keynes and others which would lead to a much more stable condition after World War II. The influence of those who realised that Say's Law was not correct, and that it was possible for economies to suffer from insufficient total demand for years on end, however, was only marginal between the wars. Their thinking had some impact in Britain and the USA, particularly on some of those involved in the New Deal, but only to a limited degree. Keynes' major influence on policy was to come later, as the institutions for the post-World War II period were established, although he also had a substantial impact on the way which World War II was financed, particularly in Britain.

By the time of World War II, therefore, much had been learnt about how to control and finance total mobilisation, and inflation in all the main belligerent countries was much less, although prices rose steeply in those countries which were defeated and occupied during the war, and in those which were eventually on the losing side as the war ended. A number of major advances had also been made in thinking about how to structure the post-war world too, laying the foundation for the great advances in living standards achieved in much of the world during the 1950s and 1960s. The period from the 1970s onwards, however, as world growth rates declined sharply, showed that still more needed to be done.

The period from 1914 to 1945 is therefore an exceptionally interesting and important one, both in terms of the impact it had on economic and political history and in the development of ideas. Much was lost in terms of output forgone or in the production of destructive military equipment, but important ground was gained, as the rest of this chapter shows, in better understanding of some of the key requirements for improved economic management.

Europe's disastrous years

World War I was a catastrophe for Europe in every way. There was huge loss of life and immense material destruction. Even worse than this, the relatively stable and secure social and economic systems which had been developed during the nineteenth century, which had stood Europe and the world as a whole in good stead, were disrupted, dislocated and dismembered. It took the passage of three decades and another world war before anything resembling the peace, prosperity and security of pre-World War I Europe would be re-established.

Approximately 10m people lost their lives in Europe prematurely as a result of World War I,[6] and a substantial additional number, harder to quantify, in the influenza epidemics which struck down a weakened population in the immediate aftermath of the war. The damage done to towns and factories, though much less than in World War II, was still considerable. The national incomes of the countries of Western Europe fell precipitately between the period just before World War I started, and the early years after it ended when the demand for war-orientated production fell away. France's industrial production dropped by over 40% between 1913 and 1919, caused partly by the disruption and damage of the war, and partly by the post-war slump.[7] It was 1927 before German GDP rose again to its 1913 level.[8] Britain did not do so badly, with the GDP staying more or less constant during the war, although it fell heavily, by about 20%, immediately the war finished.[9]

Economic instability in Europe was greatly compounded by the Treaty of Versailles, negotiated between the powers which had won the war, and the humiliated Germans. The Americans had not come into the war until 1917, and insisted on the large debts run up by Britain and France for war supplies being repaid. Britain and France, in turn looked to Germany to make huge reparations, partly to pay the Americans and partly on their own account. None of these arrangements, negotiated by political leaders under immense pressure from electorates much more interested in settling old scores than in facing up to new realities, bore any relationship to the ability of the Germans to make these payments. Leaving aside the extent to which the German economy was already languishing as a result of the damage done to it by the war, the only feasible way for the Germans to pay the reparation bill was to run a very large export surplus. In the fragile state of the world economy in the 1920s, no country was prepared to tolerate a large German trade surplus, even if it could have been achieved. Payment of reparations on the scale demanded, whatever its electoral appeal, or the requirement of the USA to see debts to it settled, was never therefore a remotely realistic prospect.

Attempts to extract reparations, however, compounded with post-war political and economic disruption, caused havoc in Germany. The government, unable to produce sufficient revenue through the tax system to meet the obligations it had undertaken to fulfil, resorted to the printing press to create the money it was unable to raise in any other way. The result was the German inflation of 1923, which ended in hyper-inflation and the total collapse in the value of the currency.[10] The Reichsmark had already lost two-thirds of its value during World War I.[11] Now all those with savings denominated in money lost everything. This experience understandably scarred the German attitude to inflation and monetary rectitude, with reverberations which are still felt today.

Gradually, however, towards the end of the 1920s, some measure of normality began to reassert itself. There was a significant boom in France, where industrial output doubled between the post-war low of 1921 and 1928, although even in 1928 it was only 10% higher than it had been in 1913.[12] Industrial production also rose in the late 1920s in Germany, peaking in 1929 at about 20% higher than it had been in 1913, while Germany's GDP grew cumulatively between 1925 and 1929 by a respectable 2.9% per annum.[13] In Germany's case in particular, however, the recovery was fragile. It depended heavily on large loans flowing in from abroad, especially the United States, to enable reparation payments to continue at the scaled down rate agreed by the Young Plan in 1929, replacing the much harsher Dawes Plan of 1924. Nevertheless, in the late 1920s, Germany's unemployment was falling and living standards were slowly increasing.

Britain remained depressed, mainly because of a repetition of the same process which had taken place after the Napoleonic Wars. The link between the pound and gold had been suspended on the outbreak of World War I, and the pressure on the economy during the war had led to considerable price inflation. Nevertheless, on the recommendation of the Cunliffe Committee, in 1918 it was decided to restore the gold value of the pound to the same parity, $4.86, which it had enjoyed in 1914. Attaining this objective meant forcing down costs in Britain, attempted by imposing severely deflationary policies. The reductions achieved, particularly in labour costs, were nothing like sufficient, however, to restore Britain to a competitive position at the new parity. As a result, Britain spent the whole of the 1920s in the worst of all worlds, suffering from a combination of lack of competitiveness at home and abroad, leading inevitably to domestic deflation and slow growth in output and living standards.

Europe therefore appeared to be very poorly placed to weather the depression which followed, beginning with the collapse of the United States stock market in 1929. The most immediate effect of the American slump on Europe was that the flow of loans from the USA to Germany dried up, plunging the German economy into a crisis of the same order of magnitude as had overcome the United States. Between 1929 and 1932, German GDP fell by almost a quarter. Industrial production dropped by nearly 40%.[14] Unemployment, which already stood at 9.3% in 1929, increased to over 30% of the labour force by 1932.[15] During this year it averaged 5.5m, peaking at 6m. In Britain, GDP fell, but by not so much as in the USA and Germany. Industrial production dropped by 5%, but unemployment, which was already 7.3% in 1929, rose to 15.6% in 1932.[16] Similar patterns to those seen in Britain were to be found in France and the Benelux countries. Mussolini's policy in Italy of keeping the lira at as high a parity as possible, mirroring the British experience, ensured that the Italian economy suffered similar disadvantages, although the proportion of the Italian GDP involved in foreign trade was much lower than that in Britain.

The crucially important lessons to be learnt from the 1930s derive from the different ways in which the major economies in Europe, particularly Germany, France and Britain, reacted to the slump which overtook all of them at the same time. The history of the years to come was indelibly stamped by the different reactions of the electorates and their leaders in these three countries.

In Germany, the collapse of the economy, coming as it did on top of the trauma of the lost World War I, the vindictiveness of the Versailles settlement, particularly the reparations clauses, the political instability of the Weimar régime, and the hyperinflation of 1923, provoked a wholly counter-productive response from the Brüning government. In July 1931, and again in the summer of 1932, the amount and duration of unemployment compensation was reduced. Instead of attempting to reflate the economy, Chancellor Brüning (1885–1970), supported by the SDP opposition, cut wages and benefits, making the economic situation worse, and precipitating the German banking crisis of July 1931, which followed the Austrian Kreditanstalt collapse two months earlier.[17] The desperate attempts by democratic, well meaning politicians to maintain financial respectability were their undoing, and that of the whole of Europe as the Nazis came to power. This mistake, on top of all the others, provided Hitler and his associates with their opportunity to take over the government in 1933.

The economic policies pursued by the new Nazi régime, however disastrous in leading Europe into World War II, and however much racist and fascist policies are to be condemned, were nevertheless remarkably successful in domestic terms. Unemployment, which stood at over 30% in 1932, was reduced by 1938 to just over 2% of the working population.[18] Over the same period, industrial production rose over 120%, a cumulative increase of 14% per annum. The gross national product increased by 65%, a cumulative increase of nearly 9% a year.[19] A substantial proportion of the increased output was devoted to armaments, but by no means all. Military expenditure, which had been 3.2% of GDP in 1933, rose to 9.6% in 1937. It then almost doubled to 18.1%, but only as late as 1938.[20] Between 1932 and 1938 consumers' expenditure rose by almost a quarter.[21] Nor were these achievements bought at the expense of high levels of inflation. The price level was very stable in Germany in the 1930s. Consumer prices rose by a total of only

7% between the arrival of the Nazi régime in 1933 and the outbreak of war in 1939.[22]

How were these results achieved? Some of the success could only have been achieved by a non-democratic régime, with access to total power. In particular, the pressure exerted to hold down wage increases, and the policies imposed to restrict trade, so as to increase Germany's capacity to supply all its essential needs internally, would have been difficult for any democratic government to implement. Unquestionably these policies also led to increasing distortions in the economy, with a price which would have to be paid sooner or later. All the same, there was plenty of new production with which to pay these costs.

The expansion of the economy was made possible partly as a result of vast increases in expenditures by the state, which nearly trebled between 1933 and 1938.[23] An increasingly high proportion of these were spent on rearmament as the decade wore on, but during the earlier years most of it went on civil expenditure, such as building a road system far superior to anything seen before, although this also had military capabilities. A substantial proportion of the rest of the rise in output, however, went on increasing the German standard of living, as rising spending power from both the public and the private sector worked its way through to German factories. Much of the initial increase in expenditure was financed by borrowing on a large scale, some of it through bonds, but much of it from the banking system. There was a large expansion in the money supply. Rising tax revenues, flowing from the greatly increased scale of economic activity, however, kept the finances of the régime in bounds, which was partly why inflationary pressures were subdued.

In Britain, the initial reaction to the advent of the slump was much in line with the economic policies previously pursued. The Labour Chancellor of the Exchequer, Philip Snowden (1864–1937), tried to persuade his reluctant cabinet colleagues that the only solution to the financial crisis overwhelming the country was to maintain a balanced budget by implementing the same sort of cuts in expenditure which had been the undoing of the Brüning government in Germany. Eventually, there was a revolt when the overwhelming majority of the Labour Members of Parliament ceased supporting the government, refusing to back any more cuts. They preferred to go into opposition, allowing a National government to be formed with the support of the Conservative opposition.

The policies then implemented were a complete break from those previously supported. The pound sterling was driven off gold, and allowed to fall in value by 24% against all other major currencies.[24] Far from the government then making efforts to restore the previous parity, as it had after the Napoleonic Wars and World War I, presaging the same mistaken response time after time to exchange rate falls in the future, policy was dedicated to ensuring that the new lower parity was retained. An Exchange Equalisation Account was established, with resources of 5% of the gross national product, to keep the pound at its new competitive level. There was a very substantial expansion in the money supply, which increased by 15% between 1931 and 1932, and which rose by a further 19% during the first half of 1933.[25] Interest rates fell to almost zero. Tariff protection was added to reinforce the protective effects of the reduction in the exchange rate.

In Britain, as in Germany, the results were dramatic and positive. Far from living standards falling, as almost all commentators had confidently predicted they would, they started to rise rapidly. Industrial production also increased substantially, if not quite as fast as in Germany. In the five years to 1937, manufacturing output rose 48% to 38% above the 1929 peak.[26] Unemployment fell sharply, as the number of people in jobs quickly increased. Over the period between 1931 and 1937, the number of those in work rose from 18.7m to 21.4m as 2.7m new jobs were created, half of them in manufacturing.[27] Unemployment fell from 3.3m to 1.8m. The poor business prospects in the previous decade had left Britain bereft of sufficient investment in the most modern technologies. Now the ground was quickly made up, with new industrial capacity employing the latest improvements, as indeed was also happening in Germany. Nor was inflation a problem. Contrary to all the conventional wisdom, the price level fell heavily, partly reflecting the slump in world prices, until 1933 after which it began a slow rise.[28] The British economy grew faster during the five years between 1932 and 1937 – at a cumulative 4.6% per annum[29] – than for any other five-year period in its history, showing clearly how effective a radical expansionist policy could be, against the most unpromising background.

Towards the end of the 1930s, the growth in the British economy began to slacken off, despite increased expenditure on armaments, a delayed response to the German threat. The reason was a further round of exchange rate changes. The Americans had devalued the dollar by 41% in 1934. In 1936 they were followed by the gold bloc countries, France, Switzerland, Belgium and the Netherlands, which had hitherto been in the doldrums with low growth and high levels of unemployment.[30] Incredibly, in the light of the experience of the previous few years, instead of devaluing with them to keep sterling competitive, the British agreed to support the new currency alignments with the Exchange

Equalisation Account. The competitiveness which had enabled the British economy to recover so quickly and so unexpectedly from the slump was thereby thrown away. In 1948, the Economic Commission for Europe estimated that sterling was as overvalued in 1938 as it had been in 1929.[31]

The French experience over the period of the 1930s was the mirror image of that of Britain. Until 1936 when, under the Popular Front government of Leon Blum (1872–1950), deflationary policies were at last abated, France, along with the other gold bloc countries, stayed on the gold exchange standard, refused to devalue, depressing the economy further and further, and reaping the inevitable consequences. French GDP dropped steadily in real terms almost every year from 1930 to 1936, falling a total of 17% over these six years. Industrial production fell by a quarter. Investment slumped. Unemployment rose continually.[32]

French crude steel production fell from 9.7m in 1929 to 6.1m tons in 1938. In Germany, over the same period, it rose from 16.2m tons in 1929 to 22.7m tons. France produced 254 000 cars and commercial vehicles in 1929, and 227 000 in 1938, while vehicle manufacture in Germany increased from 128 000 to 338 000. British crude steel production rose from 9.8m tons in 1929 to 10.6m in 1938, while vehicle output went up from 239 000 to 445 000.[33] These figures show with crystal clarity how much the French economy weakened compared to that of Britain and particularly Germany over this critical period. The results of the battles of 1940, during the early part of World War II, were very largely determined by the economic policies pursued by the three main protagonists during the previous decade.

Much the most significant contrast between the three largest economies in Europe in the 1930s was the relatively successful results, at least in economic terms, achieved by Germany and Britain, and the disastrously poor outcome in France and the other gold bloc countries. These lessons are still highly material today. The problem with the European Union in the 1990s, as a highly topical example, is that it reflected a reversion back to the same policies pursued with such relentless and misguided determination by the French sixty years ago. The difference in experience between France, Britain and Germany in the 1930s is extremely striking. Then, as now, it was not financial rectitude which turned out to be the answer to low growth, high unemployment, and overburdened public finances. The solution was expansion. The ultimate disaster for Europe in the 1930s was that it was the non-democratic Nazi régime which chose the mixture of economic policies which worked best, while most of the European democracies ploughed on into stagnation and decline.

The really interesting exemplar is the British experience, at least until 1936, combining democracy with recovery. Thereafter, reverting to type, the huge advantage of a competitive exchange rate, rapid growth and falling unemployment enjoyed by Britain for the first half of the 1930s was gratuitously thrown away. 1931 to 1936, however, showed what could be done by a democracy faced with daunting economic problems, when the right policies were chosen. Expanding the money supply, reducing interest rates, and making the necessary exchange rate adjustments were the key to success. Creating conditions where exports could boom, the home market could be recaptured from foreign suppliers, and where industry could flourish, all had an enormously positive impact on the country's economic performance.

Boom and slump in the USA

It was not until 1917, three years after World War I broke out in 1914, that the USA was directly involved in the war as a belligerent. By 1918 the US economy had grown by almost 16% compared to 1913.[34] While the 1920s saw most European economies recovering from deep post-war slumps, leaving their populations with significantly lower GDP per head than they had enjoyed before the war, the US economy soon began to surge ahead. Recovering quickly from a brief post-war set back in 1919–21, during most of the remaining 1920s a major and sustained boom developed. Between 1921 and 1929, the US economy grew by 45%, achieving a cumulative 4.8% rate of growth during these eight years.

From 1920 to 1929, industrial output climbed by nearly 50%, while the number of people employed to achieve this increase in output remained almost constant. This reflected an enormous increase in manufacturing productivity, which rose cumulatively by nearly 5% per annum as factories were automated.[35] The use of electricity in industry rose dramatically – by 70% between 1923 and 1929.[36] Living standards increased by 30%, although those on already high incomes gained much more than those further down the income distribution. Investment as a percentage of GDP rose from 12.2% in 1921 to 17.6% in 1928. Meanwhile, the price level remained remarkably stable, consumer prices being on average slightly lower in 1928 than they were in 1921.[37]

The confidence engendered by such economic success was reflected not only in an almost tripling of consumer credit during the 1920s, but also on the stock market. A bull market began to build in 1924. It surged ahead with only minor setbacks for the next five years. The Dow-Jones Industrial Averages, whose high was 120 in 1924, reached 167 in 1926, soared to 300 in 1928, and peaked at 381 on 3 September 1929, a level not to be exceeded for another quarter of a century. Speculative fever reigned in a largely unregulated market. Much of the increase in the value of stocks was financed by increasingly risky but lucrative loans. As the boom gathered strength, those buying shares often had to put up only as little as 10% of the cost themselves, the balance being provided as 'brokers' loans'. Initially, these were provided by banks, but later increasingly by corporations, which found the potential returns irresistible, resulting in many of the major American companies investing more and more of their resources in speculation rather than production. Brokers' loans, which had been about $1bn during the early years of the decade, had risen to $3.5bn by the end of 1927, $6bn by January 1929 and reached $8.5bn by October 1929. The huge demand for such loans forced the interest rate on them up and up. By the time the stock market peaked in the late summer of 1929, 12% interest rates were not uncommon at a time when there was no inflation.[38]

The initial falls from the stock market peak were modest, but by late October 1929, confidence was draining away. A wave of panic on 24 October was followed by 'Black Friday', 25 October, and a frenzy of selling on 29 October 1929. In the first half-hour that day, losses ran at over $2bn and by the end of the day they were $10bn, as the Dow-Jones fell 30 points, reducing the value of quoted stocks by 11.5%. Worse was to follow. Despite periodic rallies, the market moved inexorably downwards, until by July 1932, the Dow-Jones stood at 41, nearly 90% below its 381 peak. United States Steel shares fell from 262 to 22, General Motors dropped from 73 to 8, and Montgomery Ward plummeted from 138 to 4.[39]

The collapse of prices on the stock exchanges had a devastating effect on the rest of the economy. The huge sums which had been lost caused a wave of bank failures from coast to coast, dragging down countless businesses with them. As both consumer and industrial confidence evaporated, sources of credit dried up, and demand disappeared for many of the goods and services which the US economy was amply capable of producing. Between 1929 and 1933, US GDP fell by 30%. Industrial output went down by nearly half in just three years from 1929 to 1932. By 1933, a quarter of the American labour force was out of work. Nearly 13m people had no job.[40]

The condition of the economy reached its nadir in 1933. Meanwhile, in 1932, Franklin D. Roosevelt (1882–1945) had ousted the hapless Herbert Hoover (1874–1964) as president in a landslide vote, initiating a New Deal for the American people, designed to tackle the slump. The policies implemented by the incoming Democrat administration fell into two main parts. The first was a substantial increase in the role of the state. More financial help was provided to those hardest hit by unemployment. The Federal Emergency Relief Act provided $500m in direct grants to states and municipalities. New agencies were established, some of them designed to act in a counter-cyclical way, increasing demand by using the borrowing power of the state to provide funding. The Tennessee Valley Authority provided regional energy and flood control. The National Recovery Administration assisted with industrial revitalisation. The Agricultural Adjustment Administration had as its goal the regeneration of the weakened farming sector of the economy. The result of these initiatives was probably as much in terms of increasing confidence that something was being done by the Federal government to improve conditions than in their direct impact, although expenditure on these schemes no doubt had some reflationary impact.[41]

Much more significant in terms of causing the economy to revive were other steps taken on the macro-economic front. In 1934, the dollar was devalued by 41%, adding to the substantial protection for American industry which had already been achieved by the Smoot-Hawley tariff in 1930, a major step towards the economic nationalism which was one of the curses of the 1930s. One of the Roosevelt administration's early steps had been to stabilise the financial system by declaring a bank holiday, and then allowing the Treasury, under emergency legislation, to verify the soundness of individual banks before allowing them to reopen. Ten days later half of them, holding 90% of all deposits, were back in operation. The result was that thenceforth deposits exceeded withdrawals, as confidence in the banking system was restored, thus increasing the availability of credit. The Fed also encouraged recovery by allowing the money supply to rise as the economy picked up. M1 rose from just under $20bn in 1933 to a little less than $30bn in 1936, generating a major increase in the underlying credit base.[42]

The result was that by 1936 the US economy was in considerably better shape than it had been three years earlier. In these three years, real GDP grew by 32%, while unemployment fell by nearly a third, from 25% to 17%. Industrial output rebounded, growing 50%.[43] Corporate net income moved from being $2bn in deficit to $5bn in surplus.[44] There was little change in the consumer price level.[45] Despite these striking achievements, Roosevelt, who, notwithstanding all the New Deal rhetoric, had never felt wholly comfortable with borrowing to spend, became alarmed by the fiscal deficit, which reached $3.5bn in 1936. As a result, he ordered a cutback in Federal spending.[46] This coincided with both a reduction in the competitiveness of US exports as the gold bloc countries devalued, and the deflationary impact of the promised new social security tax, another part of the New Deal, which was introduced at the same time. The consequence was a sharp recession. GDP fell by 4% between 1937 and 1938, industrial output fell back nearly a third, and unemployment rose from 14.3% to 19%.[47]

By then, however, the start of World War II was imminent, transforming the prospects for the US economy. Although the USA did not become a belligerent until December 1941, following the Japanese attack at Pearl Harbor, the lend-lease arrangements agreed with the Allied powers at the start of the European war rapidly provided a massive stimulus to US output. Between 1939 and 1944, US GDP grew by an astonishing 75%, a compound rate of almost 12%. Over the same period, industrial output increased by over 150%, while the number of people employed in manufacturing rose from 10.3m to 17.3m, an increase of just under 70%. The difference between these two percentages reflected a huge further advance in manufacturing productivity, which rose cumulatively by some 8% per annum. Prices increased by an average of less than 5% a year, a far better outcome than had been achieved during World War I.[48] By the end of World War II, the USA was therefore in an extraordinarily strong position *vis à vis* the rest of the world. Most developed countries had suffered invasion and defeat at some stage in the war, and in consequence their economies had been severely disrupted, and in some cases devastated. Between 1939 and 1946, Japanese GDP fell by almost half, and Germany's by just over 50%. Even countries such as Britain, which had avoided invasion and had finished on the winning side, did nothing like as well as the USA. The British economy grew by only 10% between 1939 and 1946.[49] No wonder that in 1945 the US economy looked supreme.

Keynes and the Bretton Woods system

The major contribution made by John Maynard Keynes to economic thought was his perception that demand and supply would not always be in balance, as Say's Law had claimed that they would. On the contrary, Keynes maintained, while the money spent by the nation on consumption always creates an equivalent income flow for producers, there is no reason why the same should be true for that proportion of its income which the nation saves. The corresponding expenditure in this case is by companies and the state on investment goods. There is no reason why, *ex ante*, these should be the same. If there is more saving in the economy than expenditure on investment, there will be an overall shortfall in demand, which will lead to deflation and unemployment. Furthermore, if, as economic conditions become more depressed, precautionary savings rise, while investment falls as profitable opportunities decrease, the result may be an increasingly intense depression. As an accounting identity, investment and savings, or, more strictly speaking, borrowing have *ex post* to be identical in size.[50] It may well be the case, however, that equilibrium between them will be found at a level which leaves the economy as a whole heavily short of the total level of demand to keep everyone in employment, with a reasonable rate of growth being achieved.

The classical economist's response to the problem of unemployment had been to deny that it could exist, except in the case of workers changing jobs or out of work because of poor fits between skills and job opportunities, unless wages were too high or too rigid. The solution, if unemployment appeared, was therefore to ensure that wages fell until everyone was priced back into a job. A further important contribution from Keynes was to point out that this was not correct, but a fallacy of composition. What might be true of individual workers was not true of all the labour force taken together. If employers generally lowered wages at a time of unemployment, total purchasing power – the aggregate of effective demand – would diminish *pari passu* with the diminished wages,[51] thus worsening the deflationary problem.

Nor was it true, Keynes maintained, that lowering interest rates would necessarily improve the prospects for investment to provide a sufficient stimulus to pull the economy out of a depression. Worse still, lowering interest rates might increase savings, thus further aggravating the imbalance, as savers felt they needed larger cash investments to offset the lower returns which they were likely to receive. The only solution was for the state to assume a much more active role, to make up for the deficiency in demand in the private sector. If the economy was operating at below full employment, the state should offset the excess saving in relation to investment by borrowing itself, and spending the money to increase overall demand.

Keynes also had strong views about the role of the exchange rate on the performance of the economy. He had railed against Winston Churchill when, as Chancellor of the Exchequer, he had in 1925 returned Britain to the pre-World War I gold parity, realigning sterling with the US dollar at $4.86 to the pound.[52] Speaking nearly twenty years later for the Coalition government in the Bretton Woods debate in the House of Lords on 23 May 1944, he said that 'We are determined that, in future, the external value of sterling shall conform to its internal value, as set by our domestic policies, and not the other way round. In other words, we abjure the instruments of Bank Rate and credit contraction operating to increase unemployment as a means of forcing our domestic economy into line with external factors.'[53] Unfortunately, however, Keynes died in 1946, and British exchange rate policy soon regressed back to the norm.

Not only did Keynes, nevertheless, have great influence on the way in which domestic policy operated in the post-World War II period, he was also heavily involved, with the Americans, for whom Harry Dexter White took the lead, in designing the architecture for the post-war international settlement. Planning started in 1942 and culminated in the Bretton Woods agreement of 1944. Common ground between the British and Americans was the need to avoid both competitive trade restrictions and floating exchange rates, both of which, as inter-war experience had shown, could be manipulated to secure unilateral advantage at heavy multilateral expense.[54] Floating exchange rates were also believed to encourage inflation, by allowing politicians an easy escape from overheating their economies to enhance their popularity. There was more difficulty in securing a consensus over timing. It was agreed that some barriers would be required to short-term capital movements, at least in the immediate post-war period, but the Americans were also keen that trade restrictions should be removed as quickly as possible. The 'dollar gap', which manifested itself for some years after the end of the war, showed that British caution was well justified. The problem was that, with trade barriers removed, the demand from Europe and elsewhere for US exports was far higher than their dollar earnings could sustain.

Buttressed by the establishment of the International Monetary Fund (IMF), to deal with short-term international financing needs, and the World Bank, to manage longer-term development loans, and, in 1946, by the General Agreement on Tariffs and Trade (GATT), the Bretton Woods system, as it finally emerged, had a number of key characteristics. The centrepiece was agreement that exchange rates in future should be fixed, with all participating countries having to establish a par value for their currencies in terms of either gold or the US dollar. These par values could only be changed to correct a 'fundamental disequilibrium' in their balance of payments. Each country was expected to hold reserves to support its fixed exchange rate, which could be supplemented by the Fund's resources. Agreement was reached on procedures for the liberalisation of world trade by the removal of trade barriers and the progressive lowering of tariffs.[55]

The period of high growth and relative stability in the 1950s and 1960s which followed the setting up of the Bretton Woods system, once the initial dislocations of the immediate post-war period had been overcome, was unquestionably impressive, and a vast improvement on the record of the inter-war period. Between 1950 and 1970 the world economy grew by 157% compared to 97% between 1913 and 1950.[56] Nevertheless, the arrangements agreed suffered from deficiencies, which were to become increasingly evident as the years wore on. The major problem was that they contained no built-in mechanism for stopping economies which started doing better than the average from accumulating greater and greater competitive advantages. Under the Gold Standard, any country which accumulated a balance of payments surplus automatically had its monetary base expanded by the influx of gold. This tended to push up its price level, redressing, at least in part, the balance with its competitors. Under Bretton Woods, no such mechanism operated. The onus for adjustment therefore tended to fall almost wholly on the less competitive countries, forcing them into deflation to protect their balance of payments position, or to devaluation. There was no corresponding pressure on the more successful economies to share their competitive advantage with others by revaluing their currencies.

The result was that countries, such as Britain, whose exchange rate soon after the war was evidently much too high, had no easy way of securing international agreement to getting it down to a more realistic level. Germany and Japan, on the contrary, whose exchange rates had been fixed at artificially low levels after the war, were in a strong position to resist revaluing them. Towards the end of the Bretton Woods era, the USA also began to suffer from the same malaise as Britain, in more acute form, had experienced almost continuously since 1945, culminating in the devaluation of the dollar in 1971, and the break-up of the system of fixed exchange rates shortly afterwards.

The consequence of this bias in the system was that countries with competitive exports and strong balance of payments positions could grow very fast, while those which were less competitive were held back by balance of payments constraints. The result may have been to hold back overall growth from being as high as it could have been, but, nevertheless, not by much as during most of this period only a small number of countries, primarily Britain, were adversely affected. Between 1950 and 1970 the cumulative expansion in the world economy averaged 4.9%.[57] The driving force was a combination of Keynesian policies at national level and relatively minor disequilibria in trading competitiveness between the major trading nations internationally, allowing nearly all economies to expand rapidly with full employment. With comparatively low welfare dependency levels, as a result of almost all families having breadwinners, most countries had easily containable pressures on their taxation and expenditure systems, helping to keep inflation at bay.

As long as these conditions held, rapid growth could continue. When the Bretton Woods system broke up, however, the world economy began to perform much more poorly. Deprived of the constraints and discipline which world leaders had been used to working within for a quarter of a century, there was initially, in the early 1970s, an unsustainable boom. This was followed by a long period during which most of the world's major economies began to grow significantly more slowly, to exhibit much higher levels of unemployment, and to suffer far more severely than previously from inflation. As we shall see, new guidelines were forthcoming in the move in intellectual fashion towards monetarism, provided by Milton Friedman and his associate, Anna Jacobson Schwartz, in their seminal book, *A Monetary History of the United States, 1867–1960*, published in 1963. Though the ideas in this work proved to be exceptionally appealing to many people, they also turned out to be extraordinarily ineffective at dealing with the fundamental objectives with which economic policy ought to be concerned. Between 1973 and 1992, the cumulative rise in world output slowed dramatically, falling from 4.9% to 3.0% per annum.[58] At the same time, the performance on unemployment and inflation also deteriorated markedly. Nor has the record for recent years been much better. Inflation has fallen, but outside the USA there is little sign of unemployment diminishing, and, as we shall see, there are reasons for concern about the American labour market which may undermine the apparently favourable unemployment trends there. Between 1990 and 1996, world annual growth was 3.3%.[59]

The world therefore still urgently needs a framework of international economic policies which will enable the dynamism of the 1950s and 1960s to be recovered, but which can be made to operate without the fixed exchange rate régime which in the end undermined the Bretton Woods system. The history of the period between 1945 and the end of the twentieth century shows how much was lost because no adequate replacement was available to carry the Keynesian legacy forward when the Bretton Woods construct, which worked better than anything the world had ever seen previously, reached the end of the period when it was viable.

5
Post-World War II

'No nation was ever ruined by trade.'
Benjamin Franklin

World War II was an even worse disaster for the world in terms of loss of life and material destruction than World War I. Many more people were killed as a result of the hostilities. The increased destructiveness of the weapons used, particularly those involved with aerial bombardment, caused far more damage to roads, railways, houses and factories.

Of the major European economies, Germany was by far the worst affected. Constant bombing by day and night for the last half of the war had reduced most German cities to ruins. Coal production, which had totalled 400m tons in 1939, was just under 60m tons in 1945. Crude steel production, which had been nearly 24m tons in 1939, fell to almost nothing by the end of the war.[1] The currency collapsed again, and many transactions were conducted by barter, or by using cigarettes as a temporary substitute for money. During the period immediately after the war, not only was there a desperate scarcity of industrial raw materials of all kinds, but there was also a serious food shortage. The German standard of living plummeted to a fraction of its pre-war level, as the German people eked out a living as best they could amid their shattered country.

France, too, suffered severely during the war, but not as badly as Germany. The French GDP fell 17% in real terms between 1938 and 1946, and industrial production by about the same amount. Britain did a good deal better. British industrial output grew by about 5% between 1938 and 1946, while total GDP rose 16%.[2] Paradoxically, however, the British emerged from the war in many ways much worse prepared for the peace than the continental countries, almost all of which had suffered defeat at some stage during the preceding years. Britain's world pretensions were still intact, whereas those of the continental countries were greatly reduced. Germany, in particular, was allowed no more than token defence forces, whereas the British still had millions under arms, deployed all over the world. Britain had also run up substantial debts with supplier countries during the war, despite the large quantities of materiel provided by the USA, though much of this was shipped across the Atlantic without payment being required. Although substantial quantities of British foreign investments had been sold during the war to pay for supplies, large debts remained. Paying off the so-called sterling balances – debts, denominated in sterling, run up during World War II mainly to Commonwealth countries – was a major commitment for Britain, unmatched by any comparable obligations undertaken by the Germans or French.

The post-World War II settlement for Europe, after some initial aberrations, was generally a great deal more reasonable and considerate than the provisions of the Versailles Treaty after World War I. The Americans, in particular, showed outstanding generosity with Marshall Aid, which, peaking at 3% of US GDP, poured into all the economies of Western Europe, underpinning the recovery which was beginning to take place. Currency reform in Germany in the summer of 1948 was followed by a substantial, and as it turned out, largely unnecessary 20% devaluation in 1949. In the same year, an excellent harvest did much to solve the food shortage, suddenly leaving West Germany in an extraordinarily competitive position. Even though manufacturing in 1948 was still at only half its pre-war level, and output per head was even lower as a result of the large influx of refugees from the east, over the next fifteen months production rose 57% to 87% of the 1936 level. Exports more than doubled from 19% to 43% of the pre-war figure.[3]

The French economy also emerged from the immediate post-war period in a much more competitive position than it had been in before the war, and began to expand rapidly. Starting from a higher base than the Germans, increases in output were still impressive. The French economy grew by 42% between 1946 and 1950, and while some of this increase reflected recovery from the dislocations of the war years, much of the rest of it resulted from heavy investment in new industrial facilities, triggered off, as in Germany, by rapidly rising exports and home demand.[4] In Italy and the Benelux countries, too, there was a much swifter recovery from the war than had been predicted. Growth in exports and industrial output surged ahead, as all the erstwhile devastated economies in Europe began to recover much more quickly than the British and Americans had thought they would. By contrast, the British economy, whose wartime output peaked in 1943, did not regain this level of performance until ten years later, in 1953.[5]

The British, in particular, were left heavily exposed by the rapidly increasing competitiveness of the continental economies, combined with war debts, worldwide defence obligations, and major commitments on the domestic front to the creation of the welfare state by the Labour government elected in 1945. The loss of income from foreign investments, caused by sales of assets to pay for war supplies, meant that Britain had to cover a much higher proportion of its import costs than previously by export sales. This proved to be an impossible task during the early years after the war, despite strenuous efforts by the government. Britain was caught in a double pincer. On the one hand, there was a big dollar gap, caused by a major balance of payments deficit between Britain and the USA. On the other hand, British exports were unable to hold their own against competition from the reviving export industries of Europe. The British dollar gap problem was largely solved by the devaluation of sterling in 1949 from $4.03 to $2.80, but as much of the rest of Europe devalued at the same time, the continental producers retained their competitive edge *vis à vis* British exporters.[6]

The British problem was worsened by the outbreak of the Korean War in June 1950. British efforts to maintain its coveted, if rather illusory, special relationship with the USA led to Britain embarking on a major rearmament drive, pre-empting industrial resources away from exports, and adding to inflationary pressures. The economies on the continent of Western Europe, on the contrary, were largely immune from these commitments, and continued to expand both their domestic and foreign markets.

The continental European economies were thus poised for the enormous expansion in output which they achieved in the 1950s. Driven by highly competitive exports, and aided by high levels of investment and modest rates of inflation, between 1950 and 1960, the French economy grew by 56%, Italy by 80% and West Germany by 115%. The British achieved a much more modest 30%. France's industrial output over the same period grew by 89%, Italy's by 131%, and West Germany's by 148%, while Britain's grew by only 28%.[7] Significantly, this was a lower percentage than the growth in the British economy as a whole, presaging problems which would be shared by the other erstwhile successful economies in future decades.

The results of the differential performance of the major economies in Europe during the 1950s was a massive shift in their relative rankings, reflected in share of world trade, income per head and, not least, in self-esteem and self-confidence. Britain, which in 1945 had seemed to be much the most successful country in Europe, gradually began to have increasing doubts about its economic strength and its military and diplomatic position in the world. The continental economies, on the other hand, began to see each other in an increasingly favourable light, as the traumas of World War II faded in peoples' memories. Discussions about some sharing of transnational sovereignty had started early after the end of the war, culminating in the Treaty of Paris in 1951 which established the European Coal and Steel Community. Now seemed the time to embark on a more substantial and far-reaching venture.

European recovery and the Common Market

It is difficult to exaggerate the extent to which the history of Europe since World War II has been dominated by the determination of the generations which had lived through two devastating wars to make sure such a calamity never occurred again. This has been the source from which all the post-war supra-national institutions in Europe have sprung, though inevitably, once in place, the organisations established developed a momentum of their own. The key issue, from an economic standpoint, is the impact which this integration has had on the achievement of growth, high levels of employment and sustainable price increases.

The European Coal and Steel Community was the first major consequence of the vision of Jean Monnet and his associates of a Europe not only at peace with itself, but bound together by increasingly inte-grationist and federal arrangements. From the beginning, it was made clear that the intention was not just to link the countries of Europe by expanding the commercial bonds between them, but to build supra-national political structures which might eventually become the framework for a United States of Europe. The rise in power of the United States and the Soviet Union, and the divisions of Europe into East and West, made it look prudent to create a European polity as a counter-balance to the other superpowers. Furthermore, despite the successful rate at which the continental West European economies were growing, they were still divided from each other by remarkably high tariff barriers. Most of these countries had long histories of protectionism, but there were powerful arguments in favour of freer trade, with the creation of a customs union as a first step towards closer integration.

Britain was offered membership of the European Coal and Steel Community but rejected it. The ECSC was set up to support production, research and development and the restructuring needs of the coal and steel industries in the countries which participated in its establishment – the same countries as subsequently came together to form the Common Market. It fulfilled its function as a supra-national body, exhibiting for the first time the willingness of the participating states to give up some sovereignty for a common purpose, but in other ways it was less successful. The ECSC was essentially a cartel, whose primary function was to keep prices up to assist its members. Like all such cartels, the benefits to its constituents in enhanced revenues were clear enough. The cost to everyone else in the Six countries covered by ECSC, in the form of higher prices for coal and steel than might otherwise have prevailed, were not so obvious. The benefits to the coal and steel industries were bought at the expense of all their customers, some of whom, competing in international markets, were severely disadvantaged by higher raw material and energy costs.

Nevertheless, the experiment with ECSC was sufficiently promising to encourage the participating countries to convene the Messina Conference in 1955. The main agenda was to consider integration on a more comprehensive scale. The outcome was the Treaty of Rome, signed in 1957, which brought the Common Market into being on 1st January 1958. The Treaty's immediate objective was to establish a customs union. It was clear from the beginning, however, that the signatories regarded this as only a start to a process which was expected to go much further. The preamble to the Treaty spoke of those setting up the customs union being 'determined to establish the foundations of an ever closer union among the European peoples'.[8] There is no doubt that many of those involved saw the Treaty of Rome as the first step towards a much more substantial political goal.

Britain, much the largest and most important European economy not included among the original Six, was asked to participate at Messina. The British, still sufficiently confident in their world role, the Commonwealth and their supposed special relationship with the Americans, declined to join the new organisation. An alternative British proposal, to set up an industrial free trade area in Europe without the political overtones of the Common Market and without the Common Agricultural Policy régime, was decisively rejected by the Common Market founders. They were not interested in just an economic union. As with so many of the decisions taken in Europe, which shaped the way the European Community developed, Britain's rejection of membership was taken largely on political grounds, with little thought to the economic consequences. In this respect the British mirrored their counterparts in Germany, France, Italy and the Benelux countries. The motivation for setting up the Common Market was almost entirely political, as was Britain's refusal to join. In both cases, the economic arguments were treated as secondary and subordinate – a potent precedent for the future.

In fact the case for setting up a customs union in Europe was never as clear-cut as its proponents claimed it was. Nevertheless, a plausible justification could be made for it, on the grounds that the conditions required for the advantages to outweigh the disadvantages were probably, on balance, fulfilled. The arguments for and against customs unions are well rehearsed in economic literature. Essentially they turn on whether more is to be gained through trade creation within the union than is lost by trade diversion away from cheaper and more efficient suppliers who, because of the union's external tariff, can no longer compete. The proponents of customs unions generally advance two arguments. The first is that the trade creation gains will outweigh the trade diversion losses. The second is that the extra margin of competitiveness generated by a larger market will increase the average growth rate of all the participants, thus producing positive dynamic as well as static benefits.

Critics of customs unions, on the other hand, point to the fact that even if there is an overall gain from trade creation, this may be unevenly spread among the participants. Severe losses among the losers may be more important than the benefits to the winners. Furthermore, even if there are gains from trade creation, they tend to be relatively small in relation to the increase in output generated by a high overall growth rate. Trade creation benefits of the kind envisaged by the establishment of the Common Market tend, at best, to be one-off, and only of the order of 2% of GDP. This equates to the benefit of only four months' increase in output in economies growing at 6% per annum. Critics also tend to be sceptical of the claims that customs unions will necessarily increase the growth rate. They acknowledge that this may happen if all the countries comprising the customs union benefit more or less equally from its establishment. If, however, some members are in a weaker competitive position than others, they may well find that they will run into balance of payments problems, triggering deflationary measures which might otherwise not have been necessary. This will bring down their growth rate, and the resulting reduction in overall demand within

to 5.8%. Yet the most significant major influence on the relative competitiveness of the Six over the fifteen years covered by the figures were
the double devaluations of the French franc at the end of the 1950s. These
reduced the parity of the franc against the Deutsche Mark by a quarter,
following five smaller devaluations of the franc which had taken place
since 1949, evening up the competitiveness of the French and German
economies, particularly in relation to their differing inflation rates. Thus
the early success of the Common Market can be traced to a significant
extent to the exchange rate flexibility which enabled all the constituent
countries to grow at similar rates. They each preserved a broadly equal
level of competitiveness, without some countries running into balance
of payments problems *vis à vis* others. Maintaining these conditions was
one of the vital keys that was thrown away in the 1970s, when attempts
began to be made to lock Community currency parities together.

During the same periods as those in the table above, the British
economy had grown respectively by 20% and 29%, with average annual
growth rates over each of the two periods of 2.6% and 3.7%,[10] about half
the average achieved by the Six. The contrast between the performance
of the British economy and the Common Market countries was all too
striking, provoking the first application for membership by Britain in
1961. This was rebuffed by Charles de Gaulle in 1962. A second British
application in 1967 fared no better with the General, whose distrust of
British attitudes and intentions remained undiminished.

The logic, as opposed to the emotion, behind Britain's membership
application was, however, not easy to follow. It was widely assumed that
by joining a union of fast expanding countries, Britain's growth rate
would automatically be lifted to something closer to the average of those
to whom it was attaching itself. Exactly how or why this should happen
was not explained. Critics of Britain's application remained concerned
that the root problem behind Britain's slow growth rate, which was its
lack of competitiveness, would be exacerbated rather than improved by
exposing Britain to more competition inside the customs union. Between
1963 and 1973, the total Common Market GDP rose by 58%, a
cumulative annual growth rate of 4.7%, whereas the British GDP,
protected by significant tariffs, had grown by only 39%, or 3.3% per
annum.[11] These sceptical arguments failed to win the day, however,
leading to the third, and this time successful, membership application by
Britain in 1970. The European Free Trade Area, comprising Britain,
Switzerland, Denmark, Sweden, Finland, Austria and Norway, established
in 1960, had failed to provided the dynamism which Britain sought.
Britain became a Community member at the beginning of 1973, bringing

with it Ireland and Denmark, both major British trading partners, but not Norway which opted to remain outside the Community.

Up to 1973, therefore, the Common Market had been able to maintain most of the momentum established during the post-World War II recovery period. The growth rate had slowed a little since 1957, but not much. Unemployment throughout the years to 1973 was very low, averaging little more than 2% over the whole period in all Common Market countries. Inflation varied somewhat from economy to economy in the Community, but was maintained at an average of a little less than 4%.[12] Pride in the achievements of the last quarter of a century was understandable and considerable. An enormous increase in wealth and living standards had been accomplished. At the same time, generous welfare systems had been established, progress had been made towards making post-tax income distribution more equal, vast improvements had been made in housing and education, and political stability seemed assured. Few people, therefore, foresaw the scale and nature of the problems which were about to unfold.

US experience Post-World War II

The years immediately following the end of World War II saw a substantial slackening of demand on the US economy as government procurement for the war effort fell away, and US GDP fell over 17% between 1944 and 1947. Unemployment rose from 1.2% to 3.9% and the peak wartime level of output achieved by the US economy in 1944 was not regained until 1951.[13] The economy was, nevertheless, in an extremely strong position after 1945. Partly because of the dominant position in which it found itself in the post-war period, however, the USA was left facing a number of problems which tended to sap rather than reinforce its growth performance in the decades to follow.

First, its victorious position left it with heavy international commitments, which greatly increased US unilateral transfers abroad. The most substantial of these was expenditure on major military presences in Europe, the Far East and elsewhere, whose cost increased sharply with the advent of the Cold War. An additional peak was caused by the Korean War which broke out in June 1950. Significant sums were also paid out to various international programmes, not least Marshall Aid. This extraordinarily generous initiative greatly assisted the war-torn countries in Europe to recover, as we have seen.

Aid programmes also went some way towards helping to deal with the second problem with which the USA had to contend, which concerned trade imbalances. Although there was a large potential demand for US exports, which would have helped to boost the US economy, the rest of the world was extremely short of dollars with which to pay for them. Marshall Aid helped fill the gap, not only by assisting recovering economies directly with aid on soft terms, but also by providing them with payment in dollars, which they in turn could use to buy American goods and services. There was still, however, a substantial 'dollar gap' which could only be filled when the recovering economies had got themselves into a strong enough position to trade on equal terms with the USA. This was a prerequisite for the achievement of one of the major US policy goals in the immediate post-war period, which was to see artificial barriers to trade and international payments removed, allowing the world to return to something like nineteenth-century conditions as opposed to those of the inter-war period. Although, as we have seen, American tariffs in the period running up to World War I were very high, the US authorities now recognised that in the interests of the world as a whole, protectionism was not the way ahead. Freer trade and multilateral payments were not, however, achievable unless all the economies concerned could participate on manageable terms.

These considerations led to the third problem, which in the long term proved to be the most serious. After the war, the victorious Allied powers were anxious that the defeated nations should not indefinitely require succour and subsidy. Greatly underestimating their erstwhile enemies' capacity for revival, the Allies therefore took active steps to ensure that the economies of the countries which had lost the war should have some chance of speedy recovery by providing them with exceptionally competitive parities for their currencies. This affected not only the German Deutsche Mark, following the currency reforms of 1948 and the DM devaluation of 1949, but also the yen, where similar financial reforms carried out at the same time by the MacArthur administration in Japan, provided the Japanese economy with an exceptionally competitive cost base.

Germany and Japan, therefore, soon began to surge ahead with remarkably rapid recoveries. At the same time, other developed nations which had been overrun during the war also began to perform much better than they had done previously. Some of this performance was due to recovery from the wartime devastation, but other causes were almost certainly even more important. Nearly all the leaders of these countries exhibited a new determination to run their economies more successfully, learning from the mistakes of the inter-war period, fortified by the doctrines of Keynes and his associates. Old élites were swept away, discredited by wartime failure or collaboration, leaving the field free for fresh talent. Opportunities opened up by rapid growth in the post-war recovery period sucked able people into those parts of the economy where the scope was greatest, in manufacturing and exporting. As a result, strong and influential social and political groupings were established, determined to safeguard industrial and trading interests. This was a major reason why during the 1950s and 1960s the US economy grew more slowly, at 3.6% per annum, than those of either continental Europe and Japan, or that of the world as a whole which grew at 4.8% a year during this period.[14]

Again, it is important to remember that the impact of differential growth rates, which may seem small viewed a year at a time, has a huge compound effect over any reasonably long span of years. During the twenty years between 1950 and 1970, the ratio between the size of the British economy at the end of this period compared to the beginning was 1.7, for the USA it was 2.0, for the West European economies it was 2.6, and for Japan it was 6.8. Allowing for population growth, the disparities in the changes of living standards caused by these differences in growth rates were even more marked. By 1970, another massive alteration in the distribution of world economic power had taken place. Whereas up to 1945, however, the underlying trend had been to increase the relative strength of the US economy *vis à vis* the rest of the world, for all of the first quarter of a century after World War II the USA was in relative decline, a trend which has continued since.

Why did the leaders of the USA in the decades immediately after the end of World War II allow this trend to establish itself? There appear to be four main reasons, all of them to a greater or lesser extent still relevant to the condition of the USA today.

First, taken year on year, it was not so obvious that a long-term tendency towards relatively poor US growth performance had established itself. There were fluctuations in the US growth rate, and those of other countries, which made the long-term trends more difficult to confirm than would have been the case if all economies had grown at a steady pace throughout the period. Furthermore, during the 1950s and 1960s, the US economy was not only vastly more productive per head of the population than that of other countries, it was also growing richer nearly every year, even if more slowly than elsewhere. As a result, the leaders of the USA did not, on the whole, worry greatly about the overall performance of their economy in terms of its aggregate output. Their concerns were directed more to matters such as containing inflation within reasonable bounds, and all the innumerable issues concerning taxation and expenditure which determined which national interests obtained larger or smaller slices of the Federal cake.

There was some concern that the Soviet Union might be growing exceptionally fast, and could therefore pose a military as well as an economic threat to the hegemony of the USA. The time, however, at which this might conceivably happen seemed some distance away, even in the 1960s, and the Soviet bloc was never a sufficient economic threat to galvanise the US government into taking radical action to head it off. There was also some concern about the outstanding performance of Japan, which obviously was growing fast, but at least until well after 1970, the Japanese economy was still much smaller than that of the USA, with a much lower GDP per head. Furthermore, the USA had no difficulty in running a balance of payments surplus, often substantial, every year from 1945 to 1971,[15] at least before taking unilateral transfers into account. The exceptional success of other countries in building up their economies did not therefore appear to be a direct threat to American interests. On the contrary, increasing prosperity elsewhere, particularly in Europe and Japan, was welcomed as a development likely to lead to a lightening of US international burdens, providing other countries with opportunities to take a larger share in military expenditures, and other commitments such as aid programmes.

The second major reason why the relatively slow growth rate of the USA in the 1950s and 1960s was not a matter of major concern to those leading the country is that it was not a significant electoral issue, nor one which greatly stirred public opinion. The huge size of the USA, and its substantial self-sufficiency, combined with its prosperity and power, left most American citizens more than content with the country's international performance. The USA has never had a period when either imports and exports involved as much as 15% of GDP, and in this sense the US economy is much more isolated from the rest of the world than most others. Furthermore, even as late as 1965, almost 80% of US imports were still raw materials and semi-manufactures, down from 84% in 1960, and 97% in 1950.[16] Imports of this type were not a threat to US manufacturing. The hollowing out of the industrial base, which was to happen later, had hardly begun. By 1970, however, the proportion of finished goods in US imports had gone up from 21% to 39%, as American industries began to face mounting problems in competing with manufactured imports at the end of the 1960s.[17] Until this process was well under way, however, there were still plenty of high paying jobs in US industry. In 1950, 26% of the American civilian labour force was employed in manufacturing, and still 25% in 1970.[18]

Third, the USA's world leadership role put substantial constraints on its ability to make the kind of changes which would have ensured that the American economy grew faster. From the end of World War II onwards, the dollar provided the keystone to the world's financial system. The dollar was established as the world's reserve currency, and maintaining its stability was an essential component of the post-World War II financial system. In these circumstances, devaluing the dollar to make US output more competitive, thus encouraging the type of export led growth in the USA which was fuelling the rapid output increases in Europe and Japan at the time, would have been severely disruptive in the 1950s and 1960s, as indeed it was when it eventually happened in 1971.

Nor was the US lead role only concerned with financial issues. To maintain its military hegemony, procurement of materiel for the armed forces and payment for the current costs of maintaining millions of people under arms required large outlays, with much of this expenditure being incurred in foreign currencies. During the decades after World War II, the USA also undertook a high proportion of the world's aid expenditure, as well as paying a substantial proportion of the costs of a variety of international bodies. The result was that for every year from 1945 onwards, the US balance of payments had to bear a cost of billions of dollars in unilateral transfers overseas. Nevertheless, despite the relatively slow growth in US merchandise exports during the 1950s and 1960s – 6.3% cumulatively, compared to 8.4% on average for the major European economies, and 15.4% for Japan[19] – the USA did not have a major problem with its foreign payments. This was partly because imports were low in relation to the size of the economy as a whole, and partly because of a substantial and sustained surplus on investment income from abroad during this period. The result was that the drain on resources from leadership commitments, though significant, was never large enough to require a major shift in economic policy to enable them to continue to be supported.

Fourth, during most of the 1950s and 1960s, the USA was a largely conservative and contented country. At least until the advent of serious opposition to the Vietnam War, and the student campus troubles and the battles over desegregation which occurred at about the same time, American society was generally at ease with itself. The rhetoric of the Kennedy era did not do a great deal to disturb the status quo, and even the more disruptive developments of the late 1960s, in the Johnson era, affected only a minority of the population. With stability and satisfaction with existing conditions, all societies tend to become more complacent and less keen on radical change. The power and influence of those in established positions tends to grow over time. The cumulative effect of successive good years strengthens conservative financial interests. Those who have done well are not always interested in seeing changes made involving upheavals which might allow others, until then less fortunate, to catch up in wealth and status. The strong conservative bias in American society during the post-World War II period was perhaps the most fundamental reason of all why no vigorous action was taken to change the trajectory of US economic policy for a quarter of a century after 1945.

During the late 1960s, however, the prospects for the American economy began rapidly to darken. There was no one single cause. A variety of different developments occurred, all of which combined together to topple the dollar from the pre-eminent position it had enjoyed for the previous quarter of a century, and to produce a period of much greater instability, slower growth, higher unemployment and worse inflation than had prevailed for the previous decades.

A major cause of these upsets was the combination during the late 1960s of escalating expenditure on the Vietnam War with the rapidly rising costs of implementing the Great Society programme, which the Democrat president, Lyndon Johnson, had close to his heart. Successive reports from the military in charge in Vietnam, particularly General Westmoreland, each suggesting that a further comparatively modest increase in expenditure would move the outcome of the war decisively in the USA's favour, had turned out to be false. As a result, the cost of the war had steadily mounted. Total defence expenditure rose from $51bn in 1964 to $82bn in 1968, an increase as a proportion of GDP from an already high 7.4% to 9.4%.[20] The Great Society programme was both a cherished big government Democrat programme in its own right, and a response to the civil rights campaigns of the 1960s, which in turn had drawn in other disadvantaged groups. Its cost, however, was also high. Expenditure on income support, social security, welfare, veterans' benefits and family assistance, which had been $38bn in 1964, had risen by 1968 to $63bn, an increase from 5.7% of GDP to 6.9%.[21] The combined cost of both the war and rising social expenditure therefore involved an increase in expenditure of 2.6% of GDP in three years.

A shift of this magnitude might not have been a problem if taxation had been raised to pay for it, but this did not happen. Federal receipts as a proportion of GDP stayed the same between 1964 and 1968 at 17.6%.[22] The result was highly reflationary as government expenditure rose rapidly, financed largely by borrowing from the banking system, generating a fiscal deficit which peaked at $25bn in 1968.[23] This occurred at a time when the US economy was already booming. Between 1960 and 1968, the cumulative growth rate was 4.6%, a much better figure than had been achieved previously.[24] Unemployment fell below 4%, but investment nevertheless lagged.[25] Despite the more rapid growth in GDP, gross private fixed investment as a proportion of US GDP never rose during the 1960s to above a little over 15%,[26] a very low figure by international standards. By the end of the 1960s, the average age of US plant was eighteen years, compared to twelve in West Germany and ten in Japan.[27] The overall result was that the economy became progressively more overheated, and its output less internationally competitive. Consumer price inflation, which had averaged 1.3% per annum between 1960 and 1965, reached 5.7% in 1970.[28] The surplus on trade in goods and services every year since 1945, shrank to $91m in 1969 and moved into a heavy deficit in the 1970s.[29] Imports of motor vehicles and parts alone rose from $0.9bn in 1965 to $5.9bn in 1970, a real increase of nearly 450%, while over the same five years, imports of consumer goods, excluding vehicles, rose from $3.3bn to $7.4bn, almost doubling in real terms.[30]

When President Nixon took over the White House in early 1969, he therefore faced an increasingly difficult economic situation. The Vietnam War was wound down, and government expenditure cut, but inflation persisted, despite rising unemployment. The wage and price control programme, introduced by the new president, helped to bring the rate of increase in the consumer price index down from 5.7% in 1970 to 3.2% in 1972,[31] but at the cost of unemployment rising to 5.6% by 1972, up from 3.5% in 1969.[32]

Meanwhile on the external front, the situation was also deteriorating. Having moved back into surplus in 1970, the balance of trade showed a $1bn deficit in 1971, to be followed by $5bn in 1972.[33] It became clear that the dollar was seriously overvalued. The result was a conference, held in 1971 at the Smithsonian Institution in Washington DC, at which the USA announced that the link between the dollar and gold, which had underpinned the Bretton Woods system, could no longer be kept in place. The dollar was then devalued, and the Bretton Woods fixed exchange régime broke up. With the dollar no longer available as an anchor reserve currency, all the major currencies in the world began to float against each other.

By 1972, the dollar had fallen 16% against the yen, 13% against the Deutsche Mark, 4% against the pound sterling and around 10% against most other currencies.[34] As a result, by 1973 the US balance of trade showed signs of recovery. The absence of exchange rate constraints for the first time for decades, however, left policy makers throughout the world without familiar landmarks to guide them. Shorn of accustomed restraints, most countries began to reflate simultaneously. Credit controls were relaxed, and the money supply greatly increased, partly fuelled by an increasing pool of euro-dollars, themselves the product of the US deficit. World output soared, growing 6.7% in 1973 alone.[35] The impact on commodity markets was dramatic. After years of falling prices, caused by excess capacity, demand suddenly exceeded supply. The prices of many raw materials doubled or trebled. Then, in 1973, the Yom Kippur War broke out between Israel and the surrounding Arab States. It ended with a resounding victory for the Israelis, but at the cost of the West seriously alienating the Arab States, many of them major suppliers of oil to the western nations, particularly the USA, which had supported Israel during the conflict. Shortly afterwards OPEC, the oil producers' cartel, raised the price of oil from around $2.50 to $10 per barrel.[36]

The consequences of all these events for the developed world were disastrous. The increased cost of oil, although it only represented about 2% of the West's GDP, presented oil importers with a new and highly unwelcome blow to their balance of payments. Almost all tried to shift the incidence elsewhere by a process of competitive deflation. At the same time, the quadrupled price of oil, accompanied by the doubling and trebling of the cost of other commodity imports, greatly increased inflationary pressures. Growth rates tumbled, and unemployment rose all over the world, as inflation moved to unprecedented levels. Mirroring similar developments in other advanced countries, the US economy, far from growing, shrank by 0.6% in 1974 and 0.4% in 1975.[37] Unemployment rose to 8.5% in 1975,[38] while the year on year increase in the consumer price level peaked at nearly 11% in 1974.[39]

The severe economic difficulties and disruption facing the whole world – not just the USA – in the mid 1970s did not, however, only affect rates of inflation, growth and unemployment. They also had a profound effect on the intellectual climate. The consensus around the ideas of Keynes and his associates, which appeared to have guided world economic policy so successfully in the 1950s and 1960s, was shattered. Demand management did not appear to provide any satisfactory solutions to the problems faced by those confronted with the severely unstable conditions with which they now had to cope. Into the vacuum thus created, moved an old economic doctrine in a new guise, to take the place of discredited Keynesianism. Monetarism arrived on the scene in the USA and elsewhere as the intellectual underpinning of economic policy formation in a world which had lost fixed exchange rates and the discipline they provided as the anchors for taking decisions.

The rise of Japan

The countries in Asia comprised the largest part of the world economy in 1820, with nearly 70% of the world's population and nearly 60% of its GDP.[40] Three of them, China, India and Japan, accounted for 80% of both population and GDP. At this time, there was not a huge disparity in income levels between different countries in the region. By 1992, however, GDP per head was in Japan was over six times the level achieved in China, more than fourteen times that in India, and twenty-seven that in Bangladesh.[41] How did the Japanese manage to secure this achievement?

The turning point came with the arrival of the US Navy in Tokyo Bay in 1853, forcing an end to the policy pursued in Japan for more than two centuries of almost total isolation. In the 1630s the new Tokugawa shogunate, established at Edo, now Tokyo, had prohibited all travel abroad. All foreigners were expelled, except for a small colony of Dutch East India Company traders on Deshima Island, near Nagasaki, who were allowed to receive one ship a year from Indonesia. Christianity, introduced previously by St Francis Xavier, was suppressed.[42] When the Americans arrived, therefore, it is hardly surprising to find that the Japanese economy was in an exceptionally backward condition, with living standards roughly on a par with those found in Europe in the Late Middle Ages.

While the economy was undeveloped, however, Japanese political and social institutions were considerably more flexible and robust. As a result, although trade concessions were extracted by the Americans, and extended to the French, Dutch, Russians and British, and treaties were forced on Japan in 1854 which restricted its commercial and fiscal autonomy, the Japanese were able to respond far more positively to the challenge presented by western intruders than had happened elsewhere in the East. This was partly because the Japanese had always borrowed important elements of the Chinese and Korean civilisations, and were therefore not ashamed to copy a western model which had demonstrated its superior technology so dramatically.[43] The Tokugawa shogunate, humiliated by the challenge from abroad, was overthrown in 1867, and Emperor Mutsuhito assumed full powers, adopted the title *Meiji*, which means 'enlightened rule', and launched a policy of swift westernisation.

The results were dramatic. Within a remarkably short period the previous rigid stratification of society was abolished. Land could be bought and sold freely. Primary education became compulsory, and new textbooks were written with a western orientation. Large numbers of students went abroad to receive technical and higher education. Tariffs were fixed at no more than 5%, so that the economy was open to western imports. The Japanese Army and Navy were reformed and rearmed using western technology. The government then set out on a programme of economic development, much of it with a heavy military orientation, which had no parallel elsewhere in Asia, though not so dissimilar to developments elsewhere in the world where militaristic régimes were in control.[44]

The result was a steady expansion of the Japanese economy, which grew at a cumulative rate of 1.4% per annum between 1870 and 1885, accelerating to 3.1% between 1885 and 1900, and then slowing to 2.5% between 1900 and 1913.[45] This was achieved initially by the establishment of industries which, the world over, are easiest to enter with cheap labour and relative shortage of technology. By 1899, Japanese cotton mills were producing some 355m pounds of yarn, and 672m by 1913, when a quarter of the world's cotton yarn exports came from Japan.[46] This was a long way, however, from being the limit to Japan's industrial achievements. Although much copying of western techniques took place in the early phases, within a few decades, the Japanese had also established a substantial capacity to build their own machinery, and to establish a capital goods industry. By the outbreak of World War I, GDP per head in Japan was about equal to the level in Portugal and most of Eastern Europe, about a third of that in Germany, a quarter of the level in Britain and the USA, but twice that in most of the rest of Asia, including China.[47]

World War I saw the Japanese economy growing rapidly, and by 1919, Japanese GDP was over 40% more than it had been in 1913. After a sharp post-war recession, the economy continued to expand during the interwar period, checked only by a comparatively minor drop of 7% between 1929 and 1930. Starting from the 1920 low the Japanese economy grew by 3.4% per annum cumulatively to 1929,[48] aided by large exports of raw silk to the USA. When the price of silk collapsed, the yen depreciated significantly, and this undoubtedly helped boost manufactured exports as the economy accelerated sharply during the 1930s.[49] As in Germany, the advent of a militaristic régime, determined to drive the economy forward, produced a much higher growth rate. Between 1930 and the entry of the Japanese into World War II at Pearl Harbor in 1941, Japan's economy grew at a cumulative rate of 5.4% per annum.[50] By then GDP per head in Japan was approaching the level of the poorer West European countries, though it was still only half the level in Germany and 40% of that in Britain at the time.[51] Close to half of all employment in Japan – 43% – was still in agriculture, forestry and fishing.[52]

While Japanese military ventures, including, during the 1930s, the invasion and occupation of Manchuria and parts of China, followed, in 1940, by French Indo-China, had helped to stimulate the economy, World War II was a total disaster for Japan, as it was, to a similar extent, for Germany. Between 1941 and 1945, Japanese GDP fell by more than half.[53] By 1946, industrial production was down to 20% of its 1941 level, and steel production had fallen 92%. Two thirds of its large cotton textile capacity had been destroyed.[54] In 1945, Japan – before long to be the car maker for the world – produced a total of 8,200 cars and commercial vehicles.[55] Leaving aside the damage done by atomic weapons in Hiroshima and Nagasaki, American bombing raids had left all major Japanese cities in ruins. Inflation was rampant. The Japanese were humiliated and destitute.

When the American occupation, headed by General MacArthur, began, its major objectives were first to reform Japanese political institutions, to extirpate the militaristic legacy which had caused so much harm, and secondly to get the economy back on its feet, and to stop it being a drain on the American taxpayer. In 1947 MacArthur supervised the introduction of a democratic 'Peace Constitution', accompanied by demilitarisation and land reform, leading to the occupation formally ending in 1952.[56] As to the economy, the main problem, apart from general distress, was to get exports moving again, so that the country would be able to pay for the food and raw materials it needed, which in the immediate post-war period had been provided only through the Allied occupation forces, financed largely by the USA. The solution adopted was a reform of the currency, which left the cost base in Japan, measured by international standards, at an exceptionally low level, exactly as happened in Germany.

The response in Japan was very similar to what it was among all the developed countries which had been defeated at one stage or another during World War II, all of whom found themselves, in varying degrees in the same competitive position, as the victorious Allies hugely underestimated the capacity of vanquished nations to recover. Talent poured into industry, as major opportunities opened up to make fortunes on world markets. Japanese sales abroad began to soar. By 1973, Japanese merchandise exports were in volume terms 27 times as high as they had been in 1950. Germany's by contrast were 15 times as high, the USA's 4 times, and Britain's 2.4 times.[57] In 1950, Japan's share of world trade was 1.3%. In 1973 it was 16.4%.[58] Nothing shows more clearly than these figures that the history of the world, especially since the trade liberalisation that has taken place since 1945, is largely written in export competitiveness, and the alignment of exchange rates which either makes astounding success possible if the parity is favourable, or inhibits it if it is not.

Initially, Japanese post-war exports consisted mostly of comparatively simple goods in all of which Japan had an enormous price advantage because the costs of production, measured internationally, were so low. Japan had a long history of textile manufacturing and metal working. Newer industries, such as those involving the use of plastics, where the technology was comparatively simple, were quick and easy to establish. As had happened in the nineteenth century, however, the Japanese were not content to see their role solely as the producers of cheap goods. The economy rapidly developed a formidable capacity for moving up market and for making its own capital goods, as well as expanding its heavy industries in steel and shipbuilding, and its oil refining and electricity generating capacity. Crude steel production, which had been 557 000 tons in 1946, reached almost 120m tons by 1973. By then, Japan was generating over twenty times as much electricity as at the end of World War II. Perhaps the most outstanding success story of all was to be found in the motor vehicle industry. Starting from the 8,200 units of all kind produced in 1945, referred to above, by 1973 Japanese manufacturers produced over 7m vehicles, and by 1983, more than 11m.[59]

Riding on the massive growth in exports, which averaged a cumulative increase of over 15% per annum between 1950 and 1973, the Japanese economy grew extremely rapidly. Having only exceeded its 1943 peak wartime output for the first time in 1953, by 1973 it was 7.6 times the size it had been in 1950, after a cumulative average growth rate throughout these twenty-three years of 9.2%.[60] The comparatively low increase in the population – just over 1.1% per annum between 1950 and 1973[61] – avoided much dilution of the increase in GDP, so that GDP per head also rose strongly, by 8.0% per annum throughout this period. By 1973, Japanese living standards were on a par with those in Britain, and not far behind those in most of Western Europe – a massive change from the position which had prevailed a quarter of a century earlier.[62]

There is a vast literature about the reasons for the remarkable achievements of the Japanese economy, especially during the period up to 1973 when its growth rate was at its highest. Undoubtedly, a number of factors played an important role. All the countries defeated at various stages in World War II had a resurgence once the war ended, as older leaders became discredited, and new opportunities opened up for those, hungry for success, who replaced them. All of them had well educated, well trained and experienced labour forces. The disruption caused by such large-scale warfare as had taken place during the first half of the twentieth century left a substantial legacy of inventions and technical possibilities to be exploited, and the Japanese were exceptionally well placed to take advantage of these opportunities. Other characteristics more specifically orientated to institutions and culture in Japan have also been cited. The homogeneity, discipline and national pride of the Japanese people undoubtedly helped to generate a focused work ethic. Some have argued that the consensual Confucian tradition may also have assisted. The role of the Japanese Ministry of International Trade and Industry (MITI) in promoting industrial policy, and protecting the Japanese market from what it regarded as potentially excessive import penetration, may have been a positive factor at some stages. As will be argued below, however, there are good reasons for believing that much of its influence was neither successful in its own terms, or good for the economy in the longer term.

By far the strongest argument that none of these special factors was fundamentally the cause of Japanese success lies in the fact that their alleged influence evaporated as soon as the Japanese economy lost the real reason for its high growth rate, which was its undervalued exchange rate. Until 1971, this was fixed at 360 yen to the US dollar.[63] Because the Japanese export drive was so successful, and the amount of investment in production facilities available for the world market was so high, Japanese export prices rose during the 1950s and 1960s by barely 1%[64] a year, despite relatively high levels of domestic inflation, which averaged 5.2% per annum between 1950 and 1973.[65] The result was that Japanese exports became more and more competitive, thus fuelling the next stage of their expansion. Although, immediately post the 1971 move towards floating rates, the nominal value of the yen strengthened against the dollar by some 20%, followed by a slow further hardening of the yen, the competitiveness of Japanese exports continued to increase.[66]

The turning point came in the mid 1980s, when the yen suddenly strengthened against the dollar as the exchange rate moved from 238 yen per dollar in 1985 to 168 in 1986 and 145 in 1987. After staying roughly stable until 1990, it moved up again, peaking at just under 100 in 1995, before weakening to 131 in 1998.[67] The reason for the hardening of the yen was the huge balance of payments surplus which the Japanese started to accumulate from the early 1980s onwards, after decades when the Japanese current account had been in rough balance. There was a massive surplus on merchandise account, which reached over $44bn by 1984, and which averaged almost $90bn per annum in the late 1980s, partly offset by a deficit on services, but increased by a rising net income from investments abroad. Overall, the current account surplus run up by the Japanese economy between 1984 and 1994 totalled a staggering $932bn.[68]

The effect on the volume of Japanese exports as a result of the strengthening yen at the beginning of the 1990s was immediate. The price in yen which Japanese exporters could charge the rest of the world fell by about 20%, putting a severe strain on their previously buoyant profitability. The increase in volume of exports slowed to a crawl. Between 1973 and 1985, the cumulative annual rise had been 8.6%. From 1985 to 1994 it was 2.0%.[69] As the stimulus to the economy from exports died down, so did the overall growth rate, but only after a period of speculative boom in the 'bubble economy' of the late 1980s. This kept GDP rising between 1985 and 1991 at an average of 4.4% per annum, but no longer on the sustainable basis which had applied previously when exports had been growing faster than GDP. The result was that when the boom broke, Japanese banks were left holding massive uncovered debts, and the economy stalled. In 1997, Japanese GDP was only 8.5% higher than it had been in 1991, after six years during which the economy had grown by an average of just under 1.4% per annum. Expenditure on investment, previously another major growth component, was the same in 1997 as it had been six years earlier.[70]

The major mistake made by the Japanese was to allow their huge balance of payments surplus to accumulate in the 1980s. Every country's surplus has to be matched by a deficit somewhere else, and the rest of the world choked on the success of Japanese exporters, unrequited by sufficient imports to keep Japan's current account in reasonable balance. The problem was the difficulty which the rest of the world had in exporting in sufficient volume to Japan to stop the surplus accumulating. It may have seemed a good idea to MITI at the time to promote the myriad ways in which the Japanese discouraged imports, thus allowing their surprisingly inefficient non-export-orientated part of their economy to remain protected, but the price eventually paid for this error was extremely heavy.

In the end, therefore, there is nothing that cannot be explained about the Japanese economy. It was only an extreme example of the impact which an exceptionally low cost basis can achieve. As with the leaders of so many other countries, however, those in Japan appear never to have understood or appreciated the fundamental underlying reasons for the success over which they presided. If they had, it seems hard to believe that they would have allowed the conditions which were so important to the economy for which they were responsible to melt away so pointlessly and so damagingly as they did.

The USSR and command economies

By far the largest departure from the organic way in which most of the world's economy has grown was the deliberate attempt to get rid of the capitalist system undertaken by the successful revolutionaries in Russia in 1917, and their successors in subsequent régimes devoted to running their economies on non-market lines. While the writings of Karl Marx had been the basis on which communist beliefs were founded, Marx had little to say about how economies were to be run when the revolutions he advocated had taken place. Lenin (1870–1924) and his associates and successors therefore had to formulate policies as they went along, without much of a blueprint from which to work, other than the general objective of eliminating as much private ownership as they could, while getting the economy to grow as fast as possible with a crash programme of industrialisation.

The Russian economy which they inherited had expanded substantially during the late nineteenth and early twentieth centuries, with growth rates of 2.0% per annum between 1870 and 1900 and a rather more impressive 3.2% per annum between 1900 and 1913.[71] Mostly as a result of state initiatives, by the start of World War I, there was a reasonably extensive railway system,[72] and some heavy industry. The standard of living in Russia was, however, well below the level of most of the rest of Europe, although slightly above that of Japan.[73] The Russian economy was severely disrupted by World War I, and there was heavy loss of life. Another 10m died in the course of the Revolution, civil war and attacks on the new régime from western powers fearful of what the successful replacement of capitalism might presage. As a result, it was 1930 before the Soviet economy recovered the same level of output as it had enjoyed in 1913,[74] providing its rulers with a poor, backward and fractured economic base on which to build.

Although initially relatively liberal, during its New Economic Policy phase, the Soviet régime soon toughened its stance. Lenin died in 1924, to be succeeded by Joseph Stalin (1879–1953), who introduced the system of five year plans, the first two of which covered the period from 1928 to 1939. Heavy and light industries were developed, and agriculture collectivised. The country began to be transformed as industrialisation proceeded and the urban population quickly doubled.[75] The cost, however, was prodigious not only in human terms, as millions died in the Ukraine and Kazakhstan famines of 1932–4 and in political purges and liquidations, but also in economic terms as state policies drove down the current standard of living to enable more and more resources to be mobilised for investment in the future.

The result was that the Soviet economy grew during the 1930s relatively quickly, but, as a result of high capital to output ratios, much more slowly than would have been achieved if western standards of return on the use of capital had been attained. Between 1928 and 1940, Soviet output rose by an estimated 81%, with an average per annum growth rate of 5.1%.[76] Thereafter, although until 1941 the USSR had staved off being involved in World War II as a result of the non-aggression pact negotiated with Germany in 1939, once the German invasion began in August 1941, the USSR was subjected to four traumatic years of carnage and physical injury. About 25m Soviet citizens are believed to have lost their lives as a result of the German invasion,[77] and the damage done to the area occupied by the Germans was immense. As a result, in spite of huge continuing investment in new production facilities, the output of the Soviet economy was over 20% lower in 1946 than it had been in 1940.[78]

The post-World War II period, however, saw a steady increase in output, which rose every year until the end of the 1950s at an average rate between 1947 and 1958 estimated at 7.3%, a considerably higher pace than was being achieved anywhere else except in Japan and Germany.[79] This began to cause mounting concern in the West, particularly in the USA, whose growth rate was barely half that of the Soviet economy, prompting Nikita Khrushchev to promise at the United Nations that the USSR would shortly overtake the American standard of living.[80] This threat, however, gradually, became emptier. As the years wore on, it became increasingly clear that, although the Soviet economy had responded reasonably well to large investments in basic industries, running a consumer-orientated economy was much more difficult to manage without a market framework in which to do it.

Although valiant attempts were made to get the Soviet economy to produce more consumer goods of reasonable quality, after Stalin's influence had worn off and following Khrushchev's speech in 1956 denouncing his excesses, the results were remarkably unsuccessful. The Soviet economy continued to have a high proportion of its GDP devoted to investment, but the growth rate in the economy slowed, and consumers remained dissatisfied. Between 1959 and 1973 the Soviet economy grew at a still more than respectable estimated 4.9% per annum, but thereafter, during the Brezhnev era, growth slowed to 1.9% per annum.[81] During the whole of the period between 1973 and 1989, before the USSR began to disintegrate, GDP per head in the Soviet Union increased at a cumulative rate of less than 1% per annum.[82] Allowing for the military build-up which was taking place, the disposable income for the average Soviet citizen stopped rising after 1973, stabilised, of course, at a far lower level than in the USA, where nevertheless a remarkably similar stagnant real income phenomenon was to be found among most of the population.

Unquestionably, part of the reason for the relatively poor performance in the later years of the USSR was the exceptionally heavy military burden which the economy had to bear, particularly from the mid 1960s onwards when the Cold War intensified.[83] After making all allowances for this, however, the root problem with the system proved to be the impossibility of running a more and more complex economy on the basis of central plans, with market signals largely suppressed. This led not only to the rate of growth slowing down, but to more and more serious problems of resource allocation, as their appropriation became ever more complicated, reducing the real value to the final consumer of the goods and services which were produced.

The problems of the Soviet economy were mirrored in varying degrees of intensity among all the East European countries which were obliged to adopt command economies at the behest of the USSR after the installation of communist régimes following the Soviet occupation after World War II. A particularly interesting example was the German Democratic Republic, which was long regarded as being the most successful of the Soviet satellites. Prior to reunification, western estimates of East German per capita GDP levels had put them at about three-quarters of those in the Federal Republic and about two-thirds of those in the USA. When in 1990 the Berlin Wall came down, however, and East and West Germany were reunited, these estimates were found to be about 50% too high. The actual East German level of GDP per head was only about two-thirds of what it had been thought to be, confirming strongly the deep-rooted inefficiency of even a comparatively well run command economy,[84] and emphasising the weaknesses in economic performance from which the erstwhile USSR had suffered.

It was therefore hardly surprising that the process of integrating the two parts of Germany together was found to be far more difficult and expensive than had been previously envisaged. Part of the problem was Helmut Kohl's undertaking to provide parity between the Ost Mark and the Deutsche Mark which, at a stroke, made almost all of the former DDR's output grossly overpriced and uncompetitive. The condition of even those parts of the DDR's economy which were thought to be performing reasonably well, however, also generated requirements for massive remedial expenditure. The concentration on production at all costs in East Germany had left environmental considerations well down the order of priorities. The result was pollution over large areas on a scale which those used to western-style regulation found hard to comprehend. The quality of the goods which were being produced, having never been exposed to competitive pressures, was far below world standards, apart from the fact that they were now, in addition, very expensive. The legacy of command economies for those who lived in them and the states which succeeded them has not, therefore, been an easy one. Wrenching transitions were required, tending to be more pronounced for those economies longest exposed to communism. Between 1990 and 1992 alone Russian GDP fell by over 30%.[85]

The weaknesses of the command economy approach lay exposed for all to see. Yet a sense of balance is required. The record of the Soviet economy and its satellites had some points in its favour. Although achieved at horrendous cost, the growth rates for long periods were higher than those elsewhere in the world. For much of the period, they were also steadier. While the western world plunged into depression post-1929, the Soviet economy grew every year from 1928 onwards, except for a minor 1% fall in 1932. The command economies also provided employment for virtually everyone, although at a heavy cost in the efficiency with which the labour force was used. These achievements, combined with the Soviet ability to expand without assistance from outside, were sufficient to attract partial copying by many third world countries, once they had gained independence after World War II. There was no problem about maintaining a high level of demand in command economies or, at a heavy cost, in achieving high levels of investment. The difficulties, which in the end overwhelmed them, were those of allocation of scarce resources and quality of output.

The Third World

While the main emphasis in this book has been on those countries which began to industrialise earliest, and which therefore now have the highest standards of living, most of the world's population lives elsewhere. In 1992, out of a world population of 5,441m, 4,281m, or nearly 80% of the world's inhabitants were in Latin America, Asia and Oceania or Africa. If Japan is taken out of the Asian grouping and included with the other industrialised nations, in 1992 the average income per head among the remaining 76% of humanity, measured in 1990 US dollars, was $2,173, compared to $19,175 for the industrialised countries.[86]

The developing and undeveloped nations of the world are not, however, by any means homogeneous either in the absolute standards of living which they had managed to attain by the 1990s or in their growth records during the previous decades. The broad picture is that in 1992, the standard of living in Latin America was about 30% of the level in the industrialised countries, with Venezuela, Argentina and Chile well above the average, Mexico, Colombia and Brazil a little below the mean, and with Peru at about half the average level for the region. In Asian countries, the spread was much wider. Leaving aside Japan, of the larger countries, those such as South Korea and Taiwan had by 1992 reached just over half western GDP per head levels. Others, such as Thailand, China and Indonesia were spread at between a quarter and a fifth of western living standards, with India and Pakistan at less than 10%, and Bangladesh and Myanmar at barely 4%. The income levels in Africa were both lower than in Asia, and even more skewed. South Africa had a relatively high average figure, masking very large income differentials within its boundaries, but all other major African countries had GDP per head at little more than 10% of western levels at best, shading down to desperate poverty in Tanzania, and particularly Zaire and Ethiopia where the average income for the whole population in 1992 was less than $1 per day.[87]

As to the growth records leading up to the picture in 1992, the Latin American economies had all started growing fairly early. By 1913 their average living standards were a little less than half those in the western industrialised economies. By 1950, mainly because they were not involved to any significant degree in either of the world wars, they were at just over half the western level. Thereafter, they continued to perform more or less on a par in terms of growth rates with the more advanced economies, helped by the boost provided to some of them by the discovery and exploitation of large oil deposits. Between 1950 and 1973, the combined cumulative average growth rate for Latin America was 5.3% per annum. Between 1973 and 1992, it was 2.8%. High growth rates in the population, however, meant that the expansion of the South American economies was not matched by corresponding increases in living standards, which grew much less than those in the western world – cumulatively at over 1% per annum more slowly.[88]

In Asia, the growth record was more impressive, with an overall cumulative average of 6.0% between 1950 and 1973, and 5.1% between 1973 and 1992, starting from a base position which, in 1950, showed

GDP per head to be on average not much more than one-tenth of its level in the West. As the population growth rate was markedly lower than in South America, living standards rose correspondingly more quickly – cumulatively by 3.8% for the first period, and 3.2% in the second.[89] These averages, however, cover a wide disparity of performance. They include the outstanding results achieved in Japan, and the Asian Tiger countries, and, in the later period, China, but also the widespread poor achievements of other major Asian economies. A point of considerable significance, however, is that while Japanese per annum growth slowed considerably between the periods before and after 1973, most of the rest of the major Asian economies did better in the second period than the first, averaging 5.2% cumulative growth per annum to 1973 and 5.7% to 1992.[90] The improved performance included much better results after 1973 from countries such as India at 4.7%, Bangladesh at 4.5% and Pakistan at 5.9%, and China at 6.7%.

In 1950, the average standard of living in Africa was a little higher than in Asia,[91] and between 1950 and 1973, the overall growth record in Africa, at a cumulative 4.4% was only a little below the world average of 4.9%.[92] The period 1973 to 1992, however, showed the growth rate slowing to less than 3.0%. The major problem in Africa was not the increase in GDP but the very high birth rate – 2.4% per year in the earlier period and 2.9% in the second.[93] The result was a 2.0% per annum increase in living standards during the first period, but a fall of 0.1% a year in the later one.[94]

There are some important lessons to be gained from the experiences during the last fifty years of the developing and less developed countries covered in this brief survey. Unquestionably, some of the poor results achieved were the consequence of maladministration, corruption, warfare and instability, which no economic policies, however well conceived, are capable of overcoming. Leaving these factors aside, however, a number of patterns can be detected.

First, the Soviet model of forced industrialisation turned out to be an extremely poor one. Not only did it lead to large-scale waste and misallocation of resources, but the bureaucratisation and industrial favouritism which it encouraged militated against opening up the economies adopting this approach to the stimulus of international competition. The results were high import tariffs, exchange controls and restrictions on capital movements, designed to protect indigenous industries, often owned by the state or by those associated with its political leaders. Economies which adopted such policies tended to suffer from the need to service the costs of large-scale borrowing to finance investments, many of which both achieved little or no financial return, and failed to produce world class goods and services. The inefficient and uncompetitive export sectors which were the consequence were unable to launch themselves successfully on to world markets. Most countries which once modelled themselves at least in part on the USSR have now long since ceased doing so, and their economic performance has improved accordingly.

Second, there are a number of social policies which clearly favour fast growth and rising living standards. The more successful economies have tended to be those with high literacy rates and good technical training, rather than those, such as India, which have been inclined to concentrate resources on university education at the expense of the wider population. In the mid 1990s, 38% of men and 66% of women in India were still illiterate, compared to 16% and 38% respectively in China, and 9% overall in Taiwan, with much more difficult kanji-based writing to learn.[95] It is also evident that countries which have reliable legal systems, well regulated financial sectors, successfully planned infrastructures and fair and impartial tax systems, ought to have an edge on those which lack them, although it is easy enough to find examples of countries which have prospered without these advantages. None of these requirements, desirable though they may, appear to be a *sine qua non* of economic success.

Third, rising populations have clearly been a major factor in increasing the size of many of the world's economies, but the dilution of GDP caused by there being more and more people among whom it has to be shared, has held back living standards in many countries, especially in Africa, where the population is rising most rapidly. Far the most effective way to slow down population growth is to raise living standards, but this generates a difficult chicken and egg problem. The time when the richer parts of the world can afford to ignore the need to provide more direct and indirect assistance to help deal with this issue, however, may be shorter than many people realise – an issue to be revisited in Chapter 9.

Fourth, the strongest link between those economies which have achieved high growth rates, as against those which have not, is exactly the same for poorer countries as it is for richer ones. The most important requirement is a competitive export sector, which sucks in talent and investment to where they can be most productively employed, enables a cumulative increase in foreign sales to be accomplished, and thence fuels sustainable high rates of growth in the economy as a whole. It is growth in exports which drives expansion generally, as can easily be seen from the statistics.[96] It is countries whose exports, and particularly whose merchandise sales abroad, grow faster than the world average whose economies expand most rapidly, and vice versa. From Chile to South Korea, from Turkey to China, the record is the same.

Using appropriate macro-economic policies to achieve the desired end, therefore, the crucial policy variable to get right is the cost base for internationally tradable goods and services. If this is low enough to generate a buoyant export market, it is not too difficult to get a variety of complementary economic policy elements to work successfully. If the cost base is too high, however, no supplementary mixture of policies will offset this major obstacle. The inevitable result will be relative if not absolute stagnation, as scarce talent is concentrated more and more heavily in sectors of the economy which have comparatively little to contribute in terms of competitiveness and growth.

6
The Monetarist Era

'It would be a great reform in politics if wisdom could be made to spread as easily and as rapidly as folly.'

Winston Churchill

As the certainties of the Bretton Woods world crumbled away in the early 1970s, intellectual fashions in economics moved decisively away from the Keynesian orthodoxy of the previous quarter of a century. Monetarism became the theoretical and practical discipline to which the vast majority of those involved in economic affairs, both in the academic and policy making worlds, began to subscribe. It is no coincidence, however, that the prevalence of monetarism has been highly correlated with failure of economic performance. Monetarist doctrines are inclined to receive their most sympathetic hearing among political and intellectual leaders who are at the helm of the slowest growing economies. There are interlocking reasons why this is so. It is partly that monetarist prescriptions lead to slow growth, and partly that the cultural attitudes, which breed a proclivity for them, flourish especially strongly in economies with poor growth and employment records.

This was particularly the case in the Anglo-Saxon countries, the USA and Britain, but by no means exclusively so. The same ideas have also managed to get their grip on the whole of the European Union, leading to the determination, exemplified in the provisions of the 1991 Maastricht Treaty, to put monetary stability before prosperity. The loss of confidence in Keynesian policies after the rising inflation and international dislocation of the early 1970s caused policy shifts in a monetarist

127

direction, particularly in Germany and France. As we shall see, these have changed the EU bloc from being one of the world's fastest growing regions into an area of exceptionally slow increase in output, accompanied by painfully high levels of unemployment. Countries which give monetarist prescriptions less priority, on the other hand, both in Europe and elsewhere, continue to grow apace. Norway, a prime example, outside the European Union, achieved the highest rate of GDP per head within the OECD between 1973 and 1992, just ahead of Japan, increasing the population's living standards by 71%. The Norwegians succeeded in combining this achievement with one of the better OECD records on inflation, especially recently, and an unemployment rate now barely one-third of the EU average.[1] Over the same period Britain and the USA, both countries strongly influenced by monetarist ideas, achieved GDP per head increases period of only 31% and 26% respectively. The EU as a whole achieved 41%.[2]

Monetarist prescriptions, stripped of their theorising and rhetoric, are familiar to anyone who has studied economic history. Their hallmarks are relatively tight money, and high interest and exchange rates. These conditions slow down productive enterprise, and make it harder to sell abroad and easier to import. They discriminate against manufacturing investment and drain the talent out of industry. Monetarist ideas, and the devotion to balanced budgets and financial conservatism which was its predecessor, harking back to nineteenth-century classical economics, have never been far below the surface, especially in the USA or Britain. This is why, post-1973, and especially in the 1980s, macro-economic conditions prevailed in both countries, and subsequently in most of the rest of the western world, which were almost wholly responsible for the low growth and productivity increases of the subsequent quarter of a century. They were also directly responsible for the huge widening of incomes there has been over the last twenty-five years, with which the attenuation of manufacturing capacity, itself a direct result of monetarist policies, is heavily bound up.

We will turn to monetarist theory in the next section. As a precursor, however, it is worth looking at how a combination of self-interest and social attitudes can produce an environment where monetarist ideas can take strong hold even if they are weak in intellectual coherence and undermined by prescriptive inadequacies, and have such damaging consequences. Why should mature, stable, slow growing economies be particularly prone to producing a climate of opinion where such ideas can flourish?

The answer is that the implications of monetarist policies are far from unattractive to large sections of the population, especially in slow growing economies where lenders tend to be in a strong position and borrowers in a weak one. Those who have achieved success in finance rather than manufacturing tend to move into positions of influence and political power. As they do so, the monetarist doctrines which appeal to people with financial backgrounds become increasingly predominant. The attitudes of those whose business is lending money, who have an obvious stake in high interest rates and scarcity of the commodity they control, become politically significant, not least because their opinions have a self-fulfilling quality. If there is great fear that losing their confidence will lead to a run on the currency, this places those in a position to keep the parity up by their decisions in a very powerful role. Those whose incomes depend on high interest rates – pensioners and many others – are also naturally inclined to support a policy which seems so obviously in their favour. Bankers, financiers and wealth holders are the immediate beneficiaries of the deflationary policies which follow, buttressed by those who can see no further ahead than obtaining the immediate benefits from low cost imports and cheap holidays abroad. The losers are those engaged in manufacturing and selling internationally tradable goods and services.

When the economy grows slowly, the power and influence of finance increases against that of industry. This is partly a result of the process of accumulation of capital wealth, much of which tends to be invested abroad rather than at home, because slow growth in the domestic economy creates better opportunities overseas. This was the story of Britain in the nineteenth century, the United States for a long period post-World War II, while Japan has now moved into a similar role. This process produces profound effects on social attitudes and political power, particularly if these conditions prevail for a long period of time, as they have in most of the slow growing industrialised countries.

If the economy is run with relatively tight money, and high interest and exchange rates, the inevitable consequence is to produce adverse trading conditions for all output exposed to international competition. Adequate returns on investment are much harder to achieve. It becomes increasingly difficult to pay the going wage or salary rates for the calibre of employees required for success in world markets. Of course there will always be exceptionally efficient companies, or even industries, such as pharmaceuticals in Britain, which buck the trend, but they are not critically important. It is the average which counts, and here the results are impossible to dismiss. The profitability of large sections of manufacturing in the western world have become insufficient for it to be worth while for them to continue in business. This is why the proportion of GDP derived from manufacturing has fallen so precipitately in most western economies over the last three decades. By 1983, half of all US imports were manufactures, compared to just over 20% only twenty years previously.[3] By contrast, between 1960 and 1982, Japanese car production rose from 0.5m to 11m per annum, while US output fell from 6.7m to 5.0m. Over the same period, Japanese crude steel output increased from 22m to 111m tons per annum, while US output dropped from 90m to 68m.[4] The same trends affected swathes of other industries in many other developed economies. Meanwhile, in countries which gave their industrial base a better deal, fortunes were made in manufacturing, and the rest of the economy struggled to keep up.

The most able graduates from western universities nowadays go decreasingly into industry. The easiest money and most glittering careers beckon in the professions, in finance and in the media. The academic world, politics and government service look increasingly more attractive, and for those bent on a career in mainstream business, distribution or retailing generally offer more security and prospects than manufacturing. If the most able people choose not to go into industry, but instead become lawyers or bankers or television personalities, the educational system responds accordingly. The subjects orientated to those engaged in making and selling are downgraded in importance compared to those required for other careers. Practical science falls in status compared to the arts. Commercial studies come to be regarded as second-rate options compared to professional qualifications. Practical subjects, such as engineering, become perceived as less glamorous and attractive – and potentially less lucrative – than the humanities. In the USA, from the mid 1980s to the early 1990s, when an extreme example of monetarist policies was in full flight, there was a precipitate fall in freshman enrolments from the mid 1980s to the early 1990s in subjects where employment prospects had been adversely affected, particularly by the blood-letting of manufacturing which took place at the time. Those planning to pursue business studies fell from 27% to 16% of the total, while the proportion choosing engineering fell from 11% to 9%. At the same time, the share aiming for professional qualifications rose from 13% to 20%.[5] These figures provide clear evidence as to how quickly and profoundly the educational system then becomes part of cultural conditioning, as peer pressure, career prospects and the priority and prestige accorded to different subjects, determine where the nation's talent bends its energies.

A significant consequence of the social bias which runs through the whole of this process is that it determines the background of people most likely to reach the peak of their careers running major companies, especially in manufacturing. An interesting contrast between countries such as the USA and Britain, which have grown slowly, and those economies which have grown fastest, is that quite different people tend to become CEOs. In slow growing economies, chief executives are often professional people such as lawyers and accountants. Where the economy is growing fast, they tend to be engineers and salesmen. No doubt both cause and effect are operating here. If the most able people in the commercial field are in the professions, they will finish up at the top of big companies, where their particular talents will be especially in demand to deal with powerful financial interests. In fast growing economies, where financial interests are less immediately pressing and the most able people are not in the professions, engineers and salesmen tend to hold the top positions. It is hardly surprising that companies which are run by accountants and lawyers are particularly concerned with financial results, while those controlled by salesmen and engineers are more orientated to markets and products.

Nor is the low status of industry only a financial or social matter. It also has a large impact on the political weight of manufacturing interests as against those of other parts of the economy. Exercising political power requires talent, takes time and costs money. All are in increasingly short supply particularly in American and British industry, and the results are clear to see. Few Members of Congress or Parliament have any significant hands-on manufacturing experience. The role models to whom the younger generation looks up are nowadays not usually those running manufacturing industries. Those in law practice, accountancy and investment banking look more impressive and secure. In these circumstances it is small wonder that economic ideas which promote finance over manufacturing tend to find favour. It does not follow, however, that these ideas are well founded. Still less is it true that they are in the best long-term interests of the economy as a whole, or even of those in the financial community itself. In the end, those concerned with finance depend as much as everyone else on the performance of the underlying economy, and in particular on its capacity to hold its own in world markets.

Monetarist theory and practice

The appeal of hard money has a long history. Those with established wealth have always been keen that it should earn as substantial a return as possible. High rates of interest and low rates of inflation have an obvious appeal to them, a view of the world almost invariably shared by those with a banking background. A sense of prudence militates against deficit financing and easy money. The impact of high interest and exchange rates on manufacturers and exporters, whose businesses inevitably suffer, can readily be blamed on their inability to respond positively to the rigours and discipline of tougher competition.

Nor, as we have seen, is it just the well off who are inclined to favour the financial environment which monetarist policies generate. Many poorer people, particularly pensioners on fixed incomes, favour high interest rates, and therefore the relative scarcity of money which is necessary to ensure that they can prevail. A high exchange rate, which runs with high interest rates and a restrictive monetary policy, provides the benefit of lowering the cost of imports and making travel abroad cheaper, reinforcing the widely held view that people should be proud of their currency if it is perceived to be 'strong' rather than favouring a low, but competitive, international value.

Predilections of this sort were therefore widely prevalent before monetarist orthodoxies became fashionable. The change in intellectual view which occurred was the result of a number of important works, not least those of Professor Hayek and other Chicago associates, who had always had serious reservations about the Keynesian revolution. Monetarist ideas, in their standard form, would not have become accepted as widely as they were, however, without the theoretical and statistical underpinning provided by Milton Friedman and his associate, Anna Jacobson Schwartz, in their seminal book, *A Monetary History of the United States, 1867–1960*, published in 1963. In this book, they made three important claims which had a major impact on economic thinking all over the world. First, they said that there was a clear association between the total amount of money in circulation and changes in money incomes and prices, but not economic activity until approximately two years later. Changes in the money supply therefore affected the price level, but not, except perhaps for a short period of time, the level of output in the real economy. Second, these relationships had proved to be stable over a long period. Third, changes, and particularly increases in the money supply, had generally occurred as a result of events which were independent of the needs of the economy. In consequence they added to inflation without raising the level of economic activity.

The attractive simplicity of these propositions is easily recognised. The essence of the monetarist case is that increases in prices and wages can be held in check by nothing more complicated that the apparently simple process of controlling the amount of money in circulation. Ideally, a condition of zero inflation is achieved when the increase in the money supply equals the rise in output in the economy. Since both wages and prices can only go up if extra money to finance them is made available, rises in either cannot occur unless more money is provided. Thus as long as the government is seen to be giving sufficient priority to controlling the money supply, everyone will realise that it is in his or her interest to exercise restraint, reducing the rate of inflation to whatever level is deemed acceptable.

These prescriptions have attracted much support to the monetarist banner, although it has always been clear that its intellectual underpinning had severe deficiencies. To start with, the theory begged the fundamental question as to the appropriate way to measure the money stock when so many different ways of determining it were available. It was, in any event, well known that the ratio between the stock of money, however defined, and the volume of transactions could vary widely, as the so called 'velocity of circulation' altered. More recently, in addition, there has been widespread criticism of the methodology used by Friedman and Schwartz in their analysis of the relationship between money and prices in the USA, indicating that the statistical basis from which their conclusions were drawn was not nearly as sound as they claimed it was.

As with so much else in economics, there is a major feedback problem with much of the monetarist position, making it difficult to distinguish between cause and effect. It may be true that over a long period the total amount of money in circulation bears a close relationship to the total value of the economy's output. It does not follow, however, that the money supply determines the money value of the GNP, and hence the rate of inflation. It may well be, instead, that the total amount of money in circulation is a function of the need for sufficient finance to accommodate transactions. If this is so, then an increase in the money supply may well accompany an increase in inflation caused by some other event, simply to provide this accommodation. It need not necessarily be the cause of rising prices at all.

Common sense tells us that changes in the money supply are only one of a number of relevant factors determining rises or falls in inflation. Monetarists, however, reject this proposition, alleging that all alterations in the rate of price increases are caused by changes in the money supply some two years previously. They also claim that the future course of inflation can be guided within narrow limits by controlling the money stock. Empirical evidence demonstrates that this contention is far too precise, and greatly overstates the predictive accuracy of monetarist theories.

For this amount of fine tuning to be possible, an unequivocal definition of money is required. It is one thing to recognise a situation where clearly far too much money, or, more accurately, too much credit is being created. Monetarists are right in saying that if credit is so cheap and so readily available that it is easy to speculate on asset inflation, or the economy is getting overheated by excess demand financed by credit creation, then the money supply is too large. This is a broad quantitative judgement. It is quite another matter to state that small alterations in the money supply generate correspondingly exact changes in the rate of inflation. Yet this is the claim which monetarists put forward.

This claim is implausible for a number of reasons. One is the difficulty in defining accurately what is money and what is not. Notes and coins are clearly 'money', but where should the line be drawn thereafter? What kinds of bank facilities and money market instruments should also be included or excluded? Many different measures are available in every country, depending on what is put in and what is left out. None of them has been found anywhere to have had a strikingly close correlation with subsequent changes in the rate of inflation for any length of time. Often, different measures of the money supply move in different directions. This is very damaging evidence against propositions which are supposed to be precise in their formulation and impact.

Another major problem for monetarists, referred to above, is that there can be no constant ratio between the amount of money in circulation, however defined, and the aggregate value of transactions, because the rate at which money circulates can, and does, vary widely over time. The 'velocity of circulation', which is the ratio between the GDP and the money supply, is far from constant. In the USA the M3 velocity fell 17% between 1970 and 1986, but by 1996 it had risen 22% compared to ten years earlier. It has been exceptionally volatile in Britain, where it rose by 7% between 1964 and 1970, and by a further 28% between 1970 and 1974, only to fall by 26% between 1974 and 1979. Since then it has risen by 82%.[6] Other countries, such as the Netherlands and Greece, have also had large changes in the velocity of circulation, particularly during the 1970s.[7]

Some of these movements were caused by changes in monetary policy, but a substantial proportion, especially recently, have had nothing to do with the government. They have been the results of radical changes to the financial environment, caused by the effects of deregulation on credit creation, and the growth of new financial instruments, such as derivatives. Variations like this make it impossible to believe in the rigid relationship that monetarism requires. In fact, the statistical record everywhere on the money supply and inflation shows what one would expect if there was very little causation at all at work. Except in extreme circumstances of gross over-creation of money and credit, changes in the money supply have had little or no impact on the rate of inflation. The need to provide enough money to finance all the transactions taking place has, over the long term, proved to be much more important a determinant of the money supply than attempts to restrict it to control inflation, although some countries have certainly had tighter monetary policies than others. In the short term, there is no systematic evidence that changes in the money supply affect subsequent inflation rates with any precision at all.

It is not surprising, therefore, that the predictions of monetarists about future levels of inflation, based on trends in the money supply, have turned out to be no better, and often worse, than those of other people who have used more eclectic, common-sense methods. Monetarists have not kept their predictions, however, solely to the future rate of inflation. There are three other areas of economic policy where their ideas have had a decisive effect on practical policy over the last quarter of a century. These are to do with unemployment, interest rates and exchange rates.

The monetarist view of unemployment is that there is a 'natural' rate which cannot be avoided, set essentially by supply side rigidities. Any attempt to reduce unemployment below this level by reflation will necessarily increase wage rates and then the price level. This will leave those in employment no better off than they were before, while the increased demand, having been absorbed by high prices, will result in the same number of people being employed as previously. Increasing demand only pushes up the rate of inflation. It will not raise either output or the number of people in work.

At some point, as pressure on the available labour force increases and the number of those unemployed falls, there is no doubt that a bidding-up process will take place, and wages and salaries will rise. This is an altogether different matter, however, from postulating that unemployment levels like those seen over much of the developed world during the 1980s are required to keep inflation at bay. Nor is it plausible that supply side rigidities are the major constraint on getting unemployment down. There is no evidence that these rigidities are significantly greater than they were in the 1950s and 1960s, and on balance they are almost certainly less. If, during the whole of these two decades, it was possible to combine high rates of economic growth with low levels of unemployment, while inflation remained stable at an acceptable level, why should we believe that it is impossible now for these conditions to prevail again? One of the unfortunate triumphs of monetarism has been to condition people to tolerating much higher levels of unemployment or low productivity work than would otherwise have been considered economically desirable or politically acceptable.

Monetarism has also had a considerable influence on interest rates. The tight control of the money supply which monetarists advocate can only be achieved if interest rates are used to balance a relatively low supply of money against the demand for credit which has to be choked off by raising the price of money. This requirement is made to seem less harsh by suggesting that a positive rate of interest will always be required to enable lenders to continue providing money to borrowers. It is alleged that any attempt to lower interest rates to encourage expansion will fail as lenders withdraw from the market until the premium they require above the inflation rate reappears.

Yet again, we have a proposition much more strongly based on assertion than on evidence. For years on end, in many countries, real interest rates paid to savers have been negative, sometimes even before tax. Lenders, of course, have never regarded negative interest rates as fair, and frequently complain bitterly when they occur. There is, however, little that they can do about them. Their ability to withdraw from the market is generally limited. It is undoubtedly the case, however, that high positive rates of interest are a discouragement to investment, partly directly, but much more importantly, because of their influence on driving up the exchange rate.

This is particularly paradoxical in relation to the third major impact of monetarist ideas on practical issues, which has been on exchange rate policy. It is argued that no policy for improving an economy's competitiveness by devaluation will work, because the inflationary effects of a depreciation will automatically raise the domestic price level back to where it was in international terms. This will leave the devaluing country with no more competitiveness than it had before, but with a real extra-inflationary problem with which it will have to contend.

This proposition is one which it is easy to test against historical experience. There have been large numbers of substantial exchange rate changes over the last few decades, providing plenty of empirical data against which to assess the validity of this monetarist assertion. The evidence is overwhelmingly against it. As we shall see, there is example after example to be found of devaluations failing to produce sufficient excess inflation, if any, to wipe out the competitive advantage initially gained. On the contrary, there is ample evidence indicating that exactly the opposite effect has been the experience in a wide variety of different economies. Those which devalue tend to perform progressively better, as their manufacturing sectors expand, and the internationally tradable goods and services which they produce become cumulatively more competitive.

Countries which have gained an initial price advantage therefore tend to forge ahead, with increasingly competitive import saving and exporting sectors. Rapidly growing efficiency in the sectors of their economies involved in international trading gains them higher shares in world trade, providing them with platforms for further expansion. High productivity growth generates conditions which may even allow them, with good management, to experience less domestic inflation that their more sluggish competitors. In practice, monetarist policies have had pronounced effects on the exchange rates of the countries where they have been most effectively imposed, but invariably their impact has been to push them up. The economies concerned then suffer the worst of all worlds – a mixture of sluggish growth, low increases in output to absorb wage and salary increases, and sometimes higher price inflation than their more favoured competitors.

Monetarist theories start by appearing simple and straightforward, but end by being long on complication and assertion, and short on predictive and practical prescriptive qualities. They pander to the prejudice of those who would like to believe their conclusions. They lack convincing explanations about the transmission mechanisms between what they claim are the causes of economic events, and the effects which they declare will necessarily follow. Where they can be tested against empirical results, the predictions their theories produce generally fail to achieve levels of accuracy which make them worth while.

Monetarist theories have nevertheless reinforced everywhere all the prejudices widely held in favour of the cautious financial conservatism, which monetarism so accurately reflects. In practice, monetarist policies are almost indistinguishable from old-fashioned deflation. By allowing themselves to be persuaded by these misguided doctrines, it becomes all too easy for those responsible for running the nation's affairs to acquiesce in accepting levels of low growth and high unemployment which they would never have tolerated if they had realised how unnecessary they were. The result has been that policies which should have been rejected have continued to be accepted, although they failed to work. Because expectations have been lowered, the deflationary consequences of high interest rates, restrictive monetary policies and overvalued exchange rates, have not caused the outcry that might have been expected, and which they deserved.

Slow growth in Europe

During the period from its establishment in 1958 until 1973, the average rate of growth among the Common Market countries was 5.1%, the mean level of unemployment was little more than 2%, and the average rate of inflation was 3.9%. For the twenty years from 1973 to 1993 the growth rate averaged 2.1%, and the inflation rate 7.0%.[8] The rate of unemployment fluctuated over the period, but overall at least until very recently it has been on a remorselessly upward trend. The average registered unemployment level across the whole of the European Union in early 1999 was 9.6%, an almost fivefold increase.[9] Even then, the claimant count, which this figure represents, substantially underestimates the total number of people who would like to work if they had the opportunity to do so at a reasonable wage.[10] What went wrong? If the whole world had plunged to a much lower growth rate after 1973, it would be plausible to argue that Europe was part of a universal trend. It is not, however, the case, that the growth rate has fallen generally since 1973. As Table 2.1 on page 26 shows, excluding the western industrialised economies and Japan, the annual growth in world output actually rose marginally from 3.2% between 1950 and 1973 to 3.4% between 1973 and 1992.[11]

Three major developments were responsible for the substantial sea change to the fortunes of the Community economies in the 1970s. The first was the oil crisis, caused by OPEC's quadrupling of the price of crude oil, following the breakdown of the Bretton Woods system and the 1973 Yom Kippur War. The second was the change in intellectual fashion towards a much harder-line version of economic theory and doctrine, as monetarist ideas replaced Keynesian thinking among large sections of those responsible for running economic policy in the Community countries. The third was the political initiatives taken within the Community, intended to lead to closer integration by linking the currencies of the constituent economies together first of all in the Currency Snake, then the Exchange Rate Mechanism, and finally with full Monetary Union.

The effect of the quadrupling of oil prices in 1974[12] on the economies of Europe, none of which at that time was producing any significant quantity of oil, was to shift about 2% of their GDPs away from their own populations to those of the oil exporting countries. With good management, and a well co-ordinated response, this should not have been an impossibly difficult situation to contain. The problem was that the oil shock came on top of other causes of instability, including, in some countries, a crisis in the banking system as the early 1970s boom broke, and in all countries the main strain was taken on the balance of payments. The result was that everyone reined in at once, trying to shift the trade balance problems elsewhere. Growth rates fell back sharply as deflationary policies were implemented everywhere. Indeed, the economies then comprising the Common Market collectively saw no growth in either 1974 or 1975, before resuming a much slower growth trajectory than had previously prevailed.[13]

If the real world events of the oil price hike and the breaking boom were the immediate causes of the deflationary policies which checked Community growth in the mid 1970s, the willingness of the authorities to persevere with them was greatly reinforced by the spread of monetarist doctrines. This second change in direction occurred largely in response to the pressing need to bring inflation down from the dangerous heights to which it had risen in some countries during the mid 1970s. Britain's year on year inflation peaked at 24%, France's at 14%, Italy's at 19%, and Germany's at a much more modest 7%.[14]

Monetarist ideas had a particularly strong appeal in certain powerful quarters. The Bundesbank had always had a strong anti-inflation tradition, harking back to the German hyperinflation of 1923. Understandably it welcomed ideas which reinforced its collective view of monetary priorities. Nearly all Europe's central bankers followed the highly respected Bundesbank's lead. Monetarist ideas also became very much the fashion in academic circles, and these convictions were reflected in the tone of an endless succession of newspaper articles, popularising monetarist ideas to a wider audience. Despite its intellectual weaknesses, which were apparent from the beginning, monetarist ideas were extraordinarily successful in implanting themselves right across Western Europe as the norm which few people were willing to challenge.

The third and most significant long-term influence on Community policies over the last quarter of a century has been the drive to achieve further integration by locking the Community currencies together. The first steps were taken a little over ten years after the Common Market had been established. In March 1970, the Council of Ministers set up a high level group to prepare plans for full economic and monetary union, rather than just a customs union, among the original six member countries. The chairman was Pierre Werner, then Prime Minister and Minister of Finance of Luxembourg, who gave his name to the report which was produced within a few months. The report concentrated on the two principal routes which might be chosen to achieve the convergence required to make monetary union a viable proposition. This involved an uneasy marriage of Keynesian and monetarist approaches. Nevertheless, in March 1971 the Council of Ministers accepted the broad thrust of the Werner Report, and agreed that, as a first step towards its implementation, the exchange rates of the member currencies should be maintained within 0.6% of each other from 15 June 1971 onwards.

The start date for the Werner proposals came at an awkward time, though this is not an absolution for their subsequent abandonment. In May 1971 the dollar crisis began, leading to the break-up of Bretton Woods at the Smithsonian Conference, and abandonment of the existing IMF exchange rate bands. Major fluctuations in the European rates meant that that the new narrow bands for what came to be called the Snake were difficult to establish. A European Monetary Co-operation Fund was set up, operated by the central banks, to keep market rates within 1.125% either side of the central parities. In view of their impending Community membership, Britain, Denmark and Eire joined the new arrangements, as well as the original Six.

The life of the Snake, however, was relatively brief. Speculative fever in the international money markets switched from the dollar, after its Smithsonian devaluation to attacking sterling. Within six weeks of joining, the British authorities were forced to abandon attempts to maintain the agreed parity for the pound, which dropped out of the Snake, taking the Irish punt with it. Six months later, in January 1973, the Italian government abandoned its commitment to keep the lira within the required limits and withdrew. A year later, in January 1974, the French followed suit. The franc rejoined the Snake in July 1975, but the second attempt to keep to the agreed parity lasted no longer than the first. In March 1976 it left permanently. In less than four years, therefore, three of the four major Community currencies had abandoned their efforts to keep up with the stability and low inflation rate of the Deutsche Mark. The Snake had been reduced to a Deutsche Mark zone embracing, apart from Germany, only the Benelux countries and Denmark. This first major attempt to bring together all the Community currencies had failed. Phase two of the Werner plan, the originally proposed move to monetary union, was quietly forgotten.[15]

It might have been thought that lessons would be learnt from this experience, so that similar problems could have been avoided in future. It was not a convincing explanation for the failure of the Snake to say that its demise occurred because the time at which its régime was introduced was difficult and turbulent. If the Snake was worth having at all, it ought to have been more useful in times of stress than in easier conditions. The political pressures for resuming attempts to lock Community currencies together, however, proved stronger than the arguments from experience. At the initiative of the Commission's President, Roy (now Lord) Jenkins, within three years, at Summit Meetings in Copenhagen and Bremen, monetary union was back again at the top of the Community agenda.[16]

The main argument put forward for monetary union on this occasion was that the full benefits of the Community's customs union could not be achieved in an environment of exchange rate instability and uncertainty. It was alleged that fluctuating rates were damaging to trade and steady economic growth. While this may have seemed an appealing argument, there was no evidence that it was true. Indeed, a number of studies, including a particularly extensive one carried out by the Bank of England, had shown that exchange rate movements have little, if any, effect on growth rates. The fact that the Common Market countries had been growing up to then at unprecedented rates without having their currencies locked together was ignored. It was also alleged that floating exchange rates were inherently inflationary. Again, however, no concrete evidence was produced to show that this argument was correct and, as we shall see in Chapter 8, there is ample evidence to show that in most cases it is false. Nevertheless, in 1979, the Snake was reborn as the Exchange Rate Mechanism (ERM), as part of a new European Monetary System (EMS).[17]

When it began operations in March 1979, the new EMS had at its disposal a substantially more potent battery of weapons to deploy against the markets than were available at the time of the Snake. The first phase had two main objectives. The primary task was to achieve a high degree of stability in the exchange rates of the participating currencies. The second was to secure convergence in the performance of the constituent economies. Both proved difficult to achieve. In the decade following its inception, there were twelve realignments of one or more of the central rates, caused by widely different experience with inflation and competitiveness among the constituent economies. Over this period the central rate of the strongest currency, the Deutsche Mark, appreciated by 18%, while the weakest, the lira, fell by 29%. The combined impact of these changes was that the parity of the lira at the end of the decade *vis à vis* the Deutsche Mark was 50% of its value at the beginning. The effect of the ERM was not to stop exchange rate changes occurring, but merely to delay them. Nor was any greater success achieved on convergence. Living standards across the whole Community did not become significantly more equal, although the Irish economy, with a standard of living well below the EEC average, grew considerably more rapidly than the rest. Nor did variables such as inflation rates come together. For example, in 1981, the consumer price index increased by 6% in Germany, 13% in France and 18% in Italy.[18]

These variations in inflation rates highlighted the basic problem with the Snake and ERM, which was that for nearly all the period in which they were in operation, Germany's low price rises and export competitiveness made it extremely difficult for the other countries in the exchange rate systems to remain able to compete with the Germans. As their trade balances deteriorated, they were faced with the familiar choice of deflation or devaluation. With the latter being ruled out, except in extreme circumstances, they had to deflate. As about half of all Germany's exports went to other Community countries during the ERM period,[19] the consequence was that its main export markets were depressed, pulling down the German growth rate. As a result the whole of the Community's economy slowed down. Table 6.1 shows the figures. Against a long-term background of falling growth rates, each time the Community currencies were locked together, the performance of all the participating countries deteriorated – more quickly in the period of the Snake, and more slowly under the ERM.[20]

Notwithstanding these problems, further moves were afoot to proceed to full monetary union. The drafters of the Single European Act had succeeded in having the achievement of monetary union embodied in the Treaty as a specific commitment, with a target date of 1992. In 1988 Jacques Delors, the then President of the Commission, persuaded the Council of Ministers to give him the task of 'studying and proposing concrete stages leading towards economic and monetary union'.

While these proposals were being considered, and embodied in the 1991 Maastricht Treaty which set out the programme for moves to a single European currency, the ERM began to run into serious difficulties. During the summer of 1992, market pressure began to attack the weaker members of the ERM, leading to the devaluation of the lira. In September 1992 a wave of speculation against sterling swept the pound out of the ERM. The franc's parity with the Deutsche Mark only just survived, as a result of massive intervention by the Bundesbank. Finally the pressure built up against the whole ERM system to a point where it became no longer possible to hold it together. In August 1993, the narrow bands were abandoned, and fluctuations of up to 15% either side of the central rate against the ECU were allowed to take their place, while preparations went ahead for full monetary union.

Table 6.1: Growth in the EEC During the Snake and ERM Periods

YEAR	Totals all ERM Countries except Germany GDP bn 1985 US$	Annual Growth	Germany GDP bn 1985 US$	Annual Growth	Totals all ERM Countries including Germany GDP bn 1985 US$	Annual Growth		ERM Countries' Growth Rates
1966	663.5		377.1		1040.6			1950–69
1967	699.6	5.4%	375.9	–0.3%	1075.5	3.4%		Average
1968	736.5	5.3%	396.4	5.5%	1132.9	5.3%		5.5%
1969	784.9	6.6%	426.0	7.5%	1210.9	6.9%	SNAKE	Snake
1970	827.2	5.4%	447.4	5.0%	1274.6	5.3%	SNAKE	Period
1971	855.8	3.5%	461.1	3.1%	1316.9	3.3%	SNAKE	average
1972	887.6	3.7%	480.7	4.3%	1368.4	3.9%	SNAKE	3.7%
1973	939.5	5.8%	503.6	4.8%	1443.1	5.5%	SNAKE	Fall from
1974	973.9	3.7%	504.6	0.2%	1478.5	2.5%	SNAKE	6.9% to
1975	963.1	–1.1%	498.3	–1.3%	1461.4	–1.2%	SNAKE	–1.2%
1976	1014.4	5.3%	524.8	5.3%	1539.2	5.3%		1976–9
1977	1045.8	3.1%	539.7	2.8%	1585.5	3.0%		average
1978	1070.4	2.4%	555.9	3.0%	1626.3	2.6%		3.6%
1979	1123.2	4.9%	579.4	4.2%	1702.6	4.7%	ERM	
1980	1041.4	–7.3%	585.1	1.0%	1626.5	–4.5%	ERM	
1981	1156.9	11.1%	585.7	0.1%	1742.6	7.1%	ERM	
1982	1170.4	1.2%	580.2	–0.9%	1750.6	0.5%	ERM	ERM
1983	1181.6	1.0%	590.4	1.8%	1772.0	1.2%	ERM	Period
1984	1208.8	2.3%	607.0	2.8%	1815.7	2.5%	ERM	average
1985	1235.8	2.2%	619.3	2.0%	1855.1	2.2%	ERM	2.1%
1986	1267.7	2.6%	633.8	2.3%	1901.5	2.5%	ERM	
1987	1297.5	2.3%	643.2	1.5%	1940.7	2.1%	ERM	
1988	1348.5	3.9%	667.1	3.7%	2015.7	3.9%	ERM	
1989	1395.4	3.5%	691.3	3.6%	2086.7	3.5%	ERM	Fall from
1990	1432.2	2.6%	730.7	5.7%	2162.9	3.7%	ERM	4.7% to
1991	1449.0	1.2%	764.0	4.5%	2213.0	2.3%	ERM	–1.0%
1992	1467.3	1.3%	775.9	1.6%	2243.2	1.4%	ERM	
1993	1458.9	–0.6%	761.0	–1.9%	2219.9	–1.0%	ERM	
1994	1482.6	1.6%	782.2	2.8%	2264.8	2.0%		
1995	1521.6	2.6%	791.7	1.2%	2313.3	2.1%		1993–7
1996	1546.1	1.6%	801.8	1.3%	2348.0	1.5%		average
1997	1583.7	2.4%	819.5	2.2%	2403.2	2.4%		2.0%

Sources: Table 7 on pages 120 and 121 in *National Accounts 1960–1992*. Paris: OECD, 1994; and Table 0101 in *Eurostatistics* 11/95 and 4/99. Luxembourg: The European Community, 1995 and 1999.

Monetarist policies in the USA

In the USA, the problems to be faced were significantly different from those in most of Europe, although the intellectual background to the way they were tackled had much in common.

Compared to many other countries the USA weathered the 1970s reasonably well. Years of small reductions in output in 1970, 1974 and 1975 were offset by substantial growth in other years, producing erratic but, nevertheless, in the circumstances of the time, a tolerably satisfactory outcome. Real GDP growth averaged 3.2% per annum for the decade, a little below the 3.8% average for all the developed countries in the OECD.[21] US GDP per capita, however, grew by a more modest, but still respectable, compound 2.1% per annum.[22] The reduction in the dollar's post-Smithsonian parity, augmented by the USA's better than average performance on inflation, gave those parts of the American economy exposed to international trade an increasing edge. As a result, exports of goods and services, net of inflation, rose cumulatively by 7.3% per annum, compared to total imports which only increased at a compound rate of 4.9%.[23]

Unfortunately, however, this reasonably good performance was heavily undermined by adverse movements in relative costs. In particular, during the 1970s the price of oil rose hugely, with a further major price increase in 1979 following the earlier one in 1973.[24] By 1980, the USA was spending $79bn a year on oil imports, compared with only $3bn in 1970.[25] As a result the balance of trade in goods and services began an alarming deterioration. A surplus had been achieved in 1975, caused mainly by a much more substantial increase in the value of manufactured exports compared to imports – no doubt the consequence of the dollar devaluation earlier in the decade. In the late 1970s, however, the further rapid increases in the value of oil imports began to swamp the surplus earned on manufactures. From 1976 onwards, the USA has had a trade deficit every single year.[26]

To maintain a high rate of growth in the 1980s, the USA therefore urgently needed a considerably more competitive exchange rate. By increasing the country's exports of manufactured goods, it would have been possible to offset the heavy burden across the exchanges occasioned by the extra cost of oil imports. Unfortunately, exactly the opposite policy was put into operation. Under the incoming Reagan administration, heavily influenced by monetarist ideas, interests rates were raised sharply. The US Treasury Bills rate, which had fallen to just under 5% during the boom years of the late 1970s, averaged over 14% in 1981.[27] The inevitable result was that the dollar soared on the foreign exchanges. With 1973 equalling 100 as the base, and thus already allowing for the 10% post-Smithsonian devaluation, the trade weighted value of the US dollar had fallen to 89 by 1979. This trend was then dramatically reversed. By 1982 the index had reached 108, and by 1985 it was 123. In six years, the dollar had sustained a real appreciation of 38%.[28] As a result, the USA's growth in GDP during the 1980s fell back to a cumulative 2.8% per annum. Because the population was growing fast, GDP per head grew at only 1.8% per annum.[29]

Predictably, the proportion of US GDP derived from manufacturing fell heavily. Between 1980 and 1993, it dropped from 21% of GDP to 17%, a relative reduction of just under a fifth.[30] The number of people employed in manufacturing occupations also fell slightly in absolute numbers, but much more steeply as a proportion of the total labour force. Of those in employment, the proportion working in manufacturing dropped from 22% to barely 16%.[31] The problem was then the familiar one, which is that productivity increases are much more difficult to secure across the board in the service sector of the economy than they are in manufacturing. The decline in industrial output as a proportion of GDP thus contributed directly and heavily to the low growth in overall productivity which was such a key negative characteristic of this period in American economic history. Reflecting the decline in manufacturing, and the incidence of the policies pursued by the Reagan and Bush administrations on the growth rate, both the US savings and investment ratios fell heavily too, dropping from about 20% in 1980 to under 15% by 1993.[32]

Between 1980 and 1993, the first full year of the Clinton presidency, the economy grew cumulatively by 2.7% per annum, and GDP per head rose on average by 1.4% a year,[33] yet none of these benefits worked their way through to the average worker in terms of compensation per hour. On the contrary, across the board average earnings per hour fell. For the whole American economy, in real terms, income per hour peaked in 1973, at $8.55 measured in constant 1982 dollars. By 1980, the rate was $7.78. After a marginal increase to $7.81 in 1986, it dropped to $7.39 in 1993. Even in 1998 it was only $7.75. Thus, over the twenty-five years between 1973 and 1998, earnings per hour for the average American dropped in real terms by a staggering 9%.[34] Against the background of the steady rise in real earnings per hour in the US economy in the 1950s and 1960s of a little under 2% per annum – about 18% per decade[35] – who, predicting in 1973 a fall for the next quarter of a century, would have been given a hearing?

The decline in real hourly earnings, barely offset by a higher labour force participation rate and longer working hours, and aggravated by a tougher line being taken on social security payments, caused the distribution of income, even before tax, to become much more uneven. Up to 1980, the proportion of aggregate income going to the bottom 40% of income earners had been roughly stable at about 17%. By 1993 it was 14%. For the bottom quintile, the drop was even more precipitate, from 5.3% to 4.1%, making the whole of this vast swathe of the American population – well over 50m people – about 8% worse off on average in 1993 than they had been in 1980.[36] The percentage of children brought up below the poverty level rose from 15% in 1970 to 22% in 1993.[37] The number of families in poverty rose over the same period from 6.2m to 8.4m, an increase of over one-third.[38] Meanwhile, at the other end of the spectrum, those in the top 5% of income earners saw their share of total incomes rise between 1980 and 1993 from 15% of the total to 20%.[39] As a result, their total incomes increased in real terms by about two-thirds.

The period from 1980 onwards, in particular, saw an enormous increase in the wealth of the US's better-off citizens where, in very many cases, they had to do little, if anything at all, to become very much richer. The Dow-Jones index, which stood at 891 in 1980, reached 1,793 by 1986, 3,522 in 1993,[40] and in March 1999 it broke through the 10,000 barrier, subsequently peaking at over 11,000. Over a period during which the US GDP grew in money terms to a little over three times its previous size,[41] the stock market had risen to over twelve times where it had been nineteen years previously. The returns to financial institutions have risen particularly quickly, reflecting the increasing opportunities to make money out of financial activities rather than making or selling products. At the other end of spectrum, as the deflationary impact of monetarist doctrines hit hard those not already well heeled, the business failure rate rose by leaps and bounds. In 1980, there were 42 failures per 10,000 listed business enterprises. By 1986 there were 120, and still 109 in 1993.[42]

Post-tax, the distribution of income became even more uneven, as tax rates on the rich were cut. The theory behind this was that the government revenues ought to increase if tax rates were lowered, both because there would be less incentives for avoidance and because lower tax rates would stimulate more enterprise and hence more revenues. The 'Laffer Curve' approach to tax policy – one of the more egregious elements of the 'Supply Side' economic policies fashionable at the time – never came near improving the overall Federal collection rate, however, although it certainly served its purpose in justifying lower tax payments rates by the rich. The result was one of the reasons why the US fiscal deficit began to widen.

The other major reason for the deterioration in the Federal government's finances was a vast increase on defence outlays. In 1980, defence costs represented 4.9% of US GDP, down substantially from their 9.4% peak during the Vietnam War. By 1984 they were 6.0%,[43] as expenditure jumped from $174bn to $283bn,[44] a real increase of 30% in just four years.[45] The result was that the overall government's fiscal stance, including both Federal and State levels, which had been $34bn in surplus in 1979, plunged into deficit, reaching a negative $109bn by 1983. The Federal government record was even worse, with its deficit reaching $174bn in 1983. For the next eleven years it averaged $175bn a year.[46] Hardly surprisingly, an immediate repercussion from the deterioration in the fiscal balance was a large increase in the value of outstanding Federal debt. In 1980, the gross Federal debt had been $906bn, representing 33% of GDP. By 1993, it was $4,409bn, equivalent to 67% of GDP, and still rising in money terms, though stabilising as a percentage of GDP.[47]

One of the consequences of the heavy increase in military spending during the Reagan years was that a higher proportion of the relatively weakening US industrial base was drawn into defence work, exacerbating problems on the trade balance, which also hugely deteriorated over the same period. By 1980, the total US foreign payment position was back in balance, after deficits in the late 1970s, with the surplus on investment income offsetting a $19bn deficit on goods and services. From then onwards, the position went from bad to worse. By 1984 the trade deficit was $109bn, and by 1987 it was $153bn.[48] Most of this huge deterioration was the result of a catastrophic turn round in trade in manufactured goods. Even as late as 1980, the USA had a reasonably healthy $12bn surplus in trade on manufactured goods, but by 1984 this had turned into a deficit of $93bn, and $126bn by 1988.[49]

There is an inexorable accounting identity which applies to foreign trade. Any deficit on current account has to be made up by exactly corresponding capital borrowing. To pay for the multi-billion dollar deficits which accumulated, the USA therefore had to become a major net borrower from abroad, and a major net seller of investment assets to foreigners. The result was a drastic change from the USA being by far the world's largest debtor, to it being much its biggest creditor. In 1980 the USA's net international investment position at cost was a positive $392bn. By 1990 it was a negative $251bn, and by 1993 it was a negative $503bn.[50] Nor is this a trend which is currently improving. By 1995 the deficiency was $814bn, and by the end of 1997 it was just under 1.25 trillion dollars,[51] and still rising fast.

The reason why the balance of payments deficit is relevant to the huge increase in asset values which has taken place in recent years is that the gap between US domestic savings and investment has been swamped by net foreign investment. For every year between 1982 and 1997[52] the value of physical investment within the USA has been substantially lower than US domestic saving. The balance has been made up from net foreign investment. Recently, the US savings ratio has risen but, at the same time, mirroring the current account deficit, there has been a steeply rising flow of investment funds from overseas. The exceptionally high demand for US stocks and other assets has not, therefore, come only from domestic sources. It has been fuelled by the massive inflow of capital funds to the USA, which mirrors the current account deficit. For most of the years since 1985, this has been well over $100bn, and this is another problem which shows little sign of disappearing.[53] With a trade deficit of well over $100bn per annum, net unilateral transfers abroad of $40bn, and with a rapidly disappearing net investment income to act as an offset, as more and more US net assets are sold to foreigners, the total deficit in 1997 was $155bn.[54] In 1999 it may well be as high as $250bn.

During the middle years of the Bush régime, the economy had faltered, growing by only 1.2% in 1990, and contracting by almost 1% in 1991.[55] No doubt this contributed to the Republican defeat in 1992, although by then the economy was starting to pick up again. The downturn reduced the current account payments deficit, which fell from $104bn in 1989, to only $4bn in 1991, a much better outcome than had been achieved since the early 1980s. The trade deficit also fell to a more manageable $31bn from the much higher figures in the immediately prior years, aided by a fall in the value of the dollar.[56] By the start of the Clinton administration's term of office, the trade weighted value had come down a long way from the stratospheric levels of the mid-Reagan era to a considerably more realistic index of 91 in 1990 and 87 in 1992.[57] Unemployment rose to 7.5% in 1992,[58] following the impact of sharp interest rate increases in 1989 on the level of business activity. The consumer price index, which had shown a rise of 6.1% in 1990 – well above the increase in the immediately preceding years, although in line with the average experience of other OECD countries – had dropped back to 2.9% in 1992.[59] The economy inherited by the Clinton administration therefore brought with it all the structural imbalances which the monetarist era had wrought upon it, combined with considerable room for bouncing back from the shallow depression in 1990 and 1991.

Over the period between the spring of 1993, when the Clinton administration took over, and the end of 1998, there have been some improvements, but not nearly enough to counteract the impact of the Reagan and Bush policies on the American economy. Between 1992 and 1998 the growth rate averaged a compound 3.2% per annum, which is better than the 2.6% achieved between 1980 and 1992.[60] Between 1992 and 1998 the population grew by an average of almost exactly 1% per year, so that during those four years, GDP per head rose at 2.2% per annum, again an improvement on the cumulative 1.4% per annum achieved by the Republican administrations.[61]. On the bright side, the rise in consumer prices was only 1.6% in 1998,[62] a very good figure, although comparable to the outcome in most other OECD countries. Unemployment fell to 4.3% in December 1998,[63] the lowest figure since the end of the 1960s, but increased numbers of people working, accompanied by only a relatively small rise in output, indicated continuing very low increases in productivity. This outcome is borne out by average hourly earnings which, in real terms, had gone up by 0.75% per annum in the five years to the end of 1998, rising in constant 1982 dollars from $7.41 in 1992 to $7.75 in 1998.

The Clinton record on the Federal deficit was also much better than those of his two immediate predecessors. A combination of contained expenditure and rising tax revenues reduced the deficit, which had peaked at $290bn in 1992, to $22bn in 1997, with a balanced budget projected for 1999 and subsequent years. The gross Federal debt at the end of 1998 was $5,478.7bn,[64] however, and the interest charges on this large sum were an additional drain on the government's current resources.

By far the largest fundamental problem facing the Clinton administration at the beginning of 1999 was the foreign balance, for which the strengthening of the US currency *vis à vis* the rest of the world bore a heavy responsibility. The trade weighted value of the dollar rose from an index of 87 in 1992 to 98 in 1998.[65] A combination of devaluations in the Far East and the weakening of most of the major currencies in Europe had left the dollar dangerously exposed. As the US growth rate has climbed during the 1990s, so the overall balance of payments deficit on current account worsened, from $51bn in 1992 to $155bn in 1997, with well over $200bn projected for 1998, and worse to follow.[66] Without a major change in policy, this deficit will continue to widen.

The US economy, despite its travails, may still be immensely powerful, but the borrowing required to finance a deficit on this scale is beginning to look daunting. As a percentage of US GDP, the sums involved are not unmanageable, but in relation to the US foreign earnings position, they are considerably more difficult to handle. The USA is already a major net debtor to the rest of the world. In consequence the net investment income which used to buttress the US foreign payments position turned negative for the first time in 1997.[67] Other adverse developments may worsen the situation, not least a possible rise in the price of oil and other commodities, which the USA imports in large quantities, and whose prices in the late 1990s, have been at historically low levels.[68] There must, therefore, be an increasing exchange rate risk for those purchasing US fixed interest stocks, as the dollar looks more and more overvalued in relation to the USA's current and future commitments.

If the dollar does come under pressure, the US administration is going to be faced with difficult choices. If it is not going to allow the dollar to fall, the consequences are bound to be rising interest rates, and domestic deflation to try to keep the foreign payments deficit within bounds. This will inevitably threaten many of the other policy objectives which the administration has set itself, and weaken its electoral appeal. There is, of course, an alternative, which is to let the dollar fall, and the results which might be achieved by either passively allowing this to happen, or actively encouraging it to do so, will be discussed in later sections of this book.

The Tiger economies

A remarkable phenomenon in the late twentieth century was the growth rates achieved by the so called Tiger economies – Hong Kong, Singapore, South Korea and Taiwan. Table 6.2 sets out the cumulative growth rates they have achieved, their increases in population and the rises in GDP per head – a close proxy for living standards – which they have managed to secure for their populations.

A number of key points stand out from these statistics. First, the rapid growth which all these economies have managed to achieve, although checked recently, is not a new development. All of them were growing fast from the period starting immediately after the disruption caused by World War II had abated. Second, there is not much sign of a slowdown after 1973, which was about the time which clearly marked the sudden break from relatively fast growth to a consistently much slower one among the advanced industrialised economies, including Japan. Whatever caused these major countries to grow more slowly evidently did not have the same affect on the Tiger economies. Third – a rather different point – as they became very much better off than they had been previously, there was again little sign that this slowed down the Tiger

Table 6.2: Growth Statistics for the Tiger Economies

Cumulative Per Annum Growth in Gross Domestic Product

	1913–50	1950–73	1973–90	1990–7
Hong Kong	n/a	9.2%	7.6%	5.3%
Singapore	n/a	7.8%	7.4%	8.3%
South Korea	1.7%	7.6%	8.5%	7.1%
Taiwan	2.7%	9.3%	8.0%	6.5%

Cumulative Per Annum Growth in Population

	1913–50	1950–73	1973–90	1990–7
Hong Kong	n/a	3.5%	1.8%	1.5%
Singapore	n/a	2.8%	2.0%	3.2%
South Korea	1.9%	2.2%	1.4%	1.0%
Taiwan	2.2%	3.0%	1.6%	0.9%

Cumulative Per Annum Growth in GDP Per Head of the Population

	1913–50	1950–73	1973–90	1990–7
Hong Kong	n/a	5.5%	5.7%	3.8%
Singapore	n/a	4.9%	5.3%	5.0%
South Korea	–0.2%	5.2%	7.0%	6.1%
Taiwan	0.4%	6.2%	6.3%	5.6%

Sources: Tables D-1e and F-4 in *Monitoring the World Economy 1820–1992* by Angus Maddison. Paris: OECD, 1995; pages 320/321, 544/545 and 782/783 in *International Financial Statistics Yearbook*. Washington DC: IMF, 1998; and Tables 1–1a and 1–1c in the Taiwan Statistical Data Book, 1998.

economies' growth rates. It is often alleged that economic growth becomes more difficult to achieve the higher the level of GDP per head. This does not seem to have been true of the Tigers, and if they have avoided this happening, it is not clear why other economies should not be able to do the same.

Of course, the major reason why the performance of the Tiger economies was not greatly noticed until the last quarter of the twentieth century is that even as late as 1973, their combined GDPs only represented 1.2% of world output. By 1990, this ratio had more than doubled to 2.7%.[69] Even more impressive was the impact of these four economies on world trade. In 1973 their total manufactured exports (including re-exports in the cases of Hong Kong and Singapore) were 3.8% of the world total. By 1994, they were 12.9%.[70] Over one-eighth of world trade in manufactured products was being achieved by four countries containing in total only 1.4% of the world's population.[71]

It is indeed this astonishing export achievement which provides the immediate explanation of the success of the Tigers. Between 1950 and 1992 the volume of South Korea's merchandise exports rose cumulatively by 17% per annum, while Taiwan's rose by 16%, compared to 8.5% for the world as a whole.[72] The competitiveness of their exports made them extremely attractive to buyers all over the world. The opportunities thus created, as always happens in similar circumstances, sucked talent and resources into sectors of the economy where they could be most productively employed. Hardly surprisingly, all the Tiger economies, with the huge investment opportunities which fast growth opened up, had high proportions of their national incomes devoted to investment, generally averaging 30% or more.[73] As a result industrial output soared, and with it productivity. In South Korea, for example, between 1968 and 1997, industrial output increased cumulatively by an average of 13.4% per annum, while productivity in these sectors of the South Korean economy rose by 8.3%.[74] Nor was it just the Tiger economies which were following this pattern. In 1970, 4% of manufacturing output was in East Asia. By 1995 it was 11%, while over the same period the proportion in the industrialised countries fell from 88% to 80%.[75] In 1994, 43% of South Korea's GDP came from industry, and 38% of GDP was used for gross domestic investment,[76] roughly twice the ratios for the USA.

The reason why the Tiger economies were able to begin their very rapid growth rates was because each of them, for a variety of reasons, found themselves in the same situation as the other fast growing economies after the recovery period following World War II. Each had a highly competitive export sector, from which all else flowed. This is not to deny that hard work, discipline, access to world markets, good primary education, reasonably competent government and all the other characteristics of most successful economies were not important to the Tiger economies. Of course they were. The overwhelming significance of the export competitiveness factor, however, was that it provided the environment where all the other characteristics of the Tiger economies could flourish and be used to best advantage.

In a number of key respects, the rapid growth which they achieved also made it much easier for them to accomplish a number of other social and political objectives which most people would think were desirable. Unemployment rates were very low throughout the period, with all the benefits this brings. Jobs were readily available for anyone who wanted to work. The dependency ratio – that is the ratio between number of people not working, and therefore reliant on the value added of others who were – was therefore relatively low, which kept down the need for high levels of government taxation and expenditure. Money spent on education and training was seldom wasted, as most people who went through courses to improve their skills could easily find a job thereafter. The impact of rapid growth on the distribution of income was also different from what is frequently supposed. It is often thought that fast growth leads to incomes becoming more dispersed, but this is not what the figures show. The fast growing Asian economies have had more, not less, even distributions of income than is common in western industrialised economies. If the pre-tax per capita income of the top decile is taken as a ratio of that of the bottom two deciles, studies carried out around 1970 showed the ratio to be 7.6 for South Korea, 7.5 for Japan, 10.5 for Germany and the Netherlands and 14.9 for the USA. Only Sweden at 8.1 and Britain at 9.1 got close to the Asian ratios, though Australia came in at 7.2.[77] The distribution of income has widened substantially in the West over the last two decades, especially post-tax, whereas it has stayed roughly constant in most of Asia.[78]

Reflected in the relatively even distribution of income in the Tiger economies are other benefits. Almost everyone is literate. Life chances have been reasonably equal, thus helping to reduce social tensions, and to produce more cohesive societies. All of them have avoided the high crime rates, especially those involving various forms of theft, which have become an increasing problem in the West. They all have low infant mortality rates, high standards of public health and long life expectancies, generally in the mid seventies.[79]

Should the Tiger economies therefore become models for the rest of the world to follow? To some extent, the answer may be that they should, but in other respects, unfortunately the figures do not stack up. As with Japan during a similar phase of post-World War II development, the problem with the Tiger economies is that they have achieved their huge success by cornering more than their fair share of those economic activities which generate high productivity increases, and hence fast rates of economic growth. Their high concentration on industrial output, where rapid increases in output per head are easiest to secure, have been bought partly at the expense of other economies. These particularly include Britain and the USA, and now, increasingly, significant parts of continental Europe. By letting their cost bases become too high, all these areas have laid themselves open to becoming net importers of manufactured goods.

The solution to this problem, however, is not, at least as far as this can be avoided, to slow down the progress of the Tigers. It is to ensure that there is enough demand generally, especially in the western world, for industrial output to flourish in the same way as it has not only in the Tiger economies, but also round much of the rest of the Pacific Rim. As we shall see, however, for this objective to be achieved, substantial policy changes will be required.

Booms and Slumps in the 1990s

Table 6.3 a provides a combined snapshot of developments across the world in the 1990s, contrasting the hugely varied experience of success and failure that this decade has seen. A now familiar pattern emerges. Notwithstanding their high living standards, the industrialised economies of the West and Japan have not performed well in growth terms, despite some apparent evidence to the contrary in the case of the USA. Despite all the upheavals there have been in the Far East, the growth rates achieved by the economies on the Pacific Rim over the decade as whole have been very high. Western commentators who expected that the financial crises which racked the area from mid 1997 onwards would presage much slower growth rates in the future in East Asia have already found themselves surprised by the resilience the area shows.

Between 1990 and 1996, while world output rose 22%, industrialised countries grew 12% and Asia 60%.[80] The EU saw its economies' progress held back by deflationary policies associated with the introduction of European Monetary Union. The Japanese remained hobbled by the banking and financial crisis which has plagued their country since the late 1980s, and which produced an average growth rate of 1.2% between 1991 and 1997. The USA lost ground at the beginning of the decade, but has picked up since, though how long the current boom will last, built as it is on fragile foundations, remains to be seen. While this slow progress was being made, countries such as South Korea and Thailand saw their economies expanding cumulatively, at least until recently, at about 7% per annum, while China, where admittedly the statistics are rather more suspect, more than doubled its output, and the standard of living across the whole vast country rose at 10% per annum.[81]

The crucial issue, which these figures highlight, is whether the momentum in the Pacific area is likely to be maintained, or whether the recent turmoil presages a slower rate of growth in this part of the world in the future. Will the Tigers, and other economies such as Thailand and Malaysia, fall into the same trap as the Japanese, with their growth rates slowing to a crawl for years on end, or will they rapidly resume their former performance?

The reasons for the recent troubles in Thailand, Malaysia and elsewhere among the rapidly developing countries had some overlap with the problems in Japan. The immediate crises were caused by a similar mixture of incautious banking, asset speculation and high levels of investment in property, leading to widespread insolvencies and bankruptcies when an unsustainable boom broke. The major reason why the boom could not last in countries such as Thailand was that the policy goal of maintaining the parity between the US dollar the local currency in Thailand, and the bhat-allowed borrowing to take place in dollars at much lower rates of interest than prevailed domestically. Although Thai exports were growing fast, imports were growing even faster, and by 1996 the current account was $15bn in deficit.[82] When the parity could no longer be held, it fell by nearly 40%.[83] Those who had borrowed in dollars suddenly found that their debts, in local currency terms, had risen by more than 70%, at the same times as asset prices were falling. Once these problems had materialised in Thailand, they rapidly spread to other countries such as Malaysia, Indonesia, Korea and the Philippines, all of which had maintained the same kind of dollar peg to their currencies.

Herein, however, lies a critical difference between these economies and the Japanese. The root problem in Japan is that the authorities have been so cautious about expanding credit and using spending deficits to stimulate the economy. As a result, the country has remained in the doldrums for most of the 1990s despite maintaining a current account surplus which has averaged over $100bn a year for the whole of the period from 1991 to 1997.[84] In Japan, exports still represent only 11% of GDP, and the stimulus from foreign sales has not been sufficient to pull the economy out of recession. In Thailand, exports represented 47% of GDP in 1997, 38% in Korea, 46% in the Philippines, and an astonishing 94% in Malaysia, including re-exports.[85] With these far greater exposures to foreign trade, the impact of highly competitive exchange rates can hardly fail to be much more substantial. There is therefore a much greater likelihood that these economies will find themselves rapidly recovering, as their large and highly competitive export sectors provide both the stimulus and the profitability needed to restore their financial sectors to solvency.

Of course, as always, reasonably competent government will be required, and this may not be forthcoming. There may also be some counter-productive curtailment of credit and excessive interest charges, if pressures exerted by the IMF and other outsiders to bring order into their financial sectors are overdone. There are also questions as to whether the world's footloose sources of capital will behave rationally,

Table 6.3: Performance Data for Selected Economies in the 1990s

		1990	1991	1992	1993	1994	1995	1996	1997	1997 on 1990
EU	GDP at 1990 Prices	5844107	5932442	5990317	5963068	6144036	6298744	6407404	6578958	12.6%
	Increase on Previous Year		1.5%	1.0%	-0.5%	3.0%	2.5%	1.7%	2.7%	1.7%
	Population	365.2	366.2	368	369.7	370.9	372.1	373	373.9	2.4%
	Increase on Previous Year		0.3%	0.5%	0.5%	0.3%	0.3%	0.2%	0.2%	0.3%
	GDP per Head	16002	16200	16278	16129	16565	16928	17178	17596	10.0%
	Increase on Previous Year		1.2%	0.5%	-0.9%	2.7%	2.2%	1.5%	2.4%	1.4%
USA	GDP at 1990 Prices	5743.8	5687.9	5842.7	5973.1	6183.6	6308.4	6482.7	6728.8	17.1%
	Increase on Previous Year		-1.0%	2.7%	2.2%	3.5%	2.0%	2.8%	3.8%	2.2%
	Population	249.91	252.62	255.39	258.13	260.60	263.04	265.45	267.90	7.2%
	Increase on Previous Year		1.1%	1.1%	1.1%	1.0%	0.9%	0.9%	0.9%	1.0%
	GDP per Head	21658	21217	21558	21805	22360	22599	23013	23668	9.3%
	Increase on Previous Year		-2.0%	1.6%	1.1%	2.5%	1.1%	1.8%	2.8%	1.3%
Japan	GDP at 1990 Prices	430040	446371	450981	452339	455254	461951	480073	484379	12.6%
	Increase on Previous Year		3.8%	1.0%	0.3%	0.6%	1.5%	3.9%	0.9%	1.7%
	Population	123.48	123.92	124.32	124.67	124.96	125.2	125.76	126.1	2.1%
	Increase on Previous Year		0.4%	0.3%	0.3%	0.2%	0.2%	0.4%	0.3%	0.3%
	GDP per Head	18649	19288	19425	19429	19509	19758	20441	20569	10.3%
	Increase on Previous Year		3.4%	0.7%	0.0%	0.4%	1.3%	3.5%	0.6%	1.4%
South Korea	GDP at 1990 Prices	179359	195936	205860	217699	236376	257501	275792	290889	62.2%
	Increase on Previous Year		9.2%	5.1%	5.8%	8.6%	8.9%	7.1%	5.5%	7.2%
	Population	42.87	43.30	43.74	44.19	44.64	45.09	45.54	45.99	7.3%
	Increase on Previous Year		1.0%	1.0%	1.0%	1.0%	1.0%	1.0%	1.0%	1.0%
	GDP per Head	8898	9624	10010	10478	11262	12146	12880	13453	51.2%
	Increase on Previous Year		8.2%	4.0%	4.7%	7.5%	7.8%	6.0%	4.4%	6.1%

Thailand	GDP at 1990 Prices	2183.5	2370.4	2562.0	2776.8	3025.0	3292.3	3474.0	3459.1	58.4%
	Increase on Previous Year		8.6%	8.1%	8.4%	8.9%	8.8%	5.5%	-0.4%	6.8%
	Population	55.84	56.57	57.29	58.01	58.71	59.40	60.00	60.60	8.5%
	Increase on Previous Year		1.3%	1.3%	1.3%	1.2%	1.2%	1.0%	1.0%	1.2%
	GDP per Head	4104	4398	4694	5024	5408	5818	6077	5991	46.0%
	Increase on Previous Year		7.2%	6.7%	7.0%	7.6%	7.6%	4.5%	-1.4%	5.6%
China	GDP at 1990 Prices	1832.0	2000.4	2285.2	2593.5	2921.9	3230.1	3538.4	3849.9	110.1%
	Increase on Previous Year		9.2%	14.2%	13.5%	12.7%	10.5%	9.5%	8.8%	11.2%
	Population	1155.3	1170.1	1183.6	1196.4	1208.8	1221.5	1232.1	1244.4	7.7%
	Increase on Previous Year		1.3%	1.2%	1.1%	1.0%	1.1%	0.9%	1.0%	1.1%
	GDP per Head	2544	2743	3098	3478	3879	4243	4608	4964	95.1%
	Increase on Previous Year		7.8%	12.9%	12.3%	11.5%	9.4%	8.6%	7.7%	10.0%

Source: Tables D-1a and D-1e in *Monitoring the World Economy 1820–1922* by Angus Maddison, Paris: OECD 1995; and GDP and population data from *International Financial Statistics Yearbook*. Washington DC: IMF, 1998.

particularly if resumed rapid growth generates more balance of payments which need to be financed. It seems reasonable to hope that the banks will have learned – or re-learned – some old lessons about the quality of the assets on which they lend, and the risks attached to exchange rate changes. The danger for countries such as Malaysia, which imposed new restrictions on capital flows following the crisis, is that expansion may have to be held back if import deficits cannot be financed. In 1995, Malaysia had a current account deficit on goods, services and net income of $7.5bn[86]. It is nevertheless no coincidence that the countries in Asia least affected by the recent upheavals there are those such as China and India where there were more restrictions on the free movement of capital which then got used for wasteful speculative purposes.

In the longer term, the factor which is likely to be more important in slowing down the growth in the Pacific Rim countries is that their rapid output increases are so dependent on export markets, and the ability of the fast growing countries in the region to corner much more than their fair share of economic activity in which high productivity growth is relatively easy to achieve. It also depends on the willingness of the rest of the world to tolerate these conditions continuing. We have seen how the American economy has allowed its manufacturing base to become weakened by a flood of imports, generating significant protectionist pressures. The EU shows signs of heading in the same direction. Although the EU still maintains a significant overall balance of payments surplus, this would not remain the case if the economies there were to be expanded much more rapidly, at least unless significant macro-economic changes were implemented at the same time. Furthermore, while the industrialised countries still have a current surplus with those which are developing, much of this comes from the sale of capital equipment, which the developing countries will learn to make themselves before long.

The only feasible solution to this problem is a realignment of exchange rates to even up trade opportunities across the world, combined with changes in macro-economic policy to generate much higher levels of demand in the world as a whole. If this was done, then countries in the Pacific Rim could continue to grow fast without holding back others in the process. They would then continue to expand as a result of internally generated demand, however, rather than relying on the West to provide an insatiable demand for their exports. This is a theme to which Chapter 9 returns.

unemployment and related benefits. The indirect financial costs of having millions of people with no job is also high. Those who are unemployed are much more likely to need the assistance of health and social services, and to require other welfare benefits, than they would if they were in work.

Nor are the financial costs of unemployment simply to be counted in the payments to those who have no jobs. In addition, the economy forgoes the output that they could have contributed if they were working instead of being idle. In 1997, the average gross value of the output of every person in employment in the USA was about $60 000.[3] In the EU it was around $46 000.[4] Even assuming that the average output of those just coming back into a job was rather less than this, the lost production of goods and services from having people capable of working, but not doing so, is clearly very substantial.

There is also a huge social as well as personal and financial cost to be taken into account. Innumerable studies show that there is a correlation between high levels of unemployment and crime, particularly theft. It is hardly surprising that it is difficult to get the more disadvantaged teenagers to concentrate on their studies if there is little prospect of a job when they leave school. It is equally difficult, therefore, to avoid the conclusion that there is a strong association, reflected in international comparisons of educational achievement, between poor job prospects and low levels of literacy and numeracy among a whole generation of young people, many of whom have never been employed at all.[5]

High levels of unemployment cause major fiscal problems, especially in countries with substantial welfare programmes. A large proportion of the taxable capacity of the EU Member States has to be deployed into paying for unemployment benefit, and all its associated costs. At the same time, the tax base shrinks because millions of people who could be working and paying taxes are drawing benefits instead. The major reason why governments across the EU have had problems in reducing the proportion of the national product spent by the public sector, and thus to contain or diminish the overall level of taxation, has been the inexorable rise in the cost of social security payments, for which high levels of unemployment, directly and indirectly, are largely to blame.

Furthermore, having millions of people who would like to work makes less and less sense when the demographics of developed economies are considered. The position varies from country to country, but there is a marked tendency everywhere in the developed world for the number of people of working age to decline, particularly in relation to those who are retired. This inevitably means that the burden of supporting non-earning fellow citizens is going to have to rise for those who are in employment. It makes no sense at all, in these circumstances, for there to be large numbers of people of employable age who would like to work but cannot do so. Again, this is a particularly serious problem in the EU, compared to the USA.

Nor do the published figures of the numbers out of work tell the full story. The headline unemployment rate measures only those who are actively looking for a job. It excludes all those who would like to work, if the opportunity for doing so existed, but who have given up, temporarily or permanently, trying to find a job because the prospects look hopeless, or because they would be no better off in than out of employment. The ratio between active job-seekers and those who could work, but are not trying to do so, varies from country to country. The average for the European Union as a whole, according to Eurostat figures, is that for every 100 people who are registered as unemployed, about another 50 would like to have jobs if they could.[6]

The total number of people who would prefer to work, given a reasonable opportunity to do so with acceptable levels of remuneration, is therefore far higher than the number of registered unemployed. International Labour Organisation figures show that there may be as many as 30m people in the EU who could be drawn into employment if the conditions were right.[7] No doubt many of them are currently working in the black economy, so the potential gains may not be quite as large as appears possible at first sight, but they would still be very substantial. So would be the fiscal benefit from bringing them back into the tax system. Furthermore, there is considerable scope for increasing the amount done by those who count as being employed, but who only work for limited hours and who do not have a full time job. Some people, especially those with families, may prefer part-time responsibilities, but there are many others who would rather work longer hours for more pay.

When contrasted with the position in the EU, whose total economy and population are roughly the same size as that of the USA, it is therefore easy to come to the conclusion that the position in the USA is very much better than it is the other side of the Atlantic. Undoubtedly, in some important respects, this is a correct conclusion. The USA has been much better at creating new jobs over the past decades than the EU. Between 1973 and 1998, the USA employed labour force increased by 54%, from 85m to 131m, as 46m new jobs were created.[8] Over the same period, the fifteen countries now in the EU saw the total number of jobs rise from 138m to no more than 150m, an increase of just under 9%.[9] It is true that over this period, the US population increased by 28%[10] and the EU by only 8.3%,[11] but there is still a striking contrast in job creation performance. The availability of jobs in the EU increased almost exactly in line with growth in the population growth, whereas in the USA it was much faster.

The reason why the number of jobs needed across the developed world rose considerably more quickly than the size of the population was partly a function of changes in the proportion of working age, but much more significantly by the increasing willingness of women to work. This change, more than anything else, created the requirement for substantial numbers of extra jobs per head of the population. By far the most important reason why the unemployment rate is so much lower in the USA than it is in the EU is that America has been much more successful at creating new jobs than Europe. Because the proportion of the potential labour force out of work is so much lower in the USA than the EU, and because the USA has a much less comprehensive welfare system, the costs to public expenditure of supporting those without jobs is far less. There is also a persuasive case to be made for saying that even if many of the jobs in the USA are low paid, it is better for those concerned to be in work than on welfare. When anyone is in employment, the skills needed for holding down a job do not get rusty. Self-respect is maintained. Welfare assistance is not required.

It seems, therefore, that the USA has a great deal to teach the EU about how to avoid unemployment, and how to combine job creation on a major scale with stable levels of inflation. There are, however, reasons for believing that the US record is not nearly as good as it appears to be at first sight. Unemployment may be lower, but other problems may be more severe. Both the USA and the EU suffer from inadequate job opportunities, especially for their poorer and less advantaged citizens. Different fiscal, legal and welfare systems have meant that the results have materialised in varying ways, in some respects worse in the EU, but in others, as we shall see, more damaging in the USA.

Comparative experience

In the European Union, there is a major and obvious problem with unemployment. 17m people are registered as looking for work which is not available.[12] About another 11m would like to work, but have dropped out, temporarily at least, from the potential labour force.[13] The costs to the governments concerned are enormous, both in benefits to be paid out and in tax forgone. Crime rises with higher unemployment. Alienation increases. Education standards become harder to maintain. Public expenditure as a proportion of GDP tends to rise.

Although the USA appears to have avoided at least the worst of these pitfalls, the underlying realities may not be so different each side of the Atlantic. The apparently better US performance is mostly on the surface rather than underneath. This perception flows from the fact that both the USA and the EU suffer from similar root problems, for which lack of job opportunities, especially for those lower down the income scales, is a prime symptom. Growth has been slow on both sides of the Atlantic. The advent of computers, increased competition, better training and more professional management have produced distinct improvements in productivity particularly among those at managerial levels in the labour force. Slow growth, especially per head of the population, associated with productivity in much of the economy rising faster than total output, has inevitably led to job losses, including a relatively large proportion of high quality employment.

In Europe, the impact of these developments has been to increase unemployment. Over the twenty-four years between 1973 and 1997, the EU compound growth rate was 2.2% per annum.[14] Output per head among those working, allowing for a 9%[15] increase in the labour force between 1973 and 1997, therefore increased at about 2.1% a year. Over the same period, registered unemployment in the EU rose from 2.5%[16] to 9.9%,[17] a rise of 7.4%, or an average increase in registered unemployment of a little under 0.3% per annum. In the EU, as Table 7.1 shows, for every 100 people who appear on the unemployment register, something of the order of 150 on average dropped out of the employment statistics. The effect of increasing employment is to draw more people into the active labour force, whereas worsening job prospects have the opposite effect. The percentage of the potential labour force involuntarily ceasing employment each year is therefore likely to have been somewhere between 0.4% and 0.5%. Assuming that the output per head of those leaving the labour force was roughly the same as those remaining – and as we shall see later this is a reasonable approximation after making various necessary allowances – a first estimate of the shortfall in demand each year to stop unemployment rising over these years was about 0.4% to 0.5% of GDP. In fact this is likely to be too low. The average growth in productivity in the labour force would certainly have been higher if demand had been greater. Allowing for all relevant factors, an increase in GDP of probably around 3% per annum cumulatively would have been required in the EU between 1973 and 1992 to keep unemployment down to around 3% of the potential labour force. This

Table 7.1: EU and US Unemployment to Labour Force Change Ratio

Area	Date	Population Aged 15–64 mn	% Total 15–64 Population in Labour Force	Total Civilian Labour Force mn	Labour Force factored for Population Change mn	Total Civilian Employed mn	Employed factored for Labour Force Change mn	Change in Number Employed %	Employed %	Un-employed mn	Un-employed %	Employed to Labour Force Change Ratio
EU	1979	203.8	64.4%	131.4	131.4	123.8	123.8		94.3%	7.5	5.7%	
	1983	212.4	63.8%	135.5	130.0	121.5	122.7		89.6%	14.1	10.4%	
	Change		-0.6%	4.2	-1.3	-2.4	-1.2	-1.9%	-4.7%	-6.6	-4.7%	82%
EU	1991	242.0	68.3%	165.3	165.3	151.6	151.6		91.8%	13.6	8.2%	
	1994	244.1	67.6%	165.1	163.7	146.7	148.1		88.8%	18.5	11.2%	
	Change		-0.6%	-0.1	-1.6	-5.0	-3.6	-3.3%	-2.9%	-4.8	-2.9%	26%
USA	1983	155.7	71.7%	111.6	111.6	100.8	100.8		90.4%	10.7	9.6%	
	1988	162.8	74.7%	121.7	123.4	115.0	103.9		94.5%	6.7	5.5%	
	Change		3.1%	10.1	11.8	14.1	3.1	14.0%	4.1%	4.0	4.1%	22%

Note: These calculations do not provide significant results over periods with small changes in unemployment because changes in the total size of the potential workforce and other factors then usually become too large in relation to changes in the level of unemployment for the relationship under review to be seen. For all periods with big changes in the level of unemployment, however, in all developed countries, the same trend and roughly the same ratios are generally to be found.

Sources: Tables 0201, 0202, 0203 and 0301, in *Eurostatistics*, Luxembourg: European Union, 1995, and Tables 2, 5, 5.1 and 6 in *Labour Force Statistics 1970–1990*, OECD, Paris, 1992; Table B-35 in *Economic Report of the President*, Washington DC: US Government Printing Office, 1999.

would have implied an average increase in productivity of all those then working of about 2.5% per annum, or perhaps a little more.

In the USA, similar processes have been at work, but with a different outcome. Although the US economy has grown at almost exactly the same rate as that of the EU over the last twenty-five years – 2.2% compound in each case – the US labour force has increased much more quickly – by nearly 1.7%[18] per annum cumulatively, compared to 0.4%[19] the other side of the Atlantic. The result in the USA has been the exceptionally low rise recorded in output per head, or increase in productivity, averaging only 0.8% per annum.[20] With its labour force expanding as rapidly as it was, the US economy ought to have been able to grow much faster than it actually did. The reason it failed to do so, as in the case of the EU, was that there was a substantial shortfall of effective demand in relation to the level needed to soak up the rises in productivity potentially achievable. Assuming that they were roughly equal to those in the EU, allowing for a cumulative increase in output per head of the order of 2.5% per annum given reasonably favourable conditions, the shortfall in demand in the USA turns out to be even higher than in Europe, mainly because the labour force was growing so much more quickly. To achieve full potential utilisation of the labour force, mainly because of its rapid growth, between 1974 and 1998 the missing US cumulative increase in demand was closer to 1.7% per annum compound compared to 1% for the EU. The US deficiency of 1.7% each year is calculated as the difference over the last twenty-five years between the actual rise in labour force productivity, which was 0.8%, compared to the potential increase which, from experience in Europe, appears to have been at least 2.5%.

The consequences for the EU of the shortfall in demand needed to keep the labour force fully employed has been a well publicised increase in unemployment. In the USA, this has not been the outcome, but only because the welfare system is so different. In Europe, being out of work has many well known major disadvantages, but generally being on the breadline is not one of them. All European states have comparatively generous social security systems which mean that those out of work are still left with benefits on which they can survive without falling into intolerable poverty. Some EU states have even more abundant entitlements, leaving their recipients with up to 80% of their previous earnings for considerable periods.[21] Understandably, in these circumstances, those who have lost their jobs are prepared to wait, if necessary for a long time, until another position comes up which they think would suit them. The pressure to take any job, even if the pay rate is very low, is heavily blunted.

In the USA, by contrast, the welfare system is less comprehensive in scale than in Europe, and considerably less orientated, within a smaller total, to unemployment compensation than to other disbursements such as pensions, medical care and help to poor families. Of those out of work in the USA, in 1998 only 36% were covered by state unemployment insurance, down from 50% in 1980.[22] Those who are entitled to compensation for being out of work in the US receive benefits for a much shorter period of time than is generally the case in Europe. As a result, the pressure on those losing their jobs in America to find other ones quickly is much greater.

Entirely understandably, employers respond in different ways to the availability of labour, and its willingness to work, on each side of the Atlantic. In Europe, where protection for those in work is relatively high, making it expensive to lay them off, but where unemployment benefits are also high, the labour market is relatively unresponsive. Those with jobs to offer are reluctant to take on labour if they know that it will be difficult and expensive to discharge it if there is a downturn in business activity. The unemployed can afford to be relatively selective about the jobs for which they apply. In the USA, on the other hand, where the opposite conditions apply, the labour market is much more fluid. The risks involved in creating new jobs are much lower, and the competition for them correspondingly greater.

The effects of the two different systems on productivity and income distribution then become clear. In the EU, the output per head of those remaining employed has risen by about 2% per annum,[23] while those who lose their jobs make no contribution to national output at all, at least outside the black economy. In the USA, almost everyone capable of working has a job, but the extra net output achieved by many of these jobs is very low, and often negative. Labour, relatively speaking, is so cheap at the lower end of the US market that employers can afford to use it extremely wastefully. Very high manning levels in hamburger bars, plenty of employees available to clean windscreens at filling stations, and rows of people ready to clean shoes, are not signs of a highly productive economy. They are the result of the same financial pressures which force large numbers of people into these kinds of jobs in Third World countries.

To some extent at least, the availability of large amounts of cheap labour also has a self-fulfilling element to the way the economy develops. It does not pay to install so much labour saving equipment if there is a large pool of people who will work for low wages. Nor does it pay to invest heavily in skill training. The results are reflected in the depressed level of capital investment in the USA, and the poor education and training levels achieved by much of the US labour force. In Europe, by contrast, the opposite pressures apply, and investment levels are greater, and the employed labour force tends to be better educated and trained.

The distribution of income is also different in America and Europe. In both areas, there has been a marked increase in inequality of earnings during the last quarter of a century. For broadly the same reasons, the rich have become much richer than they were twenty-five years ago, while the poor have seen only a modest increase in income, and those falling through the net are in too many cases significantly worse off than their counterparts in 1973. Within these broad categories, however, there are big differences. In Europe, blue collar workers still in employment have roughly kept their share of national earnings, so that their real living standards have risen in line with GDP per head. The heavy losers have been those who no longer have jobs, or who have been dependent on benefits which have not risen in line with output per head. In the USA, on the other hand, the competition for jobs has depressed real earnings increases to levels much higher up the income scales. This is why blue collar incomes have hardly increased at all in the USA during the last twenty-five years, net of inflation.

Thus the employment record in the USA, though on the surface better than that of the EU, contains major blemishes. Average productivity growth among those in employment has been much lower. The impact of fierce competition for jobs has caused the real earnings of those in the middle ranges to rise much more slowly than in Europe, making the overall distribution of income even more uneven. Excess labour supplies have probably contributed to lower levels of investment and poorer standards of education and training on average than in the EU. There has been a vast waste of human resources in Europe during the last twenty-five years, but the figures suggest that the greatly increased labour supply in the USA has been even less gainfully and productively used than in the EU. By a very wide margin, unemployment percentages on their own do not tell the whole story.

The real problem with the labour market in the USA is not that the total number of people without a job is excessively high. On the contrary, it is quite low by international standards. The major American problem is that a very high proportion of its employed labour force is grossly under-used. This is why both its output and its growth in productivity are so low, reflected in almost static real incomes and large numbers struggling through life on minimum wages. The problem in the USA may not be unemployment, but there is underemployment on a huge scale.

Misguided solutions

Faced with the fact that in much of the developed world, there are evidently serious difficulties about providing large numbers of people with reasonably secure, well paid jobs, almost everyone's instinctive reaction is to resort to essentially supply side explanations for this state of affairs. Many different reasons are put forward to explain the difficulties which advanced economies appear to have in allowing their workforces to compete successfully with other parts of the world. In consequence a wide range of remedies is on offer. It is not at all clear, however, that any of the explanations usually put forward either at the popular or more policy orientated level to account for the low productivity of much of the US labour force, or the high level of joblessness in the EU, have any real credibility. If this is so, the solutions they entail are unlikely to do anything effective to resolve the problem.

First, there is a widespread tendency to blame poor job prospects, especially for those on low incomes, on technical progress. It is clearly the case that much modern equipment can replace men and women with machines, which can do the necessary work far more quickly and accurately than any human can manage. Perhaps the greatest fears are of computers, with their ability to replace armies of clerks, accountants and secretaries. It seems logical at first sight that if machines can replace human labour, then the result must be fewer jobs and more people out of work.

This is of course a line of argument which has been current since the beginning of the Industrial Revolution, when mechanisation started. It is wrong because it depends on the 'lump of labour' fallacy. This is the assumption that the total demand for the output of the work force is fixed, so that if part of a given amount of work is done by a machine instead of by a person, lack of good employment opportunities must be the result. There is, however, no reason why the amount of output for which demand is available should be static. On the contrary, the history of the economically developing world has been one of rising demand ever since the Industrial Revolution began. Provided there is a steadily increasing amount of purchasing power available to buy the expanding output from mechanisation and technical improvements, there is no reason why involuntary unemployment or underemployment should increase. The benefit from technical change will then appear as rising productivity and higher living standards. Problems will only occur if inadequate purchasing power is available to mop up all the new output potentially available.

Second, poor job prospects for low income earners are not caused by the social and economic changes on which they are often blamed. Neither more women in the labour force, nor more part-time workers, nor shifts away from basic industries to light manufacturing, nor from manufacturing to services, nor any other alterations in working patterns are directly responsible for low incomes, though the indirect effects of some of these changes are a different matter. It is true that many of the new jobs which have been created recently in the industrialised countries have been part-time, especially in the service sector, and that women have been in some cases more willing to adapt to them, and to work for lower pay than many men have found acceptable. It is also true that the types of jobs available have shifted away markedly from employment where physical strength was at a premium to office and service activity. This has left older male workers with skills and experience which have sometimes been difficult to redeploy in modern conditions. In this sense, there are mismatches in the labour market between the skills and abilities for which employers are seeking, and those which a significant number of applicants have to offer.

This cannot, however, be a satisfactory overall explanation for the current high levels of underemployment in the USA, or unemployment in the EU. The changes which are taking place in the labour market today are not so different from those which were occurring all over the developed world in the 1950s and 1960s when no such problems were apparent, at least to anything like the same degree. The real deficiency is a different one. It is that there is not enough work to go round. In these circumstances, employers will inevitably choose the people who are most obviously suited to the employment they have to offer, who are most adaptable and who will work for the lowest pay. With insufficient jobs for everyone, those who are least obviously fitted for the available employment, whether because of their locations, skills, ages or attitudes, will inevitably finish up with low paid employment, or with no work at all. If there was much higher demand for labour, these problems would largely disappear.

It is often argued that so many people, and particularly youngsters, are in dead end jobs or out of work because their educational skills are inadequate, they are poorly trained and lack technical capabilities, and they are not well motivated. There is little doubt that large numbers of younger people in the rich countries of the world lack good education and training. It is hardly surprising that many of them lack motivation if they are brought up in a culture where so many leaving school fail to find a steady employment with reasonable prospects. It does not, however, follow from this that they are incapable of holding down demanding jobs. As with other categories of the labour force, the difficulty is that they are not those most obviously suitable for whatever employment is on offer, so they get left at the back of the queue. The problem, again, is that there is not enough reasonably high quality work to go round, and in these circumstances the least advantaged are the most likely to finish up with poorly paid, low productivity jobs, or out of work altogether.

A different line of argument is that lack of good employment prospects for many people in developed countries is caused by their high wages compared to those in many other parts of the world. It is assumed that it is therefore impossible for labour forces in the USA or Europe to compete with workers in places like China and Malaysia, where the average standard of living is far below the level in the West. It is, however, a fallacy to believe that work always goes where labour is cheapest. It is also a fallacy to believe that rich countries and poor countries cannot trade together to their mutual advantage and in overall balance however different their wage rates and productivity levels may be. The critical factor is not the amount that labour is paid per hour, but its cost per unit of output, taking account of how productive it is and the rate at which it is charged out both to home and export markets. If the productivity of the labour force is high enough, it can compete comfortably in the world even though it is very well paid. The fact that wage rates for many Americans are not high by international standards at the lower end of the income scales, but still the companies they work for have problems competing in world markets, simply reinforces the fact that the USA has a major low productivity problem among much of its workforce. We used to be told that it was cheap labour that made the Far East economies competitive. Now, however, the Tiger economies have incomes per head approaching, and in some cases exceeding, those in the West, but their economies are still growing fast. Hong Kong currently has a standard of living which is close to that of the poorer parts of the USA and is well ahead of some of Europe, and its economy was still growing, at least until recently, at about 7% per annum.

Variations in the cost of producing different goods and services explain why rich and poor countries can trade together to their mutual benefit, even if the poor country makes everything less efficiently than the rich one. Rich and poor countries will always produce some goods and services relatively more efficiently and cheaply than other outputs, and these are the ones which they can sell abroad. For example, a low productivity Third World country may be a much cheaper place in which simple assembly work can be carried out. A rich country, in turn, may well be able to design complex products at far lower cost than might be possible even with the lowest paid labour in the poor country. It is these so called variances which make it worth while for both countries to trade with each other. Each gains, and is better off than it would otherwise have been, as a result of the exchanges which trade makes possible.

For trade of this sort to take place to everyone's advantage, however, another important condition has to be fulfilled. The trade has to be in rough balance. Of course in the modern world where almost every country buys from and sells to every other, it makes no sense to try to make sure that trade between every pair of countries is in equilibrium on a bilateral basis. It is each country's overall trade balance with the rest of the world which counts. If this is out of kilter, however, in that there are economies which are unable to sell enough to the rest of the world to pay for their imports, the inevitable result, unless there are parity changes, will be curtailment of demand to avoid balance of payments problems, and increased unemployment. This is not an argument, however, for abandoning the advantages of free trade. It is one for ensuring that exchange rates are correctly positioned to enable each economy to hold its own with the rest of the world.

A different explanation advanced for high levels of unemployment, though not underemployment, and in consequence much more applicable to Europe than America, is that generous state run welfare systems have blunted the need to work. Large numbers of people do not, therefore, try to get jobs. It makes more sense to sit at home collecting benefits, the argument runs, than incurring the costs of being at work, especially if the pay is low. There is some truth in this assertion, especially for some people on small incomes. The effects of relatively high levels of income tax on low wages, combined with benefit withdrawal, can produce high effective rates of tax on people at the bottom end of the pay scale. There are also particular problems for married couples, where one spouse working for low pay can reduce family entitlements by more than the income gained if the other remains out of work.

As a general explanation for high levels of unemployment, however, this argument is also implausible. First, large numbers of people who are out of work do not suffer from these kinds of income-trap problems. Second, at least some of these problems arise from the fact that there is so much unemployment in the first place. Many jobs are on offer at low pay because there are large numbers of people competing for the smaller quantity of unskilled jobs available nowadays. Third, and perhaps most importantly, much of the income-trap problem is itself directly the result of the huge cost to the state of having millions of people involuntarily out of work. There is acute strain on the revenue and benefit system, largely because of the massive loss of income tax revenues from unemployment, combined with the heavy costs in benefits of having millions of people without jobs. The resulting high levels of assessments on those with low earnings causes much of the overlap between taxes and benefits for people on meagre incomes.

Supply side mirages

Most people's perceptions of the reasons for poor employment prospects for low income earners are that large numbers of people appear to be marginal candidates in the job market for the 'supply side' reasons set out in the previous section. It is therefore hardly surprising that the government's response, in almost all countries with apparently inadequate job opportunities, is to tackle supposed supply side deficiencies. The objective is to make the economy more efficient, and thus better able to secure enough of the world's purchasing power to keep a higher proportion of the labour force employed. This activity is frequently devoted to efforts to improve productivity in the hope that this will make the economy more competitive.

The scale of much of this activity is enormous. In the USA, this is reflected in major current initiatives on education and training,[24] though these are dwarfed by actions in some other countries. France, recently afflicted by unemployment rates of more than 12% of its labour force, peaked at spending almost 0.75% of its entire gross national product on training schemes. Sweden and Denmark spent even more – over 1% of their GNPs.[25] Nor do efforts to improve competitiveness cover only training. Higher levels of investment are also perceived to be a key factor, especially if it can be orientated to producing products with high value added. This often shades into claims that high technology is the key to improving productivity and competitiveness, generating initiatives to move advanced economies away from relatively 'low-tech' activity to the 'higher-tech' end of the spectrum, where it is thought that it would be easier to compete with producers in less developed parts of the world.[26]

Because this approach generally requires substantial capital expenditure, another plank in the policy platform is then to encourage more savings to finance increased investment, particularly in manufacturing industry. Fast growing economies reinvest a much higher proportion of their national incomes than the relatively slow growing economies of the West. It is therefore assumed that if investment were increased, this would tend to lead to high rates of growth. It is also argued, although again more in Europe than in America, that the state has a major role to play in enhancing the infrastructure to make the economy more competitive. Improving the road and rail system and developing more advanced telecommunications, proponents of this type of investment claim, will improve the capacity of any country to export and to compete in the world.

Unfortunately, evidence for the overall efficacy of any of these policies is almost totally lacking. Of course, more training gets some people into jobs which they might not otherwise have been able to secure, and it is certainly the case that wilting levels of investment weaken any economy's capacity to compete in the future. This is a different matter, however, from being able to show that all these state-driven supply side efforts to cope with poor employment prospects have been successful. On the contrary, the evidence strongly suggests that they have failed to provide the sought for solutions in all the advanced western countries which have spent large sums of money on them.

These policies have failed to work because none of them begins to cope effectively with the real reason why there are so many people across the developed world in the West with poor job prospects. This has little to do with supply side problems. On the contrary, it has everything to do with lack of sufficient demand for the goods and services which western economies are capable of producing. When looked at in this light, it becomes comparatively easy to see why all the huge efforts currently being put into employment measures are not going to work in the absence of changes in overall economic environment.

The fundamental problem with trying to use education and training programmes, and increased investment to make any slow growing country more competitive, is that it is much easier to run such programmes successfully in economies which are already growing rapidly. Advanced western economies are not the only ones with education and training programmes. Every developed country has them, and so, too, do developing countries. Furthermore, in countries which are growing quickly, with buoyant tax revenues and rapidly expanding and profitable enterprises, high quality education and training can be afforded relatively easily both in academic and on-the-job environments. The incentive for everyone to improve his or her skills is also clearly evident. With a tight labour market, everyone can find a job, so time devoted to training courses is seldom wasted. As a result, the effort and money spent on education and training has an immediate pay-off for almost everyone concerned.

In countries with sluggish growth, the cards are stacked the opposite way. First, it is impossibly difficult to raise the skills of the labour force as quickly in a slow growing economy as in one which is growing fast, because the opportunities for using increased training are so much less. Slow growing economies thus progressively slip further behind, and become even less competitive. Second, because there is still not enough work to go round, much of the education and training that takes place is wasted, since those on the courses cannot obtain work where they can use their new-found skills once their training is completed. Even if they can, all too often they do no more than displace someone else, who then finds his or her way either on to the dole queue, or back to another training course. This is much too close to being an expensive and dispiriting zero sum game.

Nor is the encouragement of investment any more of a panacea in the absence of overall economic changes. As with education and training, it is far easier to implement successful investment projects in economies that are already growing fast than in ones which are static or growing slowly. Profitability is much greater, making them easier to finance. Wages and salaries in the enterprises making them are relatively high, attracting able entrepreneurs and managers, who are likely to make good decisions. When mistakes are made, which inevitably they will be, it is easier to pay for them. As wave after wave of investment takes place, so the experience in managing the highly skilled process of organising a successful investment strategy becomes honed. It is extremely hard to succeed against competitors who have accumulated this kind of expertise. Far from it being easier in high-tech industries, furthermore, it is likely to be more difficult. Running high-tech operations successfully usually involves accumulating years of experience in managing rapid technical change. The chances of companies anywhere being able to move into these fields from scratch and to compete successfully are not good. Logic and experience strongly suggest that it is generally easier to compete in industries where the technology is well established, and where the risks and skill requirements are lower, provided that the overall cost base is favourable.

The reality is that it is not high levels of savings and investment which produce high growth rates. It is high growth rates which produce high levels of savings and investment. The key to better economic performance is not to subsidise and cajole reluctant investors into putting more money into new projects than they would if left to themselves. It is to create the macro-economic environment where high rates of growth are strongly encouraged by rising effective demand. Investment will then follow, as profitable opportunities open up. The reason for relatively low levels of capital expenditure in much of both US and European manufacturing, compared to the fast developing areas of the world, is that the prospects for making money out of new plant, machinery and factories in fast growing economies tend to be much better than in those in North America and Europe which have a much lower average growth rate.

There is, nevertheless, a broad issue as to what strategies are the right ones to pursue when there are millions more people available for work than the economy really needs to achieve its current output. Does it not make sense to try to improve productivity in conditions where there are very large numbers of people with no jobs, as is the case in Europe? Have we no alternative but to move towards the American solution, reflected in Britain, which is to generate welfare and employment conditions which drive productivity down to a point where output per head is low enough for nearly all the potential labour force to be employed? This is where the current enthusiasm for deregulation and flexibility will eventually lead. Simply posing questions in this form, however, exposes how far many government policies in the western world may have drifted from providing effective solutions to pressing problems. They also point the way to some important and widely believed fallacies about productivity and supply side remedies, and the link between competitiveness, improved economic performance and better job prospects. If asked what needs to be done to improve growth rates in the West, the stock answer from most quarters is that the only solution is to raise investment, productivity, quality, innovation and value added. Is any of this true?

As we have already seen, productivity is not at all the same as competitiveness. If it were, the richest countries would always successfully out-strip the poorer ones competing more successfully in international markets, and growing faster. This is clearly, however, not the experience of much of the world today. Nor has it ever been in the past. The reason is that output per head has everything to do with the standard of living, but almost nothing to do with competitiveness. It is the exchange rate – or more accurately the prices each country charges the rest of the world for the combined cost of all its factors of production – which determines whether the economy grows fast, or slowly, or remains static. Increasing productivity to make the economy more competitive will only work if it can be done quickly enough to reduce prices more rapidly than the world average, without reducing profit margins. Achieving this objective from a position where economies are growing more slowly than the rest of the world is an impossibly difficult task, and attempts to achieve it are virtually bound to fail.

Of course quality and innovation are important. No doubt, the better the quality the higher the price which can be charged. What can be done, however, if any economy starts from a position where quality is poor, and the products sold are old-fashioned? Making them better is expensive, and everyone else in the world is trying to improve product quality at the same time. The companies which are likely to succeed are those which are already profitable and expanding – in fast growing countries. Those in economies which are expanding slowly are likely to be growing less rapidly, to be less profitable, and with lower levels of investment, and therefore not in a position to afford and implement improvements nearly so easily. This is why fast growth is the easiest and fastest route to product enhancement. Trying to use increasing quality and innovation as ways of raising competitiveness and growth, rather than seeing them as by-products of an expanding economy, is again to set an impossibly difficult target which will almost certainly not be achieved.

Value added has similar characteristics to productivity. The total value added in any economy is more or less equivalent to its GDP. If the economy does not expand, total value added will stay the same. If productivity then increases in some parts of the economy, it will have to fall in others. This is the root problem with trying to raise value added and productivity without tackling the macro-economic environment. Even if successful in those parts of the economy where the policies are effective, if there is no overall output increase, the result has to be a corresponding reduction in performance in other parts of the economy which the policies have not touched. Rising average productivity in some areas, while the economy stays the same size, does no more than guarantee worsening job opportunities somewhere else. In particular, if productivity increases among those with already high output, but the level of demand on the economy remains the same, those already worse off are bound see their employment prospects deteriorating.

The truth is that the connections between productivity, quality, innovation, value added and improved economic performance are indeed significant, but different from those normally perceived. It is not improved productivity or any of the other quality measures of output which produces more growth. The sequence is the other way round. This does not, of course, mean that productivity and related measures of economic performance are unimportant. On the contrary, they determine the standard of living, and are thus of vital significance. It is the output per member of the labour force which multiplies up to the gross domestic product. Whether an economy has a high or low standard of living, however, tells us nothing about the ability of its producers to compete in the world and whether, therefore, its total output, and with it productivity, quality, innovation and value added will increase or not. The economy's growth is determined by an altogether different factor, which is whether its output is competitively priced in the home and export markets. This is an exchange rate issue, and not one where any realistic policies on improving productivity, quality, innovation and value added, in isolation from macro-economic policy changes, have a chance of being successful on their own.

As with so many other economic matters, feedback makes it difficult to distinguish between cause and effect. In this case, as elsewhere, it is all too easy to confuse symptoms and root causes. Determining the direction of causation is, however, critical to formulating proposals which are going to work. Many billions of dollars or euros can be spent on supply side policies designed to improve competitiveness and growth by increasing investment, productivity, quality, innovation and value added. Little or nothing will be attained. No money needs to be spent, however, on implementing the policy which will actually achieve the results which otherwise appear so elusive. Bringing down interest rates, increasing the money supply, and positioning the exchange rate correctly, so that effective demand is raised, all cost nothing. Much more rapid growth will then follow, bringing enhanced investment, higher productivity, improved quality, innovation and greater value added effortlessly in train, as market forces drive the economy to expand. Job opportunities, especially for those on relatively low incomes, will then progressively cease to be a major problem. As happened to the US labour force during the world wars, in Europe in the 1950s and 1960s, and as, at least until very recently, was the experience in the Tiger economies, once the labour market gets tight enough, it becomes worth training almost everyone. This is the only secure and certain route to the increases in productivity and wages among the less well off, which are otherwise so easy to advocate, and so difficult to achieve.

Growth and the trade balance

The most important reason why so many western economies suffer unemployment or low productivity among a high proportion of their labour forces has nothing to do with any supposed deficiencies which supply side policies might be able to cure. The real reason so many people are unemployed in Europe, and earn such low wages in the USA is that there is insufficient demand for what they could otherwise produce. Until this deficiency is remedied, these problems will main intractable and insuperable. The only solution both sides of the Atlantic is to raise demand. How much demand is missing? The calculations are not particularly difficult to follow, and they are set out below.

It is easiest to start from a hypothetical country to illustrate the principles, and then to apply them to real economies. It is also simpler to exemplify the position in a country where the impact of insufficient demand has led to unemployment, which is easily measurable, and then to extend the conclusions to the USA where the effect has been primarily on productivity and wage levels – that is, on underemployment – instead of on joblessness. The simplest method is therefore to consider the problems faced by European countries, and then to relate their policy change requirements back to those of the USA.

The starting point is to consider a country whose level of unemployment is higher than is regarded as acceptable. If the reason for lack of jobs to keep everyone in work is insufficient demand, total demand within the economy will have to be increased until unemployment has been reduced to a level which is regarded as reasonable. How much extra is needed? If the potential output per head from those out of work was the same as those in employment, the answer would be easy to calculate. The increase in effective demand would have to be proportional to the increase in employment that was needed. For example, to reduce 10% unemployment – close to the EU average in recent years – to 3% would require an increase in demand to lift the proportion of those in work from 90% to 97% of the potential labour force, an increase of 7 divided by 90, or about 8%.

It is clear, however, that this is much too simple, even if we are only looking for broad approximations rather than exact figures. There are three significant adjustments which need to be taken into account to produce acceptably reliable results.

First, there is substantial evidence that to reduce the registered unemployment rate by, say, 100 000 people, much more than 100 000 new jobs need to be created. The reason for this is that increased employment opportunities attract back into the labour force people who would not otherwise register as out of work, and the converse tends to apply when unemployment increases. The ratio fluctuates, and is difficult to pin down accurately because changes in the size of the labour force are affected by many other factors than the level of unemployment. Table 7.1 on p. 164 showed examples of the ratios thrown up both sides of the Atlantic during periods when there have been marked changes in the percentage of the workforce which was unemployed. These figures suggest that a reasonable approximation is that for every 100 000 people taken off the unemployment register, roughly 150 000 new jobs need to be created.

Second, increasing demand is bound to lead to higher remuneration for existing employees, as the labour market tightens, even without hourly wage rises. More shift work will be needed, increasing overtime and payments for operating during unsocial hours. People now counted as employed, but involuntarily working part-time, may take on full-time jobs. As a result, the average remuneration for all the existing labour force is likely to go up. Clearly the larger the rise in demand, the more pronounced this tendency will be.

Third, it is unlikely that the output per head of those currently unemployed will be as high as the average if they are reabsorbed into the active labour force. It will almost certainly be lower by a significant margin. Furthermore, the higher the level of unemployment from which we start, the larger this discrepancy is likely to be.

We are not dealing with exact figures here, but within reasonably narrow limits the evidence suggests that these last two adjustments are likely to cancel each other out. Making this assumption then provides a relatively simple formula for calculating in a reasonably accurate way the approximate rise in effective demand needed to increase employment by any given percentage. If registered unemployment is 10% and the target is to reduce it to 3%, effective demand has to be increased by the 8% already calculated, multiplied by an estimated additional 50%, to take account of the extra people drawn into the labour force. The total rise needed, therefore, will be approximately 8% times 1.5, which comes to about 12%.

How can demand be stimulated to achieve much lower levels of unemployment? It has to be done both by increasing the money supply and by expanding import saving and export led demand. The credit base needs to be increased sufficiently both to stimulate greater activity and to accommodate the new and higher volume of transactions which will need to be financed as the economy expands. The ratio between the money in circulation and the volume of transactions tends to fall as money becomes cheaper and more plentiful, and more idle balances materialise. As a result, the increase in the money supply is likely to have to be significantly greater in percentage terms than the proportionate rise in domestic demand which will be needed.

It is not possible for any economy to increase demand by a significant percentage without regard to the impact this change would have on its balance of payments position. The next stage is therefore to calculate the balance of payments and exchange rate implications of a large increase in domestic demand. Again, it is easier to consider a hypothetical economy first, and then to apply the conclusions to the real world.

Suppose that the economy we are considering had a trade balance within acceptable limits before domestic demand was increased, and by way of illustration, suppose that the increase in demand needed was 12% – the same figure considered a few paragraphs above. Again, as an approximate estimate, the result is likely to be that exports of goods and services would stay the same as they were before, but imports would rise by the same proportion as the increase in domestic demand. A balance of payments deficit would therefore be created. To correct this, there would have to be a devaluation. How much depreciation would be needed? Again, it is not difficult to calculate the broad magnitude required.

Large numbers of studies have been conducted into the sensitivity of the imports and exports of developed countries to price changes. All these studies show results that cluster round the same values. These are referred to as the price elasticities of demand, and the studies show that both imports and exports have elasticity values (ignoring their signs) of about one.[27]

This means that if any economy, with these elasticities, devalues its currency, the volume of exports will rise by about 1%, while the volume of imports will fall by 1%. If, again as an approximation, but not far from experience, import prices are set by world prices, and export prices are set in the domestic economy, a devaluation of 1% will have the following effects:

The value of imports, measured in the domestic currency, will stay the same as it was before. This will happen because they will rise in price by 1%, but fall in volume by 1%, these two changes cancelling each other out.

The value of exports, measured in the domestic currency, however, will increase by 1%. This happens because their price, measured in domestic currency stays the same, but their volume increases by 1%.

The overall effect of these impacts on imports and exports taken together is that a 1% depreciation will improve the trade balance of the devaluing economy by 1%. This ratio then feeds straight back to the change in the trade balance required from the increase in domestic demand. If a 12% increase in demand is needed to reduce unemployment to acceptable levels, as a first approximation, this will need to be accompanied by a devaluation of the same size. This will both provide the stimulus needed to trigger off more growth and investment to sustain it, while also ensuring that there is no balance of payments constraint to check progress. Although this is not obvious, in fact these relationships remain the same whether the economy concerned has a large or a small proportion of its output involved in foreign trade. The sums of money involved in financing a trade deficit, compared with total GDP, however, would obviously be smaller if the economy had less of its GDP concerned with the import and export of goods and services.

Looking first at the EU, it is clear from the different levels of unemployment across the EU that, if exchange rate changes were to be used to deal with joblessness in Europe then major parity adjustments between Member States would be needed to bring unemployment down to an acceptable level across the Union as a whole. The first column in Table 7.2 shows the levels of registered unemployment in the EU states as of July 1998.[28] It is clear from these figures that some countries, particularly Spain, Finland, France and Italy, have a far more serious unemployment problem than others, especially some of the smaller countries such as Luxembourg, Austria and Portugal. If, because of the euro, no exchange rate alterations can take place within the Union, it is certain that some of the EU economies will become overheated before others bring unemployment down anywhere near 3%. Assuming for the moment, that the Single Currency had not come into being, however, it is possible to calculate the parity changes required in the EU, if its impact was to produce a general reduction in unemployment across the Union to about 3%. The third column of figures in Table 7.2 shows the parity changes which would have had to have been made in the summer of 1998 *vis à vis* the Deutsche Mark to enable all the EU economies to reduce unemployment to about 3% together. The final column shows the parity changes required, country by country, against the rest of the world, and the EU total, which is a devaluation of about 11%. Interestingly, the early part of 1999 saw a reduction in the trade weighted value of the euro which was remarkably close to this percentage.

Turning now to the USA, because the labour market there works so differently from in Europe, an alternative approach is needed to estimate the parity change needed to the US dollar to achieve full utilisation of the US labour force. In the US case, the simplest approach is to calculate the trade weighted value of the dollar required. We have seen from a previous series of calculations, starting on page 162, that the cumulative shortfall in demand on the US economy for the decades following 1973 to achieve full utilisation of the labour force was approximately 1.7% per annum compared to 1% for the EU. As Table 7.3 shows, for all the

Table 7.2: Registered Unemployment Rates in the European Union by Country in July 1998 and the Approximate Parity Adjustments Required Against Both the Deutsche Mark and the Rest of the World to Achieve 3% Unemployment Throughout the EU

Country	Parity Against US$ in Dec 98	Unem- ployment %	Parity Adjustment needed against DM	Parity Adjustment needed against Rest of World
Austria	11.7	4.4%	8%	–3%
Belgium	34.4	8.5%	1%	–9%
Denmark	6.4	4.6%	7%	–4%
Germany	1.7	9.2%	0%	–10%
Greece	280.5	9.6%	–1%	–11%
Eire	0.7	12.3%	–5%	–15%
Finland	8.1	7.5%	3%	–8%
France	5.6	11.7%	–4%	–14%
Italy	1654	12.3%	–5%	–15%
Luxembourg*	34.4	2.6%	10%	–1%
Netherlands	1.9	3.6%	9%	–2%
Portugal	171.2	4.3%	8%	–3%
Spain	142.1	18.0%	–16%	–25%
Sweden	8.1	7.5%	3%	–8%
United Kingdom	0.6	6.2%	5%	–6%
All the European Union		9.7%	–1%	–11%

* Luxembourg uses the same currency as Belgium.
Source: Tables 0601 and 2403 in *Eurostatistics*. Luxembourg: The European Union, April 1999.

years between 1977 and 1998 the arithmetical average trade weight for the dollar was 96, with the base year, 1972, being 100. The dollar's trade weighted value in 1998 was 98.[29] Table 7.2 indicates that to get back to 3% unemployment, the value of all EU currencies together needs to fall, relative to the rest of the world, by about 11%. Previous calculations show that, as a first sighting shot, to have the same impact on achieving full utilisation of the labour force, the dollar needs to fall by roughly 1.7 times the EU parity change required. In 1998 this would have been by approximately 2% to get back from a trade weighted 98 to 96, and then by a further 1.7 times 11% – a total of about 21% from its average 1998 value against all currencies. When President Clinton was elected in 1992 the broad trade weighted value of the dollar stood at 87.[30] It needed to fall to about 75. The fact that it has risen 13% instead of falling the 14% which was really needed will have the same profound effects on the future of average American living standards as did the overvaluation between 1973 and 1992.

Table 7.3: Trade Weighted Value of the Dollar: Broad Index

Year	Value	Average
1977	94.1	
1978	88.2	
1979	89.4	
1980	91.5	
1981	98.0	
1982	107.6	
1983	111.6	
1984	118.2	
1985	123.3	
1986	108.6	
1987	99.1	
1988	92.4	
1989	94.0	
1990	91.2	
1991	89.7	
1992	86.8	
1993	88.3	
1994	86.4	
1995	84.0	
1996	85.9	
1997	90.5	
1998	98.4	96.2

Source: Table B-110 in *Economic Report of the President*, Washington DC: US Government Printing Office, 1999.

It is important to stress again that the calculations set out above are approximate, and that they involve assumptions and simplifications which mean that the conclusions drawn are rough and ready rather than exact. These qualifications do not mean, however, that the orders of magnitude have been wrongly assessed, or that, allowing for margins of error, it is unsafe to rely on these results within broad limits. On the contrary, they point clearly to the direction in which policy needs to be moved, and they provide a reasonably reliable quantified indication as to the size of the changes required. It is significant that they are by no means out of line with the scale of the exchange rate adjustments which have occurred frequently in the past, or indeed, the change in the trade weighted value of the dollar – albeit in the wrong direction – over the last five years. This is a further indication that the orders of magnitude have been correctly calculated.

A major complicating factor, of course, is that both for the EU and the USA, the dollar and the euro respectively are highly significant components in the trade weight of each other's currencies. This highlights the problem the world economy faces. If the older industrialised economies are going to have to lower their cost bases *vis à vis* the rest of the world, to enable them to get back to full employment and reasonable growth rates, this can only be done by a relative rise elsewhere, particularly in the Pacific Rim. If the Asian economies are not to be slowed down, however, world demand has got to increase considerably more rapidly than it has in the past.

Wider perspectives

It is now possible to see the problems of slow economic growth, high levels of unemployment and low increases in productivity in the same context. The solutions to all three overlap. Policies have to be changed in two vital respects. The internal level of demand has to be expanded to a point where their labour forces are fully stretched. Exchange rates have to be repositioned at a level which makes it possible to shift to a much higher rate of growth. We need now to explore in more detail the conditions required not only to achieve an increase in output while the labour force is used more effectively and under-used resources are brought back into commission, but also to maintain an optimum growth rate for the foreseeable future.

The only way to do this is for a high and rising level of demand to be sustainable at whatever growth rate is considered desirable, without any economy concerned running into either capacity constraints, or – the other side of the same coin – unacceptable inflationary problems. These conditions can be achieved, but to understand how to attain them, we need to revert to some of the issues discussed in Chapter 2. Bringing exchange rates in Europe and the USA down to a level which gets productivity to rise at around 2.5% per head each year is certainly a very important first step. Accomplishing this objective is not, however, a sufficient condition for ensuring that the economies of the West grow with the vigour still exhibited in many countries in the Far East, or by Japan and most of Europe in the 1950s and 1960s. Other steps will have to be taken to ensure that these conditions are achieved.

A major move in the right direction would have been taken if western economies could be made to grow at around 4% on average each year, though even this would require substantial changes to current macroeconomic policies. At least they would then hold their own with the world average growth rate. Western living standards would then cease growing more slowly than the world average, as they have done over recent decades. To do this, the western economies would have to obtain and keep a sufficient share of the investment and production which has the falling cost curves and large returns characteristic of international trade. This means that the costs of output in the West, allowing for appropriate productivity levels, would have to be as low as the world average. If this does not happen in future, footloose investment and production of both goods and services – primarily in light industrial man-ufacturing – will continue to migrate to other parts of the world where overall costs, measured internationally, are lower.

It is, however, possible to predict with a high degree of certainty what will happen to the competitiveness of the western economies if they continue to grow much more slowly than the world average. If their growth rates are less than that of the rest of the world, it is inevitable that this will be reflected in rates of gross investment below those of the economies which are expanding more quickly. It is then equally inescapable that the proportion of the investment which takes place of the highly productive internationally tradable kind will be lower than in rapidly growing economies. The unavoidable consequence is that the West will become progressively less able to compete in the world, unless, eventually, exchange rate adjustments take place.

Indeed, a general rule can be promulgated which applies to Europe and the USA as much as to anywhere else. Any economy which is growing at less than the world average rate, which has recently been close to 4% per annum, will find its ability to compete falling away, while any growing faster than the world average will find its competitiveness increasing. This is a direct consequence of the self-reinforcing tendency for economies with exceptionally low cost international tradable sectors to grow more rapidly than the average, as they attract more and more investment, and their competitiveness increases. Exactly the reverse happens to the weaker economies whose ability to compete steadily diminishes, a reflection of rising costs, making them progressively less attractive sites for more investment.

There is thus a universal tendency for fast growing economies to develop currencies with a tendency to appreciate, as a result of their inter-national competitiveness increasing, while those of slow growing economies come under threat as their balance of payments position weakens. The latter are then faced with the all too familiar choice in the West – to deflate or to devalue. If devaluation is ruled out, the deflation which follows will progressively worsen their condition, as their investment ratios and competitiveness fall further and further away.

Even a consistent growth rate of about 4% per annum, close to the world average, is still quite low by the standards of the Pacific Rim countries, or in comparison with the achievements of many European economies in the 1950s or 1960s. Would it be possible for the western economies to move up to growth rates of 6% or even 8% or more, if they wanted to, as are regularly achieved in the Far East? It might be, but still greater downward movements in the exchange rate would be required, to enable the major economies in the West to achieve the super-competitive status that would be needed to promote them to the same growth league as Taiwan, South Korea and China. For a number of reasons, as we shall see, this might not be possible, as important constraints started to bite. Nevertheless, if only to show how 8% or more rates of growth could be achieved, it is worth exploring the structural changes which would be required to bring the western economies up to the Pacific Rim level of performance, to see how such high growth in output could be obtained. Table 2.2 in Chapter 2 suggests that western exchange rates might have to drop perhaps another 20% *vis à vis* those in the Far East to do it. How would the returns on investment then produce the very high growth rates which the Far East economies achieve?

Consider again the total returns achieved by different types of investment projects, encompassing all the increases in income received by everyone in the economy as a result of investment. These include higher wages, better products, greater tax receipts, and higher profits, as well as the returns to those who put up the money. Recall the important point that returns on investment projects vary enormously. In some of the private sector, and much of the public sector, they are little more than the rate of interest, and sometimes lower. This is typically the total rate of return obtained on investments, for example, in housing, and many roads and public buildings. At the other end of the spectrum, in some light manufacturing and parts of the service sector, the total rate of return is often far larger. It can be as great as 100% per annum in favourable cases. In the middle are investments in heavy industry, which typically produce total rates of return of around 20% or 25%.

Investment projects with exceptionally high total returns are charac-teristically those involved in international trade in goods and services. They therefore tend to be heavily concentrated in countries with low exchange rates and competitive cost bases, and are strongly discouraged by over-strong currency values. Furthermore, the high total returns on these investments both produce large resources for reinvestment, and ample opportunities for new profitable projects. The result is that a much greater proportion of the national income goes into investment than in slow growing economies. Now consider two examples:

Country A has total gross investment of 15% of GDP. Two-thirds of this – 10% of GDP – produces an average total return of 10%, and one-third – 5% of GDP – produces an average total return of 20%. This economy will have a growth rate of (10% times 10%) plus (5% times 20%) – a total of 2% per annum.

Country B has a total gross investment of 35% of GDP. In terms of GDP share, 15% produces an average 10% total return, 10% produces a 20% total return, and 10%, in the highly competitive internationally traded sector, produces a 50% total return. This economy will have a growth rate of (15% times 10%) plus (10% times 20%) plus (10% times 50%) – a total of 8.5% per annum.

Of course this is an oversimplified model, but this does not prevent it from demonstrating an important insight into how economies produce different growth rates, and how their structures adapt to, and reinforce the opportunities which their foreign trade relations open up for them. With an 8.5% growth rate, and gross investment running at 35% of GDP, productivity rises rapidly. The competitiveness of the internationally tradable sectors grows fast. Education and skill levels increase exponentially. The problem which these economies have is to avoid the growth of export surpluses, and the appreciation of their currencies, eroding away the competitiveness which makes such high increases in output possible.

Should the West aim for as high a growth rate as this? Almost certainly not. The size of the western economies, taken together, would make it hard for them to secure a sufficient proportion of the world's high return investment for a growth rate as ambitious as 8% or more to be sustainable, even if they captured much more than their fair share of the world's output where productivity gains are easiest to secure. Table 7.4 provides estimates of a more reasonable balance, showing how a 3.5% per annum sustained growth rate in GDP per head could be spread round the whole of the developed world. For this to be achieved, manufacturing industry, where productivity increases are most easy to attain, would have to be given much higher priority by adjusting exchange rates to get the cost base right. This table also shows how in the USA, over the twenty years from 1977 to 1997, 60% of all the increase in GDP per head came from manufacturing, which comprised less than 20% of the

Table 7.4: Estimated Sources of Growth in the World Economy: GDP per Head

	USA 1977–97 Actual			Western Economies Estimated			Tiger Economies Estimated			The Developed World in Balance Projected		
High Productivity Growth Sectors												
Manufacturing	18.8%	3.0%	0.6%	22%	4%	0.9%	30%	12%	3.6%	25%	10%	2.5%
Mining	1.7%	3.1%	0.1%	1%	3%	0.0%	0%	3%	0.0%	1%	3%	0.0%
Agriculture	1.6%	5.7%	0.1%	8%	4%	0.3%	10%	6%	0.6%	9%	4%	0.4%
Wholesale Trade	6.3%	3.2%	0.2%	6%	3%	0.2%	6%	3%	0.2%	6%	3%	0.2%
Medium Productivity Growth Sector												
Transport and Utilities	8.6%	1.6%	0.1%	8%	2%	0.2%	10%	2%	0.2%	10%	2%	0.2%
Low Productivity Growth Sectors												
Construction	4.2%	−0.7%	0.0%	3%	0.5%	0.0%	5%	0.5%	0.0%	4%	0.5%	0.0%
Retail Trade	9.3%	1.0%	0.1%	9%	0.5%	0.0%	8%	0.5%	0.0%	9%	0.5%	0.0%
Financial Services	17.6%	0.4%	0.1%	13%	0.5%	0.1%	10%	0.5%	0.1%	11%	0.5%	0.1%
Other Services	18.3%	−0.9%	−0.2%	16%	0.5%	0.1%	13%	0.5%	0.1%	15%	0.5%	0.1%
Government	14.0%	−0.2%	0.0%	14%	0.5%	0.1%	8%	0.5%	0.0%	10%	0.5%	0.1%
	------			------			------			------		
Totals:	100%		1.0%	100%		1.8%	100%		4.8%	100%		3.5%

Note: For each group of countries, the first column represents estimated proportions of total output derived from each activity, the second column provides an estimate of average productivity growth per annum, and the the third column is a calculation, based on the first two, of the contribution to the total average growth in GDP per head made by each activity.

Sources: Table 3, pages 221 *et seq* in *World Employment Report*. Geneva: International Labour Office, 1998, supplemented with estimates from a number of other sources.

economy's output. Almost all the remaining sources of increased living standards were in agriculture, mining, wholesale trade, utilities and transport, which together made up less than another 20%. All the remaining 60% and more of the US economy made no net contribution at all to increasing real incomes over the whole of the period.

With faster growing economies would go a corresponding ability for the West at least to retain, and probably to enhance, its international power and influence, rather than seeing it slowly whittled away as other parts of the world grow much faster. The point to grasp is that it is possible for at least some of these kind of choices to be made. It is not inevitable that western economies should be left to languish near the bottom of the growth league, while other countries take advantage of opportunities which they could seize. If the West's leaders wanted to see their economies growing at a rate of at least 4% per annum, they could achieve this objective.

8
Inflation

'Good order is the foundation of all good things.'
Edmund Burke

Few topics are as loaded with ideological baggage as consideration about whether inflation, at least in moderation, is desirable or a scourge. It is also clear, at least in nearly all the western world, which side has won this particular battle of ideas. It is now the conventional wisdom almost everywhere that one of the most significant objectives of economic policy – perhaps the most important of all – is to maintain the average increase in the price level to no more than 2% to 2.5%.

There is, however, remarkably little reason to believe that inflation rates as low as this are a particularly worthwhile goal, if the interests of society as a whole are taken into account. In particular, there is very little evidence that they can be combined with other targets, such as full employment and a growth rate of 4% or 5% per annum. Of course there are strong arguments against allowing very rapid increases in the price level to occur, and nobody wants hyperinflation. This is an entirely different matter, however, from it being worthwhile tolerating some extra inflation to secure much better growth and job prospects, if such a trade-off exists. In fact, nearly all competently run economies which are growing fast and which have full employment do not have very low increases in the price level. They nearly all have inflation rates year on year bunching round about 4% per annum[1] – as did nearly all of Western Europe in the 1950s and 1960s[2] – for good reasons, as we shall see. Indeed, an important study carried out by the International

Monetary Fund in 1995 showed that there was no systematic evidence that inflation rates of anything less than about 8% per annum caused enough disruption to slow down growth or to increase the number out of work.[3]

The widely exhibited determination in the western world to keep inflation down to very low levels is not, therefore, a sign of economic wisdom. It is much more convincingly seen as another sign of the dominance in the West of the culture and outlook of banking and finance over manufacturing and industry. Low inflation – and the high real interest rates which go with it – favour old money *vis à vis* new; lenders as against borrowers; established wealth holders as opposed to *parvenus*; those who have already made a success of their lives *vis à vis* those coming up to challenge them. All these powerful groups, typically with deeply conservative instincts, have a vested interest in promoting inflation as being a major affliction. In fact, in moderation, it is nothing of the kind. On the contrary, it is an almost entirely unavoidable, but relatively harmless, concomitant to any policies seriously orientated to pushing up the growth rate and getting everyone back to work.

A particularly strong link in the chain of inflationary demonology has been firmly established in the public mind – and in the academic and policy orientated literature – in relation to any downward change in the exchange rate. There is a widespread fear that devaluations automatically generate inflationary pressures in economies where they occur. It has always been a major tenet of the monetarist position that any benefits secured from depreciation will at best be temporary. They will soon be lost, it is argued, as a result of increasing price rises in the devaluing country, leaving the economy concerned in no more competitive a position than it was before, after a short adjustment process, but also with the legacy of an enhanced level of inflation.

It is also widely believed that a devaluation necessarily produces a reduction in the living standards of any economy where the external value of its currency is falling. There are two reasons usually advanced to support this proposition. The first is that if a country devalues, there will inevitably be an adverse movement in its terms of trade. This means that, after the fall in the parity, the amount of imports which can be purchased for each unit of exports is bound to fall, depressing the national income. The second, which overlaps with the first, is that to make up for the reduction in the terms of trade, more room will have to be found for goods and services to be sold abroad. The only way of achieving this objective is to shift resources out of current living standards into exports, thus lowering average real incomes, and depressing the real wage.

There can be little doubt, however, that the almost axiomatic strength of these monetarist arguments has persuaded large numbers of people that devaluations are inflationary, reduce living standards, disrupt business plans, discourage investment, and ought to be avoided if at all possible. This is the standard case for fixed parities. Even a brief look at economic history, however, shows that these views are almost entirely unfounded. There have been large numbers of exchange rate changes in recent decades which can be used to test the validity of the widely believed monetarist case, and several of the most prominent are set out in Table 8.1. Without exception, they show that even large exchange rate changes generally make little or no difference to the rate of inflation, unless the economy concerned was already operating at full stretch, as was the case in France, for example, at the end of the 1950s. Even then, however, the sharp increase in prices, to which the double devaluations under Charles de Gaulle undoubtedly contributed, quickly abated.

Table 8.1: The Effects of Exchange Rate Changes on Consumer Prices, the Real Wage, GDP, Industrial Output and Employment

| | | Year on year percentage changes | | | | | |
	Year	Consumer Prices	Wage Rates	Real Wage	GDP Change	Industrial Output Change	Unem-ployment %
Britain – 31%	1930	–6.0	–0.7	5.3	–0.7	–1.4	11.2
Devaluation	1931	–5.7	–2.1	3.6	–5.1	–3.6	15.1
against the US	1932	–3.3	–1.7	1.6	0.8	0.3	15.6
dollar in 1931	1933	0.0	–0.1	–0.1	2.9	4.0	14.1
	1934	0.0	1.5	1.5	6.6	5.5	11.9
France – 27%	1956	2.0	9.7	7.7	5.1	9.4	1.1
Devaluation	1957	3.5	8.2	4.7	6.0	8.3	0.8
against all	1958	15.1	12.3	–2.8	2.5	4.5	0.9
currencies in	1959	6.2	6.8	0.6	2.9	3.3	1.3
1957/58	1960	3.5	6.3	2.8	7.0	10.1	1.2
	1961	3.3	9.6	6.3	5.5	4.8	1.1
USA – 28%	1984	4.3	4.0	–0.3	6.2	11.3	7.4
Devaluation	1985	3.6	3.9	0.3	3.2	2.0	7.1
against all	1986	1.9	2.0	0.1	2.9	1.0	6.9
currencies over	1987	3.7	1.8	–1.9	3.1	3.7	6.1
1985/87	1988	4.0	2.8	–1.2	3.9	5.3	5.4
	1989	5.0	2.9	–2.1	2.5	2.6	5.2

continued

Table 8.1: *continued*

	Year	Consumer Prices	Wage Rates	Real Wage	GDP Change	Industrial Output Change	Unem ployment %
				Year on year percentage changes			
Japan – 47%	1989	2.3	3.1	0.8	4.8	5.8	2.3
Revaluation	1990	3.1	3.8	0.7	4.8	4.1	2.1
against all	1991	3.3	3.4	0.1	4.3	1.8	2.1
currencies over	1992	1.7	2.1	0.4	1.4	–6.1	2.2
1990/94	1993	1.3	2.1	0.8	0.1	–4.6	2.5
	1994	0.7	2.3	1.6	0.6	0.7	2.9
Italy – 20%	1990	6.4	7.3	–0.9	2.1	–0.6	9.1
Devaluation	1991	6.3	9.8	3.5	1.3	–2.2	8.6
against all	1992	5.2	5.4	0.2	0.9	–0.6	9.0
currencies over	1993	4.5	3.8	–0.7	–1.2	–2.9	10.3
1990/93	1994	4.0	3.5	–0.5	2.2	5.6	11.4
	1995	5.4	3.1	–2.3	2.9	5.4	11.9
Finland – 24%	1990	6.1	9.4	3.3	0.0	–0.1	3.5
Devaluation	1991	4.1	6.4	2.3	–7.1	–9.7	7.6
against all	1992	2.6	3.8	1.2	–3.6	2.2	13.0
currencies over	1993	2.1	3.7	1.6	–1.6	5.5	17.5
1991/93	1994	1.1	7.4	6.3	4.5	10.5	17.4
	1995	1.0	4.7	3.7	5.1	7.8	16.2
Spain – 18%	1991	5.9	8.2	2.3	2.3	–0.7	16.3
Devaluation	1992	5.9	7.7	1.8	0.7	–3.2	18.5
against all	1993	4.6	6.8	2.2	–1.2	–4.4	22.8
currencies over	1994	4.7	4.5	–0.2	2.1	7.5	24.1
1992/94	1995	4.7	4.8	0.1	2.8	4.7	22.9
	1996	3.6	4.8	1.2	2.2	–0.7%	22.2

Sources: Various editions of *International Financial Statistics Yearbook*, Washington DC: IMF, various editions of *Eurostatistics*, Luxembourg: European Union, 1931 British devaluation data from *Economic Statistics 1900–1983* by Thelma Liesner, London: *The Economist*, 1985.

Furthermore, far from the average standard of living falling after a devaluation, it almost invariably rises, because the GDP of all devaluing countries tends to increase significantly shortly after the currency has depreciated. There is also a marked tendency for industrial output to rise sharply soon after a devaluation, triggering increased investment, while the experience of Japan, after the yen's major revaluation in the early 1990s, shows the opposite outcome equally strongly. In most cases, the real wage tends to rise as well, shortly after the exchange rate falls. This is calculated in Table 8.1 as being the difference between the change in average wage rates and the change in the consumer price level. The increase in the real wage is not so pronounced as the rise in GDP, because devaluations tend to increase employment, thus reducing the numbers out of work, but also diluting average earnings. This bias can be seen in the US experience after the dollar fell in the second half of the 1980s as the GDP rose, but the number of people in work increased very rapidly. The table also shows the opposite results occurring in the major case of Japan's revaluation of the yen during the early 1990s. There the growth rate went down, the real wage stayed static, and unemployment began to creep up.

These may well be unexpected results to many people who have been led to expect a very different outcome. In particular, the figures in Table 8.1 provide no justification at all for the widely believed monetarist view that it is impossible to secure a permanent advantage in terms of competitiveness and growth by exchange rate adjustments. Perhaps the widespread conviction that devaluation will have the damaging results so frequently anticipated stems from the fact that many people might like these predictions to be true. Everyone who has a stake in seeing interest rates kept high and money tight might be inclined to share such a view. This tends inevitably to include a large proportion of the banking and financial community. Those doing well out of importing goods into economies with overvalued exchange rates, because the costs of production are so much cheaper elsewhere than in the home market, may also tend to find the same opinions particularly acceptable. Undoubtedly the monetarists have helped support the case, with appropriately impressive theorising, which neatly underpinned what many people, from simple motives of self-interest, were only too pleased to hear. All the same, it is extraordinary that so many believe these propositions to be true when there is so much simple and incontrovertible evidence easily to hand to show that the assumed relationships between depreciation, inflation and the standard of living are wrong.

On the contrary, if, as Table 8.1 shows, it is possible for any industrial economy to devalue, especially when the economy concerned has substantial unused resources, without any significant inflationary penalty being paid, this is a very important policy matter. It means that long-lasting adjustments, which are highly beneficial in terms of growth, productivity and employment prospects, are in fact entirely feasible, even although their possibility may be denied by monetarist theory. It can then no longer be claimed that economies stuck in the doldrums lack any practical way out of their predicament. On the contrary, the way is open for any country which is having difficulty competing and keeping all its resources employed, especially its labour force, to remedy the position by making appropriate exchange rate adjustments to allow demand to be expanded. As we shall see, this can be done without any disbenefits to the rest of the world. Far from the gains from devaluations being only temporary, shortly to be eroded away by extra-inflation, they tend to be self-reinforcing, as arguments in previous chapters have shown.

This is not to say that inflationary problems can be ignored if parity changes continue to take place. Good management of the economy is required in all circumstances. The evidence in Table 8.1 makes it clear, however, that many of the widely held opinions about the relationship between devaluation, price rises and the real wage are at variance with the facts, and therefore cannot be well founded in theory. There is much evidence that the problems with inflation are more diverse and more manageable than is often recognised. We turn now to see what these may be.

Devaluation and the price level

Those who believe that exchange rate changes will affect prices are right in at least one sense. Any parity reduction is bound to exert upward pressure on the costs of all imported goods and services in the devaluing country. While the prices of both imports and exports will almost certainly rise measured in the domestic currency, there may also be a tendency for import costs to increase faster than export prices, worsening the terms of trade. In this sense, too, there is a direct cost to the economy. Furthermore, there is no value in a policy of depreciation unless it makes imports more expensive relative to home market production. A major objective has to be to price out some imports by making it relatively cheaper than it was previously to produce locally rather than in other countries. It follows that there will have to be price increases for imported goods and services, otherwise there will be no new bias towards production from domestic output.

The evidence presented in Table 8.1, however, clearly indicates that other factors have to be taken into account. If, as is commonly supposed, it is only import prices which are significant, the figures in the table would show increasing inflation and declining living standards after a depreciation, and not, generally speaking, the opposite. How are the figures in the table to be explained? The answer is that the impact of a devaluation on the price level is more complicated than is often recognised. Many of the effects are disinflationary rather than the reverse, and tend to increase the national income rather than reduce it. Obviously, the more exposed any economy is to foreign trade, the greater the immediate impact of exchange rate changes will be on living standards and the price level. Even in economies with comparatively small exposure to foreign trade, such as the USA, however, it is still easily large enough to make the consequences significant.

First, one of the immediate impacts of a devaluation is to make all domestic production more competitive in both home and export markets than it was before. Within a short period of time, this leads to increased output. Of course there are time lags and not all the potential increases in sales will be realised immediately, but almost any rise in production will help to reduce average costs. Increased capacity working spreads overhead charges across more output. We have seen that production and service industries involved in international trade typically have falling cost curves, a reflection of the fact that the marginal cost of production is well below the average. Enterprises of these sorts cannot fail to benefit from a depreciating currency. Obviously, some of their input expenses, if they include either imported goods and services, or a switch to a domestic producer who has now become competitive, will rise. This is part of the price that has to be paid for devaluing. The increased volume of output which can now be obtained, however, is clearly a substantial factor weighing in the balance on the other side.

Second, some of the policies which have to be associated with bringing the parity of the currency down also directly affect both production costs and the cost of living generally. One of the most important of these is the rate of interest, which almost invariably comes down with the exchange rate. Indeed, lowering the cost of borrowing is part of the mixture of policy changes needed to get parities reduced. High real rates of interest are a heavy and expensive burden on most firms which produce goods and services. They are also an important component of the retail price index, particularly in countries where a large proportion of personal outgoings are on variable rate loans, such as mortgage payments. A substantial reduction, designed to bring down the parity to a more competitive level, itself makes an important contribution to holding down inflation.

Third, rising productivity, which flows from increased output, not only has the immediate effect of reducing costs. It also makes it possible to meet wage claims of any given size with less impact on selling costs. Nor is this just a factor which applies for a short period until those responsible for formulating wage claims adjust to a new situation and then increase their claims. The international evidence strongly suggests that economies with rapidly expanding output have a better wage negotiation climate generally, and thus achieve rises in remuneration more realistically attuned to whatever productivity increases are actually being secured.

Fourth, one of the major objectives of reducing the parity is to switch demand from overseas sources to home production. While the price of imports is bound to rise to some extent, there is strong evidence that the increase in costs from exchange rate changes are seldom passed on in full. Foreign suppliers are inclined to absorb some of the costs themselves, calculating that what they lose on margin they may make up by holding on to market share. Furthermore, if demand is switched from imported goods and services to home production, this purchasing power will not be affected – at least not directly and in full – by the increase in import prices. It will benefit in cost terms from the fact that domestic output is now relatively cheaper than purchases from abroad.

Fifth, it is possible to employ the much improved fiscal position which higher growth produces to have a directly disinflationary impact, using the tax system. It is often argued that if there is a depreciation, the government of the devaluing country necessarily has to deflate the economy to make more room for exports. This argument cannot hold water, however, if there are large numbers of unemployed or underemployed people, and considerable slack in the economy. In these circumstances, it is not difficult to combine increasing output, stimulated by a lower exchange rate, with an expansionary monetary and fiscal policy. It is then possible to structure tax changes so that they have a positive disinflationary impact. Reducing taxes on labour, where this is possible, is particularly effective, because it both directly cuts production costs and encourages more employment.

Taxation policy may help to secure a further crucially important objective to avoid price increases if there is a devaluation, not only immediately after the parity has come down, but subsequently as well. If the first-round effects of higher import prices can be neutralised by greater output, rising productivity and tax changes, then there will be no second and subsequent rounds of price rises flowing from the change in parity. This is clearly an extremely desirable state of affairs to achieve, making it much easier to manage the economy in a way which protects erosion of the increased competitiveness flowing from devaluation.

When each of these disinflationary factors is taken into account, all of which apply in varying degrees whenever the parity comes down, the figures in Table 8.1 become much easier to understand. It is evidently not true that devaluation necessarily increases the rate of inflation. Still less is it true that it must always do so to such a degree that any extra competitive advantage is automatically eroded away.

At the cost of a few more calculations, it is possible to set out in quantified form why this should be the case. Suppose that the currency is depreciated by 25%, and that on average import prices rise by two-thirds of this amount, while foreign suppliers absorb the rest. Assume that imports of goods and services make up around 30% of gross domestic product – a fairly typical ratio among developed countries – so the impact on the price level from increased import prices in these circumstances is likely to be about two-thirds of 25% times 30%, which comes to 5%.

On the other side, consider all the factors which work to reduce the price level when the external value of the currency falls by 25%. First, the output of all enterprises in the domestic economy is likely to rise substantially on average. Suppose that the growth rate rises by 3% per annum. If two-thirds of this increase in output could be achieved in the period immediately following the devaluation by using the existing capital stock and labour force more intensively and efficiently, the benefits from economies of scale of this type would amount to around a 2% contribution to reduced prices in year one.

Second, the total money supply currently represents about 85% of GNP across the developed world.[4] All of it is essentially debt of one kind or another, and nearly all of it is interest bearing. If base rate borrowing costs were reduced from, say, 5% to 2%, not all interest charges would be affected, but a significant proportion would be. If half were reduced on average by 3%, the borrowing costs on the whole of the money supply would fall by about 1.7%. This would produce a reduction of around another 1.5% in the retail price index.

Third, one of the most important reasons for a depreciation is to switch demand from abroad to home production. Suppose this happens to 10% of all demand. Allowing for an import content of one-third, the remaining two-thirds of this new output would, broadly speaking, not be affected by increased costs as a result of the exchange rate changes. Perhaps half of it, however, would only become economical to produce at rather higher world prices than applied previously. These ratios multiply up as 10% times 25% times ⅔ times ⅔ times ½. This factor reduces the inflationary impact by a little more than another 0.5%.

Fourth, another major impact on the economy from reducing the parity would be vastly to improve the public sector's finances, as tax receipts rose and calls on public expenditure for welfare benefits fell away. If some of this improvement were used to reduce taxation on items sensitive to the consumer price index, it should not be difficult for the government to bring down inflation by a further 1%, by reducing taxes by this amount. Adding this 1% to the other disinflationary factors set out in the preceding paragraphs produces a countervailing total of 5%, which equals the impact of higher input prices.

These calculations are again broad brush, and subject to margins of error. They nevertheless show that the disinflationary impacts that can be garnered from a well managed devaluation are likely to counteract, quite possibly in full, the impact of higher import costs, even if the depreciation is substantial. This is why a devaluation is not necessarily inflationary at all, as ample empirical evidence shows is the case, except perhaps when resources were already fully employed, as in the French example at the end of the 1950s. This is clearly an extremely important conclusion, and one with major policy implications.

Nor does depreciation lower the standard of living. In fact it quickly does exactly the opposite in almost all circumstances. It is easy to see why this should be the case. If the domestic economy expands after the exchange rate has gone down, as the figures in Table 8.1 show that it almost invariably does, the standard of living, on average, is bound to go up. So, sometimes after a time lag, does the real wage. The proposition that lowering the exchange rate necessarily impoverishes the devaluing country is the reverse of the truth. Again, this is an outcome of great policy significance, making it politically much easier to implement a reflationary and expansionary policy than is generally supposed.

These conclusions do not mean, of course, that inflation is no longer a problem. A well managed devaluation may not cause an acceleration in price increases, but there are other reasons why inflation may increase. They all need careful management, but with reasonable judgement they are all containable. They are leading sector inflation, external shocks, 'demand pull' price rises caused by bottlenecks and overheating, excessive growth in the money supply which may in particular lead to asset price inflation, and 'cost push' wage and salary increases outstripping productivity gains. Many of these are closely related to other elements of the policies confronting all developed economies, and the following sections of this chapter consider them in turn.

Leading sector inflation

While almost everyone agrees that, in general, lower rates of inflation are desirable, there is considerable evidence that very low, and especially zero, rates of price increase are impossible to combine with any significant rate of economic growth. At some stage a trade-off between inflation and growth has to be faced. The higher the priority given to stabilising prices, the less likely it is that the economy will grow rapidly. Certainly the notion that squeezing inflation out of the economy altogether is the way to prosperity flies in the face of universal experience. On the contrary, although there may be some inflationary price to pay for considerably higher growth, it is not likely to be a large or a dangerous one. Furthermore, recent developments, particularly the gains in efficiency from computers and increasing world competition, suggest that the risk that faster growth will produce price rises at unacceptable rates is even less than it was previously.

Table 8.2 shows the rates of inflation and economic growth in ten OECD countries, and the OECD as a whole, during the sixteen years from 1953 to 1969, a long period of continuous growth in world output. This table indicates that, during these years, not one of these countries managed to avoid a steady increase in the price level, albeit a relatively moderate one. It also shows a tendency for those economies growing most rapidly to have rather higher inflation rates than those growing more slowly. Obviously other factors were at work than those solely concerned with the differing growth rates, but the correlation between higher inflation and growth is clearly there.

Table 8.2: Growth and Inflation Rates in Ten OECD Countries between 1953 and 1969

Country	Cumulative Growth Rate	Cumulative Inflation Rate
Japan	10.0%	4.0%
Spain	6.0%	6.3%
Germany	5.8%	2.7%
Italy	5.5%	3.4%
France	5.4%	4.5%
Netherlands	4.9%	4.3%
Switzerland	4.5%	3.3%
Belgium	4.0%	2.5%
United States	3.6%	2.4%
United Kingdom	2.8%	3.4%
OECD Average	4.4%	3.0%

Source: *National Accounts of OECD Countries 1953–1969*. Paris: OECD, 1970.

At first sight this seems the reverse of what one would expect. How did Japan manage to achieve a cumulative compound growth rate of 10% if the Japanese rate of inflation was above the average for the whole of the OECD, and well above the rate at which consumer prices rose in a number of countries, including the United States and Britain? Why were British exports not becoming more and more competitive with those of Japan? Clearly this cannot have been the case, judging by the slow British growth rates over the period, contrasted with the high performance of the Japanese economy.

This paradox is easily resolved. In all the major countries of the developed world, increases in productivity were enabling sustained economic growth to take place, while growth in turn generated rising output per head. These increases, however, were neither spread evenly throughout any of the individual economies concerned, nor between them. In all countries there were some parts of the economy where productivity growth was slow, non-existent, or even negative. If the number of children taught by each teacher goes down, each child may be better taught, but the output of teachers measured in economic terms tends to fall. If legal aid is extended to people who could not otherwise afford to obtain justice, society may be fairer, but there is no increase in GDP which corresponds fully to the extra skilled manpower required to make the legal system work more fairly. The really high rates of productivity growth were to be found in those parts of industry, agriculture and the service sectors, especially in fast growing economies, where mechanisation, falling unit costs with longer production runs, and much more efficient use of labour were possible. The results were costs which dropped rapidly in real terms, and often in money terms too, even though average prices in the economy were rising. These are the sectors which are the familiar generators of fast rates of economic growth.

This phenomenon was seen markedly in Japan, with one of the fastest growth rates, but also above average increases in the consumer price level. It was caused by leading sector inflation. Those employed in parts of the economy with rapidly rising productivity secured large wage rises, which were offset by increased output. Those working in jobs where such improvement in economic performance were unobtainable also pressed for, and received wage rises. The prices of the goods and services produced by those where no significant increase in output could be achieved therefore had to go up. The faster the economy grew, the more marked these price increases were. The overall inflation rate was a result of the averaging process which took place between the high and low productivity growth parts of the economy. In Japan the results were truly astonishing. Despite the relatively large Japanese overall domestic inflation rate, for many years their export prices barely rose at all. Indeed over the whole of the period from 1952 to 1979, while the general price level in Japan rose by 364%, the average price of Japanese exports rose by only 33%. In Britain, over the same period, the general price level rose by 442%, and export prices by 380%.[5] No wonder Britain kept losing more and more markets to Japanese competition.

The initial competitiveness of Japanese exports, and those of most of the economies of Western Europe after their recovery from World War II, enabled all of them to break into the virtuous circle of rapid growth. Once established, all these countries maintained high growth for years on end, concentrating economic activity in those areas where productivity increases were at their greatest. We have seen the same process at work in the Far East, not only in countries such as Taiwan, Malaysia and Korea, but also, perhaps most conspicuously of all, in China. The American and British experience has been exactly the opposite. Starting from uncompetitive positions after World War II, both the US and Britain, and now much of the rest of Western Europe, followed by Japan, have allowed the costs of their exports compared to the world average to rise and rise.

Despite all the indications to the contrary, it is still said that price stability is the condition needed to maximise growth on a sustainable basis. There is no evidence from round the world that this is true. Nor does economic history provide any support for such a view. During the period when the Gold Standard operated, just as much as subsequently, prices were constantly changing. Only the price of gold remained fixed. It is argued that low inflation allows interest rates to be kept down too, and in nominal terms this may be correct. Unfortunately, however, it is not the nominal but the real rate, with inflation subtracted, which is the true cost of borrowing. Squeezing price rises down with monetarist policies has a dismal record of producing much higher real borrowing costs than more accommodating strategies, thus pushing up the exchange rate and discouraging investment and growth, by making real interest costs greater than they would otherwise be.

The lessons from international comparisons and economic history indicate that rapid growth is associated with price changes in all directions, some upward, particularly where productivity increases are hard to achieve, and some downward, especially where there are falling cost curves. Nor has experience shown that nominal interest rates have been particularly low in fast growing economies, although real rates have often been negative, at least after tax. With rapid growth – 8% to 10%

per annum – rises in the price level tend to be above the world average, mainly because of leading sector inflation, but in most cases the rate at which prices increase is still relatively stable. As Table 8.2 shows, in the 1950s and 1960s, the Japanese economy grew at 10% per annum with average inflation running at 4%. In economies growing at 5% to 6% per annum, the optimum combination of rapid productivity growth without too much leading sector inflation seems to be achieved. This was the experience of most countries in Western Europe during the 1950s and 1960s where, over a long period, inflation rates averaged just under 4%, with similar nominal base interest rates. If the objective is to get the western economies to grow faster, perhaps at 4% or even more per annum, it is likely that we will have to expect a similar experience with price rises and interest rates as prevailed in other economies achieving growth results of this order.

Shocks to the system

Seen from the vantage point of the late 1990s, the 1950s and 1960s look like a period of remarkable stability and growing prosperity in the western world. At least until 1968, low and quite stable levels of inflation were combined with rapidly increasing standards of living almost everywhere. After the adjustments of 1949, there were few exchange rate changes among the major economies of the time, the most significant being the double French devaluations in 1958, the British devaluation in 1967, and the German revaluation in 1968, followed by some consequential parity changes in other countries. By the standards of what was to follow, price increases were low, although they attracted a good deal of concern at the time. All the advanced economies were helped by the falling cost of raw materials, many of which came from the Third World. The biggest shock to the system, albeit a temporary one, was the Korean War at the beginning of the period, which led to a sharp increase in commodity prices. These quickly collapsed, however, as the war ended. Inflation then fell away as the long boom in the 1950s and 1960s got under way. No period of economic history of any length is devoid of inflationary shocks, however, and at the end of the 1960s a much more turbulent period began.

The rate at which prices increased in the world's mature industrial economies during the thirty years from the late 1960s to the late 1990s, following the calmer period which preceded it, exhibited upsurges when major inflationary shocks materialised, followed by declines back to more usual levels within two or three years. The end of the 1960s saw the year on year increase in consumer prices peaking in 1970, as a result of the inflationary pressures generated by the Vietnam War and the implementation of the President Johnson's Great Society programme, but the index was back to a 4.8% increase by 1972.[6] The next peak, at 13.4% year on year came in 1974, as a result of the early 1970s boom and the quadrupling of oil prices, but the index had fallen back to a 7.5% increase by 1978.[7] The third major shock came at the end of the 1970s with the next oil price rise, causing a further year on year peak of 12.4% in 1980, but by 1983, the index was back to 5.2%.[8] These average figures, of course, masked a wide range of experience country by country. In particular there was a substantial variation between the overall rises in the domestic price level over this period between long-standing low inflation countries and others which had already had much more difficulty in containing price increases. Between 1975 and 1995 consumer prices rose 84% in Germany, 183% in the USA, 322% in Britain, and 640% in Spain.[9]

Looking back over the whole period since World War II, the ups and downs which have taken place in inflation have clearly been caused by a wide variety of different factors. From the world's point of view, only one of all the major events pushing up inflation – during the early 1970s – appears to have been the direct result of excessive credit creation, in this case initially in the USA during the late 1960s. With appropriate policies, the rest of the world could have avoided much of the inflation which followed, as indeed happened in some countries. Germany's year on year price rises in the mid 1970s never rose above about 7%, compared to a 24% at peak in Britain.[10] In most of the developed world, the real money supply, that is net of inflation, remained remarkably stable, although it fluctuated much more than the average in Britain and the Netherlands.[11] In the USA, it has also been much less constant than elsewhere. The widest money supply measure, 'L', as a percentage of GDP, rose from 80% in 1971 to a peak of 93% in 1986, and then fell heavily to 77% in 1994. By 1997 it was back to 82%, still, historically, a relatively low percentage.[12]

Other causes of rises in prices had little or nothing to do with changes in the credit base. All of them, however, because they caused higher inflation and thus pushed up the requirement for money, had to be accommodated by increasing the money supply if more deflation was to be avoided. When the supply of money fell in real terms, as for example it did during the period of the 1974–9 Labour government in Britain, when it was reduced by 27%,[13] the deflationary effect was very powerful. Interestingly, during the Reagan era in the USA, although interest rates were raised to exceptionally high levels, the restrictions on the money supply were modest. Much the heaviest squeeze has been recently, particularly in the late 1980s and early 1990s. Both the M3 and L measures of the money supply fell in real terms every year from 1987 to 1994,[14] pushing the US money supply ratios down well below the international average. There is little doubt that this is one of the major reasons why the dollar is currently so strong.

The history of the last fifty years therefore shows a remarkable ability by all countries in the developed world to absorb inflationary shocks, from wherever they have come, despite the variety of different events which, over the years, have been responsible for initiating rapid increases in the price level. Once the initial cause of the surge in inflation disappeared, however, the rate at which prices rose soon fell back, given an absence of further shocks and reasonably competent management of the macro-economy. This ought not to cause surprise. Rapid rates of economic growth are powerfully effective at absorbing inflation.

If this is so, however, it removes the underpinning for a major component of economic policy employed in varying degrees by almost all major western governments since the 1970s. They have all tended to assume that the best way to counteract inflationary shocks has been to deflate their economies, rather than to absorb the disturbances by increasing output. The monetarist argument that all increases in inflation are caused by antecedent rises in the money supply, and that only monetary discipline will stop prices rising more and more rapidly, is only a more precise formulation of a view which has underlain conservative economic policy making for a long time before monetarism became fashionable. On the contrary, the international evidence shows that the resulting deflation has been both damaging and destructive, and not particularly effective at keeping inflation rates down. If most of the events which have generated upsurges in inflation are not caused by anything to do with the money supply, and the international experience is that rapid rises in the price level nearly always recede once their immediate cause has been removed irrespective of the monetary stance in the economies concerned, what indeed is left of the argument that the money supply is both the cause and the cure for all inflationary ills?

Moreover, the picture is even worse than this if the prospect for the coming period is one of continuing slow growth. The historical evidence suggests that economies which have used growth to dampen down inflation have done at least as well at restraining price increases as those which have used deflation, and perhaps better. Table 8.3 shows the record for the major western economies for the period 1973 to 1978, when all of them were suffering in various degrees from the upsets of the 1970s, and for the following five years from 1978 to 1983. Japan, with much the highest growth rate, was far the most successful in bringing down inflation. All the remaining countries, whose growth rates fell between the first and second periods, had similar or higher rates of inflation in the later period compared to the earlier one. This evidence reinforces the view that economies which have reasonably strong growth rates are better at absorbing external shocks than those which are growing more slowly.

Table 8.3: Economic Growth and Inflation Rates in Selected Countries between 1973 and 1978, and 1978 and 1983

Country	1973–8		1978–83	
	Average Growth Rate	Average Inflation Rate	Average Growth Rate	Average Inflation Rate
Japan	3.7%	12.8%	4.1%	4.2%
France	3.1%	10.8%	1.4%	11.8%
United States	2.8%	8.0%	1.3%	8.8%
Italy	2.1%	16.6%	1.5%	17.3%
Germany	2.1%	4.7%	1.2%	4.7%
United Kingdom	1.7%	12.4%	0.7%	11.2%

Source: *Economic Statistics 1900–1983* by Thelma Liesner. London, 1985. *The Economist*

Without doubt, there will be more random shocks and policy changes in the future which will cause upsurges in inflation. The issue is whether, when they come, the best policy to pursue is one of cautious deflation, or whether the safest solution is to keep economies growing to absorb pressures for rising prices with increased output. The evidence from international experience shows that in both the short and the longer term a reasonable measure of boldness pays. Restricting the money supply and deflating the economy is not the most efficient way to contain inflation. Rising output is at least as efficacious an agent for slowing down increases in the price level, and generally more so. If this is the case, in large measure the poor job prospects for many people, the lost output and the social strains caused by the deflation and slow growth which so many western economies have been through during past decades, primarily to fight inflation, have been unnecessary, and could have been avoided.

Excessive demand

If a much more expansionist policy was adopted by the western economies, it would require a significant devaluation of their exchange rates *vis à vis* those of the rest of the world, particularly those of the Pacific Rim countries. It is not likely that the parity changes required, of themselves, would necessarily lead to any great inflationary problems during the early or later stages. The causes of inflation, however, are not only those already discussed. There is a further potentially substantial generator of prices increases of a different sort. This is to over-expand demand, so that overheating occurs. Once demand on any economy outstrips its capacity to supply, prices will start to rise. This is a prospect which must be taken seriously, and avoided.

'Too much money chasing too few goods' is the classic definition of inflation. While one of the central propositions in this book is that the solution to this problem should, wherever possible, be found by expanding the supply of goods rather than restricting demand, there must inevitably be a point where too many local shortages and bottlenecks have an increasingly serious effect on the price level. This problem has not been a significant one among western economies for almost all the period since the Korean War, but it could become one in the future.

There are, however, good reasons for believing that these difficulties are likely to be relatively easy to contain. There is a vast reservoir of unemployment in Europe, and under-utilised labour in the USA. Years of low demand have taken their toll on both European and American manufacturing capacity, but plant utilisation of what remains leaves room for significant increases in output before capacity constraints start to bite hard. Some labour will have rusty skills. Much of the plant and machinery may not be as modern or efficient as it should be, as a result of relatively low levels of investment over recent decades. All these resources, however, are much better than nothing, and there is no doubt that substantial extra output could be obtained from them.

While there is a significant reserve of unused or under-used resources to draw on, these will not last for ever, and the problems of sustaining economic growth without over-stretching the economy will then become more acute. One of the major disadvantages which decades of unmanageable competition have inflicted in the developed world is not just the closed plants and the fall in manufacturing employment, but the break-up of teams of people with design and production experience. The West has still managed to retain a lead in a number of the newer industries, such as the advanced use of electronics and biotechnology, but there is still a wide swathe of production where foreign imports dominate the market – in toys, giftware, household and hardware products, for example – many of which could and would be made in the Europe or the USA, given suitable exchange rates. Although most of these products are comparatively straightforward to manufacture, which is why the West could easily produce them competitively if it had the appropriate international cost base, it still takes time and skill to achieve high quality standards, and to market them efficiently. Building up successful industrial operations is not achieved in a day. The damage done by the weakening of the West's manufacturing base is not going to be put right in a few months. These problems can, however, be solved over a reasonably short period of years, and meanwhile they can be contained or minimised.

First, we have seen that the more the resources of the economy are deployed into those sectors concerned with falling cost curves and foreign trade, the easier it is for self-sustaining growth to be achieved. The faster the western economies are to grow, the more vital it is that wages and salaries in the import saving and exporting sectors of the economy should rise relative to those everywhere else. There will be a pressing need to attract the most talented people, capable of making good quickly the management deficiencies that are bound to exist after years of slow growth. The large returns on investment which are obtainable in these sectors should be able in turn to provide enough new output to finance all the additional investment required, without calling on the resources of the rest of the economy. There is thus an extremely strong case for fostering this kind of self-sustaining growth, and avoiding unnecessary obstructions to its taking place. There will also inevitably be pressure to expand expenditure in other directions. To avoid overheating, however, it is important not to siphon too many resources away from those parts of the economy which are achieving large increases in output towards those which cannot do so, by poorly judged taxation or public investment policies. The ways to fast growth are to let wealth be created before it is taxed too heavily, and to allow as much investment as possible to be concentrated in projects which have short pay-off periods and high returns.

Second, for at least some shortages, there is considerable scope for importing inputs not available from home production. One of the strongest arguments against the strategy of reflating the economy behind the shield of import tariffs or quotas, and protectionist policies generally, is that they would reduce or preclude the availability of alternative sources of supply at competitive prices to cope with domestic shortages. This is not an advantage which the West should throw away. Not all materials, however, can be imported in practice. Nor, in particular, is there an inexhaustible supply of skilled labour, much of which has been drained away from manufacturing industry by relatively poor wages, bad working conditions and uncertain prospects. Too many skilled engineers have now turned their hands to other ways of earning a living outside the industrial sector. They need to be attracted back with improved wages and conditions.

Third, any serious attempt to reflate the West's economies, designed to bring the labour force back to full stretch again, faces a major training, retraining and educational task, particularly for all forms of engineering and technical work. One of the consequences of the decline of manufacturing in the West has been that a far smaller proportion of the university-level students take engineering courses than is the case in other countries. In America, in 1995, 78 000 students gained batchelor's degrees in engineering, 6.7% of the total degrees awarded, down nearly 20% from the number ten years previously.[15] In Germany, with a population less than one-third of that of the USA, but with a much stronger manufacturing tradition, around 50 000 students begin university-level engineering courses every year, representing over 20% of all students.[16] This is a similar ratio to Japan where around 100 000 engineering graduates are produced per annum, forming more than 20% of all graduates.[17] Typically, in other countries with a longer history of manufacturing decline, the position is much worse. In Britain only a little over 20 000 students graduate in engineering annually.[18] Training courses may nevertheless have little value if there is insufficient demand available to provide work for those who have been through them. They are, however, a vitally important component of success once new opportunities for employment come on stream. Undoubtedly, they will be supplemented by large amounts of on-the-job training as employers need to upgrade the skills of their workforces.

The unemployment figures in all of the western economies would clearly be much higher if they were to include those not registered as unemployed, such as housewives and those who have been involuntarily retired early, who would like to work but have given up the prospect of finding a job as hopeless.[19] There is also a major problem with lack of skills among those who are unemployed in Europe or in menial, low output positions in the USA. Nearly all would require at least basic skills such as the ability to drive a motor vehicle or to use a keyboard, and the scope for employment for those who cannot read or write properly would inevitably be limited. Long years of poor job prospects may have sapped the motivation of a generation of children, especially in deprived areas, and in many cases their educational attainments are poor, and considerably worse than they were a few years ago. Similar problems of outdated or rusty skills apply to those who are older. The West cannot afford either for social or economic reasons to fail to get a high proportion of its unemployed or underemployed labour force back into much more productive jobs. It owes it to them to provide them with the training to enable them to hold down the better paying jobs which could be created in the future. The experience of the years during both World War I but particularly World War II shows that it is possible to find worthwhile employment for almost everyone, if the will and the determination is there.

Fourth, governments everywhere need to be wary of trying to contain problems of shortages of either raw materials or labour, especially skilled labour, by implementing wages and price freezes. The fact that prices and labour costs rise when shortages occur are signals that more resources in these areas are particularly needed. The changes in the economy which are required would involve considerable shifts in relative wage and salary levels, to attract high quality labour into the those sectors concerned with international trading, and away from other sectors. In particular, there would have to be substantial increases in remuneration for those involved in manufacturing industry. Suppressing the necessary price and wage rate signals will only aggravate shortages, leading quickly to even more pressure on prices and wages to rise. With inflation generally as quiescent as it is at present, controls over prices and wages are not currently on the agenda anywhere in the West, and this condition needs to be maintained.

Even if prices were to start rising much more rapidly than seems likely in the near future, there are better ways of dealing with profiteering and excessive wage increases than centrally imposed freezes. They have never worked for any length of time in the past in any country, and are unlikely to do so in future. Far the best alternative is not to expose the economy to strains which cause excessive bottlenecks and shortages in the first place by a two-pronged approach. The first is to create conditions where output can expand quickly in those sectors of the economy which are capable of achieving fast self-sustaining growth. The second is to refuse to allow overall demand to increase more rapidly than the rate at which even rejuvenated economies are capable of responding. Achieving this balance is not an impossible task.

Labour costs

In the end the most important determinant of inflation trends is the rate of increase in wages and salaries. Payments to labour represent an average of some 60% of total costs in the world as a whole, but tends to be considerably higher in the slower growing western economies. In the USA and Britain it is nearer to 70%, mainly because the savings and investment ratio is so much lower in countries which are growing slowly than in those expanding more rapidly. If the wage and salary bill rises faster than output, the extra costs are bound to be reflected in higher prices. If economies are run with a much greater level of demand which is intended, among other things, to produce a very substantial reduction in the level of unemployment, is it inevitable that high levels of wage inflation will be the consequence?

Before attempting to answer this question, it is worth looking again at the historical record and current experience in countries throughout the developed world. A glance at the unemployment percentages among developed countries and across different periods, as an indication of the tightness of the labour market, and the rates at which the consumer price level rose, must surely cause some concern even to those who are most convinced that wage inflation is inevitable. Table 8.4 provides some of the relevant figures. Those for the earlier period, before the general increase in inflation in the mid 1970s, show a wide range of countries with low rates of unemployment with moderate rates of inflation. At the beginning of the 1990s, countries as varied as Japan, Austria, Norway and Switzerland all managed to combine nearly full utilisation of their labour forces with low increases in the price level.

Much of the argument about the level of unemployment in developed countries has centred round the concept of the non-accelerating inflation rate of unemployment, or its acronym, the NAIRU. It is argued that, unless there are sufficiently large numbers of unemployed people, the pressure for wage increases will tend to outstrip the growth in output which the economy can provide, necessarily leading to increased inflation. The NAIRU, it is said, is higher in countries which have more inflexible labour markets, with more rigidities in the form of restrictive practices both in the way the workforce is deployed and in wage bargaining. While training and improved economic performance clearly have a role to play, the only fundamental solutions to the problem of unemployment, it is argued, are to reduce supply side rigidities by making wage rates and the labour market more flexible, to reduce job security, and to weaken the power of trade unions to fix wages which are unrelated to productivity gains.

There may well be substantial economic advantages for countries with non-rigid labour markets – offset, in many cases, by significant social costs – but even in these circumstances there has to come a point where there is a trade-off between fuller and fuller employment and rising

Table 8.4: Unemployment and Inflation in Ten OECD Countries at Selected Periods between 1963 and 1993

Country	1963–73		1974–9		1980–9		1990–3	
	Unemployment Rate	Inflation Rate	Unemployment Rate	Inflation Rate	Unemployment Rate	Inflation Rate	Unemployment Rate	Inflation Rate
United States	4.8%	3.2%	6.7%	8.5%	7.2%	5.5%	6.5%	3.9%
Japan	1.3%	6.2%	1.9%	9.9%	2.5%	2.5%	2.2%	2.5%
Austria	1.7%	4.2%	1.7%	6.3%	3.3%	3.8%	3.6%	3.6%
Norway	1.3%	5.1%	1.8%	8.7%	2.8%	8.3%	5.6%	3.0%
Switzerland	0.5%	4.2%	0.5%	4.0%	0.6%	3.3%	2.2%	4.6%
France	2.0%	4.6%	4.5%	10.7%	9.0%	7.3%	10.0%	2.8%
Germany	0.8%	3.4%	3.4%	4.7%	6.8%	2.9%	7.3%	3.6%
Italy	5.3%	3.9%	6.6%	16.7%	9.9%	11.2%	11.0%	5.5%
Spain	2.5%	4.7%	5.3%	18.3%	17.5%	10.2%	18.1%	5.8%
United Kingdom	1.9%	5.1%	4.2%	15.6%	9.5%	7.4%	8.3%	5.1%
OECD Average	3.2%	4.1%	5.0%	10.8%	7.2%	8.9%	7.2%	5.5%

Source: OECD *Historical Statistics*. Paris: OECD, 1995.

inflation. To argue, however, that the NAIRU requires a level of registered unemployment as high as that presently seen in most western economies, even before any allowance is made for underemployment, appears to be completely incompatible with all the international and historical evidence. Evidently, it was possible to combine relatively high rates of growth and low levels of unemployment with moderate inflation for twenty-five years after World War II in most of Europe, but more particularly in Japan, when supply side restrictions of all kinds were at least as prevalent as they are now, and in many cases much more so. Why should it therefore not be possible to achieve low levels of unemployment now? It might take some time to get there, but arguments about the NAIRU provide no convincing reason to believe that it would not nowadays be possible to achieve an unemployment rate in the industrialised countries of about 3%. This should be achievable within perhaps four to five years, if appropriate policies were implemented, with almost all the labour force in jobs which stretched their holders' talents, and in most cases paid much better than they are now. There is a great deal that can be done to achieve this objective.

First, wage determination is in the end as much a political as an economic process. The wage increases for which people are prepared to settle are not decided by a totally mechanistic process. Persuasion also counts. Even more difference may be made by the prospect of a rational economic policy which is capable of delivering results, and which is therefore seen to be one where some sacrifice of current wage and salary increases is worth while to obtain more in the future. Certainly a major objective must be to create a climate for wage negotiation which is conducive to average money increases at as low a level as possible, hopefully with the support of trade union leaders, to secure larger real rises as soon as practical in the future.

A complicating factor in wage determination, if a transition is to be made towards much faster rates of economic growth, is that it will not be possible to have the same increases for everyone. There needs to be a substantial relative adjustment. If talent at every level is going to have to be switched to those parts of the economy capable of producing high productivity increases, and rapid investment pay-off periods, rises in pay will have to be considerably higher in these areas of economic activity than elsewhere. This suggests that aiming for relatively low general increases, but with substantial wage drift at the level of individual enterprises, is the most realistic policy.

Another problem is that there are going to be shortages of certain types of skilled labour, and also a pressing need for a considerable amount of retraining to enable the labour force to be adequately prepared for the new types of jobs which will become available. Government programmes have a major role in providing training and retraining to enable there to be a sufficient response to this challenge, supplementing what is carried out on the job. If bottlenecks in the form of skilled labour shortages are to be avoided, the places where these are likely to occur need to be identified as far in advance as possible, and training put in hand as early as it can be to provide the manpower needed at adequate skill levels. Generally, this will need to be fairly precisely orientated towards specific job opportunities. Improving general standards of education and motivation in schools is another vital component, but takes much longer to pay off. Preparing those already of working age will almost certainly have to be given higher immediate priority.

There clearly is potential for wage pressure if these changes are taking place, and all the dampening effect of increasing output in absorbing whatever wage increases there are will be needed. There is no reason, however, why the major disinflationary influence of increasing production should not be supplemented where possible by government actions on the price level. There is much to be said against prices and incomes policies if they can be avoided, but there are other steps which the state can take apart from freezing or limiting increases in prices, wages and incomes. Lowering interest rates, which has many other advantages, reduces the cost of living. If the economy needs reflating, there are several ways which have already been mentioned in which this can be done which actually reduce costs, such as lowering taxes on employment to keep down the price level. All this should help to produce a more helpful wage climate in addition to acting directly on both the cost of living and of producing output of all kinds.

When all these factors are put together, it becomes clear how some countries have managed with a NAIRU which allows much fuller use to be made of their labour forces than has been achieved for many years in others. Faster growth makes larger money wage claims possible without inflationary consequences. Rising output in an economy run in a way which appears rational and sustainable makes a degree of wage restraint seem a sensible policy. Flowing from this comes something closer to a consensus. This should make economically unjustified wage claims look irrational and greedy, instead of being the only way available to buck trends which never seem to end, as has been the experience too often in the past in countries with a longer record of slow growth such as the USA and Britain. If some countries can operate with 3% or 4% rates of unemployment, with all the rest of their labour forces in jobs which stretch their members' talents, there is no reason why others should not be able to do so too.

Summary

There is little doubt that a major reason why many people who might otherwise be willing to contemplate using exchange rate changes to improve economic performance oppose such a policy because they believe its use would both push up the price level and reduce the standard of living, at least in the short term. They treat it as axiomatic that inflation must rise in any economy where the currency is devalued, and that in consequence the real wage would fall. It therefore seems worth summarising at the end of this chapter the reasons for believing that these fears are misplaced. On the contrary, the evidence shows that even major devaluations do not lead to any significant rise in inflation, while almost invariably quickly increasing the standard of living in economies whose currencies have depreciated. If this is true, it then becomes far more feasible and attractive than is generally assumed to use macro-economic policy and exchange rate changes to provide both the stimulus and the flexibility to allow the economy to grow faster, and vastly to improve employment and compensation prospects for the labour force, without taking undue risks with inflation.

The proposition that increasing the money supply within reasonable bounds, lowering interest rates, and encouraging the exchange rate to fall will necessarily lead to an immediate increase in inflation may be widely believed. There is, however, very little empirical evidence from the history of the developed world to support it. On the contrary, the record of all the devaluations over the nearly seventy years since the break-up of the Gold Standard in 1931 shows the opposite tendencies manifesting themselves to a greater or lesser extent on almost every occasion. The expected impact of a depreciation on the price level does not materialise because lowering the exchange rate involves disinflationary factors which are as powerful, and sometimes even more so, than those tending to push prices up. Furthermore, if policies are implemented which assist these tendencies, such as reducing taxes where this is not only possible but desirable on other grounds, then the influences working against inflation become even more pronounced. In the medium term, with a much higher growth rate, the prospects are for fairly low but sustainable levels of inflation, the main generator of price increases being leading sector inflation if the rate of expansion is very high. There should be no reductions in average living standards at any stage.

The evidence from across the world shows that many of the causes of prices rises have had little directly to do with the money supply, though some inflationary upsurges have been caused by monetary mismanagement and excessive credit creation. Most of the increase in the money supply in all countries has been the result of the need to accommodate economic growth. Inflation has then occurred for non-monetary reasons. Recent developments, particularly deregulation and the growth of new forms of money, have tended to increase the requirement for credit. This makes precise monetary ratios even more unreliable than they were before. Especially in conditions like the present, therefore, where inflationary pressures requiring any kind of deflationary solution are not a serious threat, the risk of price rises from excessive money supply is low. The problem in the West at present is not too much credit creation, but too little.

There are bound to be more random inflationary shocks both to the world and to the advanced industrialised economies, and governments everywhere have to be prepared to deal with them. They ought, however, not to cause undue difficulty. The international evidence strongly indicates that there is a universal tendency for inflation to die back in advanced economies which are reasonably competently run, once the causes of individual upsurges have been removed. This is best achieved by using increasing productivity and output as a sponge to soak up inflationary pressures, and, in particular, as the way to accommodate wage and salary increases which might otherwise push up the price level.

There is no evidence for the view that all increases in prices are ultimately due to one sole cause, and therefore only amenable to one solution. On the contrary, the causes of inflation are varied. The way to deal with any particular inflationary problem depends on careful diagnosis of the specifics rather than the application of general monetary theories which may not be relevant, and which may indeed be counter-productive. Different causes of inflation require different policies to deal with them.

Overall, however, the problems associated with ensuring that price rises stay at relatively low levels, at least for most of the time, even if the economy is growing very quickly, do not look particularly daunting. With a sustained growth rate of around 4% – or even 6% – it ought to be possible to keep inflation at no more than around 4% per annum, as it was for years on end in the fast growing economies of Europe in the 1950s and 1960s. Between 1954 and 1969 the French economy grew cumulatively at 5.4% per annum, with an average annual inflation rate of 4.5%. Over the same period, the German economy grew at 5.8% per annum, with average per annum inflation of 2.7%. Even Japan, which grew at 10.0% per annum over this period had an annual inflation rate of only 4.0%.[20]

If mistakes are made, or external shocks are experienced, either of which push up the rate of increase in the price level, it is not usually difficult to get it down again without plunging the economy into deflation. In advanced economies, the main causes of inflation which are subject to policy control appear to be far from unmanageable, though all require self-discipline and good government. Allowing the economy to become overheated, tolerating the creation of an excessive money supply, mishandling the wage bargaining process, and using the tax system to pay for wasteful public expenditure, are all avoidable provided that relevant policies are implemented reasonably efficiently. Whatever the institutional background, whether nationally or internationally, if mistakes or misjudgements are made in these areas, rising inflation and falling living standards will be the consequences. There are no short cuts to responsible behaviour and political maturity. The cushion of increased output and productivity provided by a fast rate of economic growth, however, ought to make all these policy issues easier, and not more difficult to handle.

Even if events were to prove this thesis wrong, however, which the evidence does not suggest they would, and there was some significant extra-inflation as a result of downward parity changes and the western economies grew much more quickly, there is still a strong case for believing that it would be worth it. The standard of living is, in the end, far more important than the cost of living. It would be worth paying a modest inflationary price to raise growth rates from their current level to the world average or beyond, and vastly to improve the job prospects and productivity of the European and American labour forces. In any event, such an inflationary surge would almost certainly be temporary, and quickly absorbed. This does not, however, appear to be the real choice. It is not necessary to choose between more growth with significantly more inflation or less growth and much lower price rises. In the short, as well as the medium and long term, high rates of growth and manageably low rates of inflation can and should be made to go hand in hand.

9
The Future

'No great improvements in the lot of mankind are possible, until a great change takes place in the fundamental constitution of their modes of thought.'

John Stuart Mill

The previous chapters provide a vantage point from which it is now possible to assess the policy changes which need to be made to deal with the low growth rates and high unemployment from which the West suffers. The issue is whether there is a common cause for these deficiencies which could be rectified by nothing more complicated than altering macro-economic policies in entirely manageable ways.

Although western economies, by world standards, have performed in many respects exceptionally well over the half-century since the end of World War II, they have nevertheless substantially underachieved in relation to their potential. The standard of living in the world's industrialised countries has been well above that in other parts of the world, mostly by a wide margin, but this does not mean that it could not have been higher still. Nor would this would have been to the disbenefit to less developed countries. In fact, the prosperity which is so evident in much of the West is the main reason why it may be hard to persuade most people of the scale of the opportunity which has been missed. This may be particularly so as the richest and most influential sections of the West's population have generally suffered least in relation to the extra increases in output and living standards which could have been achieved, but which have in fact been forgone. The major losers have been all but the most well off. Their losses, in many cases, have been substantial. Over a wide swathe of those on lower incomes, especially for those who have become unemployed, they have been huge.

The root problem for the West's major current malaises all lie in the same place. The basic cause lies in the macro-economic policies which all the major industrialised countries have pursued, particularly during the last quarter of a century. Without ever seriously considering what the alternatives might be, their governments have allowed the value of their currencies to become too strong, and their cost bases too high, especially in relation to the Pacific Rim economies. The results of this general overvaluation have been to make exporting more difficult and importing more profitable than it should have been, manufactured goods being, by value, much the largest component. As Table 9.1 shows, nowadays, about 65%, on average, of all industrialised countries' exports, are manufactured goods, as are about the same proportion of all their imports. Just over 20% are services, the remainder being raw materials, agricultural products and fuels. Advantages of climate, soil, and the availability of mineral and other natural resources are largely irrelevant to where manufacturing output is located. Overwhelmingly the most important determinant is the overall costs of all the factors of production, with labour charges adjusted for productivity being the largest component. As between different countries, by far the biggest influence on overall competitiveness is the exchange rate.

Because the cost of manufacturing a vast range of products has been allowed to become much higher than it needed to have been in the West compared to elsewhere, investment in manufacturing plant has been much less than in other countries with a more favourable cost base. Because it was much easier to make money out of producing and selling products in these other countries than it was in the West, more able people there went into producing and marketing goods rather than services. A combination of high investment levels, talent and profitability then set these economies into the upward, self-reinforcing spiral of export led growth, mostly unconstrained by balance of payments problems, which were generally held in check because domestic production was highly competitive with imports. By their very nature, because they all tend to share falling unit costs as production volume increases, the goods and services which are internationally traded are exactly those where productivity gains are easiest to achieve. Any country which manages to corner more than its fair share of this kind of economic activity will therefore tend to grow faster than the average.

Table 9.1: Analysis of Imports and Exports of Industrialised Countries, 1997

Mio ECU	EU	USA	Japan	Totals
Total all Exports:	100%	100%	100%	100%
Made up of:				
All Goods	79%	73%	85%	78%
All Services	21%	27%	15%	22%
Total all Imports:	100%	100%	100%	100%
Made up of:				
All Goods	78%	84%	71%	79%
All Services	22%	16%	29%	21%

Billions of 1991 US dollars	All OECD Countries	
	Exports	*Imports*
All goods:	1000.4	994.3
Manufacturers	858.9	798.7
Manufacturers as a percentage of all goods	86%	80%
Manufacturers as a percentage of all trade	67%	63%

Sources: Tables 2801, 2802, 2804 and 2805 in *Eurostatistics*, Luxembourg: EU, December 1998, page 37 in *OECD Main Economic Indicators*, July 1999.

Because the demand for labour was high in these fast growing economies, it paid everyone to make sure that the labour force was educated and trained to a high standard, and then used to the full. Skill levels and productivity rose exponentially. Unemployment barely existed. The societies created by this kind of experience – recently mostly in the Far East, although much of Europe had two decades of very high growth in the 1950s and 1960s – then exhibited far more equal distributions of income, educational attainment and life chances than in the much slower growing economies now typical of the West. It is hardly surprising then to find that social bonds are stronger, crime rates are lower and expectations for the future are higher. Because real incomes are rising fast, the domestic as well as the corporate savings ratio tends to be much greater, so financing rapid expansion and a high reinvestment level is generally not a problem.

In the West, especially over the last twenty-five years, all the opposite tendencies have manifested themselves. Because, for large volumes of tradable goods and services, but particularly for manufactures, it has been cheaper to produce elsewhere, the West's share of this kind of production has fallen steadily, and with it the West's share of world trade. The industrialised countries have, as a result, forgone a large proportion of both the scope for productivity increases from this source, and some, especially the USA, their ability to pay their way in the world.

Rising productivity does not, however, occur only in the internationally tradable sector of the economy, although, given favourable conditions, rapidly rising output per head is much more likely to be found here than elsewhere. It also tends to increase in other parts of the economy, but not so fast. During the last few decades, world trade has become freer, competition has increased, the pressure for better management has grown, job training has become more focused and the computer revolution has transformed activities of all kinds. As a result, output per head has gone up, particularly in the more favoured areas of the world's economies, allowing the same or an increasing volume of goods and services to be produced by fewer people. If overall demand had been rising fast enough, this might have generated large increase in incomes for everyone. In the West, however, this has not happened. Relatively tight monetary policies have kept increases in demand well below the true output potential. The result has been that the productivity gains achieved among those capable of taking advantage of them led to millions of people losing good jobs and being pushed out into the labour market where only much lower quality employment was available, or none at all. Alternatively, they retired or dropped out of the job market altogether.

The labour forces in western countries have thus been caught in a pincer movement. On the one hand, western economies failed to take sufficient advantage of the productivity increases typically found in internationally traded goods and services, which could have been shared throughout the labour force. On the other hand, the generally available benefits from computers, training, and better management were used to improve the prospects of those already most advantaged at the expense of thinning out the job opportunities for everyone else. The results are then clear to see. They have materialised as stagnant real incomes for twenty-five years for the vast mass of blue collar workers in the USA, high levels of unemployment in the EU, far more divided societies throughout the West than they ever needed to be, and, since the beginning of the 1990s, stagnation in Japan.

There is a series of links in a chain of causation, therefore, which, when taken together, explain the major problems from which the West suffers, now including Japan. All of them stem from the same source, which is the extent to which the operation of the West's economies have been skewed by allowing their cost bases to become too high in relation to other parts of the world, particularly on the Pacific Rim. This is the single most important economic policy issue which the West needs to address.

Changing the environment

If the West wants to improve its economic performance, to enable it to grow at least as fast as the world average, and to keep all its workforce at full stretch, it could do so. The solution to all the major problems holding back western economies from doing so lie in the same area of macro-economic policy. A combination of changes would be required. Across Europe and America, there would need to be lower interest rates, a much more accommodating monetary climate, and there would have to be a substantial downward movement in the value of western currencies *vis à vis* those particularly in the Pacific Rim. All these changes would be needed together to enable the West's economies to grow more quickly and to make the exchange rate changes acceptable to those countries currently enjoying unduly low cost base advantages.

Could other countries, particularly in Asia, stop the value of western currencies falling against theirs, if the authorities in the industrialised countries were determined to see this occurring? The answer is clearly 'no' as far as the USA and Japan are concerned, but more problematic for the EU. No external government could stop the USA from lowering its interest rates and increasing its money supply, if that is what the US authorities decided to do. Nor could other countries stop the Fed selling US dollars to help push down the exchange rate. In Japan, the problems and solutions are different, but still, in principle, well within the control of the government. There, the requirement is to flood the country with purchasing power. The government needs to maintain a lax monetary stance, while liberalising imports, including the removal of informal restraints, to bring down the value of the yen. In the EU, the situation is made much more difficult by the locking together of currency values in the euro. The problem, as we have seen, is that the depreciation now required by the euro is likely to generate overheating in some parts of the EU economy, while others remain operating at well below full capacity. As long as the EU Single Currency remains in being, the only solution to this problem is greatly to increase the fiscal powers of the EU at the expense of national governments, thus providing sufficient tax raising and spending powers across the EU to even out disparities in performance between its constituent economies. Whether the Member States will be willing to give up this much sovereignty remains to be seen. If they do not do so, but the Single Currency remains in being, the result is all too likely to be a reiteration of the poor growth and employment performance exhibited during the Snake and ERM periods.

Could the Pacific Rim countries retaliate against those in the industrialised West, supposing they were minded to do so? Perhaps, but given a liberal trading régime in the industrialised countries, such a response would not be one which made much sense for those which felt themselves threatened. They could try raising tariffs, but the risk of retaliation would be high, and such a policy would go against recent experience of the best way of promoting sustainable growth. They could attempt to devalue themselves, in competition with the West, but this might not be easy if their economies were already expanding fast, and in danger of overheating.

Much would depend on the policies pursued by the industrialised countries both in terms of how liberal they were with their imports, and how firm they were in resisting any temptation to run large balance of payments surpluses. If the western economies were to expand considerably more rapidly than they have done during the last quarter of a century, this ought to benefit rather than harm Asian countries. Because western markets would, in these circumstances, be growing much more quickly, Pacific Rim economies should then see their exports to the West increasing faster, and not more slowly, than has been the case in recent decades. Provided exchange rate adjustments continue to be made to avoid any of the world's major economies accumulating large balance of payments surpluses – as countries such as Germany, Japan and Taiwan have done so damagingly during recent decades – corresponding deficits should not materialise elsewhere, generating the need for deflationary policies which hold back growth. In conditions of full employment in the industrialised countries, it ought to be much easier to maintain low barriers to imports, whether formal or informal, than when there are large numbers out of work, and protectionism appears to be the only way of safeguarding jobs.

Some countries might have more difficulty than others in adjusting to the new trading environment which would then be produced, particularly those which have become accustomed to running large bilateral trade surpluses with the USA, pre-eminently Japan. Here again, however, the changes which would need to be made are by no means necessarily to the disadvantage of America's trading partners. In many ways, the Japanese economy is the mirror image of that of the USA. It combines extremely competitive, high productivity export industries, based largely on manufacturing, with an often surprisingly wasteful and inefficient domestic economy. If the US trade deficit disappeared, of course not all the adjustment would be with Japan. The USA has multilateral trading relations with the whole world. There is little doubt, however, that the general impact of a much more competitive dollar would be to confront the Japanese with the economic and political imperative of accepting a substantial reduction, if not elimination of their trade surplus. No doubt this would present the Japanese government with some difficult political choices. Faced with the necessity to respond, however, the thrust of the decisions which would need to be taken are obvious. The solution would be a combination of domestic reflation and liberalisation of imports, both of which would benefit the Japanese, while also helping the rest of the world away from being hobbled by the Japanese trade surplus. If the Japanese refused to adjust their policies along these lines, the alternative would be for the yen to become even more overvalued as the US dollar and European currencies fell. It is true that there would then be a danger of Japan plunging into a major recession. The fact that the Japanese authorities would then be faced with this prospect may, however, be the way the rest of the world has to force their country to make long overdue changes which everyone else urgently needs to see being carried out as much as the Japanese themselves.

Would a substantial downward change in the value of western currencies, particularly the dollar, upset world trade, removing the convenience and readiness with which they are used to finance the buying and selling of goods and services of all kinds all over the world? Again, the answer is 'no'. No such disruption occurred when the value of the dollar fell by over 30% on a trade weighted basis between 1984 and 1988. Nor were there any significant problems as the index rose 15% between 1992 and 1997. Most business people would prefer prices not to change, because dealing with alterations in costs involves extra work and produces less certainty. There is no evidence, however, that changing prices and exchange rates deter business activity, as has been shown by study after study by international organisations. Manufacturers and traders simply have to tolerate the instability which surrounds them all the time.

Another objection which might be put to western economies growing much faster is that the world ecology might be put under increasingly unacceptable strain if this happened, since the older industrialised countries still represent so substantial a share of total world output. A different concern might be that the standard of living in the West is already so high that it might be difficult for it to go on rising rapidly before some kind of ceiling was reached. Both of these fears, however, seem wholly misplaced. All the available evidence suggests that greater wealth and disposable incomes increase humanity's capacity to deal with environmental problems rather than reducing it. Most environmental programmes are expensive, and much more easily afforded out of incomes which are high and rising rather than low and stagnant. The consumption of raw materials and the generation of waste tends to fall rather than rise as a percentage of rising incomes, while the money available to deal with their ecological impact increases. As to the notion that the desire for additional goods and services in the West has reached the point where satiation is in prospect, surely few people can be convinced that anything approaching this situation has been reached. The rich show no problems at all in spending their hugely increased incomes, while the poorer sections of society work longer and longer hours to try to keep their living standards from falling. At some point all economic wants may be satisfied, but we seem to be a safely long way off this state of affairs at the moment.

Perhaps the most telling question of all, however, is that if there is a comparatively simple answer to the West's most serious economic problems, as this book suggests there is, why has it not been more widely canvassed before? This is a fair question, which deserves a full response.

Reassessing the past

This book has argued that the macro-economic policies which nearly all western economies have pursued at least since the 1970s, and in some cases since World War II, have led to their currencies being consistently overvalued, particularly *vis à vis* the Pacific Rim economies. It has suggested that the consequence has been that both the USA and Europe have under-performed in relation to their potential to a much greater extent than is commonly realised. The conclusion is that there is a relatively simple way in principle of overcoming these problems, which is to bring down the value of the West's currencies as against those in the Asian economies, while at the same time adopting much more expansionist domestic policies. Both of these objectives require lower interest rates and a more accommodating monetary strategy.

If the argument in this book is essentially correct, however, it clearly is at variance with almost all of what Professor Kenneth Galbraith has aptly described as the conventional wisdom. A major reduction in the value of the dollar, the euro and the pound against the Pacific Rim currencies is not a policy prescription found in newspapers, best-selling books about western decline or in the academic literature. It is not a plank in any major political party's manifestos. Those reading the proposals set out in this book may therefore be tempted to presume that the monetary and exchange rate changes proposed cannot be an effective remedy, otherwise it would have been much more generally recommended in the past. Before reaching this conclusion, however, the reader is invited to consider the following powerful reasons for believing that the remedy on offer, though effective, might be surprisingly difficult to see.

First, it needs to be said yet again, the western economies, whatever their deficiencies may be, have done extremely well for a long time. They have provided their citizens, on average, with a higher standard of living than elsewhere in the world, mostly by a large margin. They still comprise a major proportion of the world's economic output. Most of the major industrial and commercial developments have been pioneered in the West, and this seems to be a trend which is likely to continue. Their economies, by world standards, operate far more efficiently than the average. Their culture, management techniques and values, not least in the form of the liberal democratic political forms they all share, permeate and set standards for the rest of the world. With this record of achievement behind them, in an imperfect world, it has been hard to comprehend how vulnerable in some important respects their economies have become.

Nor have the countries which have challenged the West's hegemony over the past decades been successful in denting its apparent invincibility. In the 1950s and 1960s, there were real concerns that the Soviet bloc might overtake the West in economic power and living standards, but this threat was steadily reduced during the stagnation of the Brezhnev years, and disappeared when the Soviet Union broke up following the Gorbachev era. Later, there were fears that Japan would dominate the standards of living in Europe and perhaps overtake the USA, at least in terms of GDP per head, and even perhaps in terms of the total size of its economy. These have become a good deal less pressing during the 1990s as Japan's fabled growth has melted away. There may be a threat from China, and perhaps from some of the other Tiger economies, either in terms of their absolute size or their living standards, but it is hard to envisage this risk materialising in the course of the next few years, even though, unless there are changes, it may become more visible within decades. In the meantime, however, America's ascendancy looks as secure as it ever has done, though some of Europe is now beginning to look rather more vulnerable.

Second, it may well be that the sheer efficiency with which so much of the West's economies run has blinded people to their competitive weaknesses. Perhaps understandably, there is a vast amount of confusion between productivity, efficiency and competitiveness. It is very easy to assume that because the West's factories are much more productive than those almost everywhere else in the world – which they are – that therefore they must be competitive internationally. This is, however, certainly not necessarily a correct conclusion. Even if output per head is much higher in the West than in China, the average Chinese product may still be more competitive – and indeed generally nowadays it is, if it involves reasonably straightforward and widely available production techniques. This has nothing to do with productivity, because Chinese output per head is far below that of the West in almost every branch of economic activity. It has everything to do with exchange rates and the cost base in China compared with western countries for generally available production techniques.

Third, there have been serious misunderstandings about the role and importance of manufacturing. It is true that as economies become more advanced, and the standard of living rises, there is a tendency for the proportion of the GDP involved in the production of services to rise in relation to the ratio involved in manufacturing. This happens partly because of a price effect. Because productivity increases are so much more difficult to achieve in services, the relative cost of manufactured goods tends to fall, making them look less significant than in volume terms they really are. No doubt, however, there is also an important inclination for those with rising incomes to spend more of their money on services. The result is that it is easy to assume that as any economy becomes increasingly advanced, the proportion of its GDP devoted to manufacturing will fall away exponentially, and that this is inevitable and does not really matter.

A vital theme running through this book is that this perception is misplaced. This does not imply that services are of no significance and that industrial output should always be given priority. A sense of balance is obviously required. It does entail, however, recognising that manufacturing, and indeed all those activities whose outputs particularly lend themselves to international trading, have a peculiarly important role to play in two critical regards. One is that they comprise the parts of the economy where productivity increases are most easily achieved, and hence they are critical to the growth rate. The second is that they provide most of the output to be sold abroad to pay for imports, and it is therefore critically important that there should be enough available at competitive prices. If not, balance of payments problems and constraints on economic expansion will be the inevitable outcome. The implication is that if the

West is to grow at the same rate as the rest of the world, it needs to have an appropriate proportion of the world's manufacturing capacity functioning within its own borders.

Fourth, a large majority of those who are most influential in forming opinions are now in the top earning brackets. In nearly all western economies, the distribution of income has become markedly less even over the past quarter of a century, but this has not diminished the living standards of most of those who write books or newspaper articles, who appear on television, or who get elected to positions of political power. The rapidly increasing wealth and income of those with most influence may have been responsible for creating a widespread illusion that everyone is much better off than was the case twenty or thirty years previously. Perhaps this is the case because much wider access to higher education in the early post-war period left far fewer able people dissatisfied with their life opportunities, and therefore inclined to identify their interests with the less fortunate in whose ranks they found themselves. Whether or not this is the case, however, neither in the USA nor in Europe is it true that the rich variety of life for those who are very well off reflects the reality for everyone else. In the USA, living standards have stagnated for all but roughly the top 10% of income earners during the last quarter of a century, while those at the bottom of the pyramid have seen their life circumstances significantly deteriorate. In Europe, the increase in living standards has been higher than in the USA for those in work, but millions of people have either dropped out of the labour force altogether, or have had, and still have, major problems finding employment.

Fifth, although there have been large numbers of books published about the problems which the West is perceived to have – some of them, particularly in the USA, best-sellers – coupled with a vast profusion of academic articles and publications, on these and related topics, their recommendations have been remarkably confusing and muted. The best-selling books are – or were – full of spine-chilling statistics about the advance of Japanese manufacturing techniques and anecdotes about relatively poor western performance in response, but their recommendations as to how to overcome these problems are generally unconvincing, if not plain wrong. Some have advocated various forms of fairly straightforward protection, apparently without seeming to recognise that this is just a backdoor and relatively inefficient way of changing the exchange rate. Others favour a variety of confrontational 'get tough' policies, mainly with the Japanese, which are really protection in another guise. A different school has seen the solution in industrial strategies, concentrating resources on 'high-tech' industries, mostly, it appears, without bothering to look up the statistics to see whether their recommendations had any foundation in economic reality. The notion that high-tech industries produce higher value added per employee is simply not correct. In the USA, for example, as Professor Paul Krugman has pointed out,[1] the average hourly earnings in 1997 of those in the long established and relatively low-tech cigarette producing industry (SIC 211) were almost twice as high as those manufacturing electronic components and accessories (SIC 367), and 31% higher than those producing aircraft and parts (SIC 372).[2]

Nor has the academic economic world been much help, despite the vast amount of publications produced. Perhaps the most serious attempt to find a solution to the inability of western companies to compete successfully in the world has consisted of the extensive studies carried out in the USA on Strategic Trade Policy.[3] They have involved investigations as to whether a temporary period of protection for specific industries would provide them with permanent long-term advantages. The conclusion reached is that in certain circumstances such a policy might work, but in the real world convincing examples have been hard to find. Even if specific cases could be located, fitting the criteria required, the difference which would be made to the USA's overall economic performance would be so small as to be virtually imperceptible. Apart from Strategic Trade Policy, the American economic establishment has had little of substance to say about how to improve US economic performance, most of its members apparently believing that there is little in practice that can be done. The same attitudes prevail widely in Europe. Despite the talent attracted to the study of economic affairs, its proponents have been remarkably unsuccessful throughout the western world at producing convincing explanations of the causes of economic growth, the conditions needed to ensure it occurs, and prescriptions on related issues where there are obvious trade-offs, such as full employment and inflation.

Sixth, and perhaps most fundamentally of all, there are the many social and cultural forces which bear heavily on the framework of ideas which shape both public opinion and the menu of policy options viewed among those whose opinions matter in the West as being practical and acceptable. Ideology permeates economics, and establishment views heavily influence opinions on what choices are within and without the pale. Most countries in the West are broadly contented and proud. Their social structures are stable. The rich and established have done exceptionally well, and generally do not want to see policies which have served them so satisfactorily being changed. While those on the left might be happy to see the distribution of income becoming more equal, though perhaps provided, that their own pockets were not hit, this is not necessarily the case with those of a more conservative turn of mind. Those on the right of the political spectrum may therefore not be inclined to favour a change in policy which would make the poor richer, even if it did not make the rich poorer. There is also the fear of inflation to be taken into account. The monetarist creed, which appeals so strongly to those in established positions because it produces such a wonderfully persuasive justification for the circumstances which suit them best, states as a catechism that expanding the money supply, reducing interest rates and lowering the exchange rates will invariably produce more inflation. All the evidence suggests that all these canons of the monetarist faith are false, but many millions of people believe that they are true all the same. As a result, expansionist policies involving depreciating the currency, with its supposed although illusory risks of inflation, are regarded as policies to be strongly avoided if possible, rather than encouraged.

All of these sentiments are wrapped up in the rhetoric about exchange rates which is so widely used. When the value of the currency is high it is strong. When it is low it is weak. When it depreciates its value falls. When it appreciates it rises. All these loaded terms colour everyone's perceptions. The reality, however, is different. If any country's currency is too strong, its exports wither, its manufacturing declines, investment and the savings to pay for it falls, living standards for most people stagnate, life chances deteriorate, the fiscal balance tends to go into deficit, and its relative power and position in the world falls away. This is a terrible price to pay for misconceptions which need to be exposed, and which ought not to prevail.

Choices for the future

The period from about 1500 to the end of the second millennium has been a long success story for the West. Quickening economic development, precipitated by the Renaissance, led on to the Industrial Revolution, and provided Europe, and then those parts of the world largely populated by people of European stock, with a huge lead. Spain was probably the richest country in the world in the sixteenth century, followed by France in the seventeenth, the Netherlands in the eighteenth, and Britain in the nineteenth. The years from 1900 to 2000 have seen the USA pre-eminent. The extent to which the most-favoured position passed from one country to another, however, gives no grounds for supposing that in future the West's lead in living standards will automatically remain secure.

No governments in any of the countries which allowed their leads to slip away permitted this to happen deliberately. In all cases, no doubt, they tried their best, judged by the knowledge and information available to them, to provide conditions which would allow growing prosperity to continue, maintaining their relative position. History shows, however, that in each case that they failed to do so, allowing some often previously disdained rival to overtake them. As we have seen, a difference in growth rates of quite a small percentage makes a huge difference over two or three decades. If one economy grows at 2% per annum and another at 6% cumulatively for twenty-five years, the first will grow by 64% over this period and the second by 329%. If living standards were 50% lower in the second economy at the beginning of this quarter-century than the first, by the end they would be over 30% higher. If the West were to allow the growth rate of its economies to be only a cumulative 2% per annum, which is not an impossible outcome by any means on present trends, its current lead would almost certainly be under threat before very far into the twenty-first century.

It might be argued that this is unlikely to happen because other countries would not be able to sustain an expansion in output of 6% a year cumulatively for long enough to enable this to occur. Perhaps this will turn out to be correct. Certainly the Japanese, long held up as models, have allowed their economy to perform exceptionally badly in the 1990s, as their growth rate has slumped. If the argument in this book is correct, however, this need not have happened. The Japanese lost their way in the growth stakes not because of any historical inevitability, but because they have made avoidable mistakes. During the years when their growth rate was high, they allowed export surpluses to pile up, instead of letting their domestic market have the benefit of import competition. When the size of these surpluses became intolerable, and the value of the yen was driven up, the Japanese government failed to take the action it could have done to increase the money supply to stimulate domestic demand. Instead, the export surpluses continued, driving up the yen still further. When, eventually, interest rates were brought down to very low levels, the yen fell, but not sufficiently to take up the slack. As a result, the values of Japanese assets have remained in the doldrums and many banks and other financial institutions have been on the edge of insolvency. Some have failed. Neither consumption nor exports nor domestic investment have risen significantly in recent years, and the cumulative Japanese growth rate between 1991 and 1997 was 1.4%[4] per annum.

It may turn out to be correct that all rapidly growing economies will eventually make the same sort of mistakes, so that their growth rates slow. This book has explored some of the social and political pressures which have tended to make this happen. It is not the case, however, that policies necessarily have to be adopted which slow down the growth rate. The success which some countries have achieved in continuing to grow for long periods attests that this must be true. The message in this book is that the conditions which create and sustain growth, which achieve the full use of the potential of the labour force, and which can be combined with tolerable levels of inflation, are not determined by blind history. On the contrary, they are the subject of policy choices which any government, democratic or otherwise, is free to take. The risk to the West can then be simply stated. If other countries make the right decisions, and the leaders of the western economies make the wrong ones, then the West's long-lasting lead will be eclipsed.

Of course, this is not the only reason why the West should get its growth rate up. There are other reasons too, of greater importance to the millions of Americans and Europeans who may have enjoyed a high standard of living compared to the rest of the world during past decades, but who could have done better. There is a huge amount of potential waiting to be unleashed. There is no reason why living standards in western countries should not rise at least as fast as the world average, and perhaps faster, if that is the democratic choice, which it almost certainly would be. This should not only make the average person much better off, but it would also relieve other strains which currently scar western societies, particular the condition of the worse off. Hopefully, richer countries, with less unemployment and more even distributions of income, wealth and life chances, would also be more contented, less divided, less prone to violence, racism and xenophobia, and more at ease with themselves.

For the failure of economic policies in the West to generate enough growth to keep everyone fully employed, and to raise living standards reasonably rapidly, except for the well off, has had deeply corrosive effects. For many people in the industrialised world, life is much less secure than it was a quarter of a century ago.[5] Average living standards may have risen, but many people are worse off than their equivalents were in the 1960s. Some of these changes may have been difficult to avoid, but many of them stem from the need to compete with goods and services produced in other countries where the cost base is so much more favourable that too many of the more civilised ways of organising businesses and productive relations have had to be jettisoned. It is not a sign of progress that millions of people in rich western economies have to work absurdly long hours on extremely low pay to make ends meet.

A major part of the malaise in the West, reflecting trends which have tended sooner or later to envelop all societies which have had a period of successful growth, is that the result of rising prosperity is disproportionately to favour the economic, political and social status of groups of people who are least inclined to favour the changes needed to improve economic performance. Whatever the importance of the rule of law, it is not lawyers who generate increased wealth. Nor, except to a surprisingly limited extent, is it bankers, government officials, politicians, the military, church leaders, academics or those in the media. However much the services provided by all these groups are valued, and however much many of them get paid, their contribution towards increasing prosperity is remarkably small. Worse than this, it may be negative. The service sector's record on increasing productivity and output is, as we have seen, on average, remarkably low. Those whose contribution to future rises in living standards, on the contrary, are much more likely to be found in industry, especially in manufacturing. Shifting talent in this direction is going to require major changes in perception in most western countries about what types of careers are most worth while. Only when those which are actually the most productive are also those which are the best rewarded will this transition be achieved.

The Industrial Revolution changed the course of human history more fundamentally than any other development since humankind first emerged into civilisation. It has transformed all our lives. It has had a massive influence on the way events have developed over the last two centuries. It has shaped the way the world is run. Yet the opportunities it has presented humanity for bettering its lot have only partially been grasped. Much more can be done with the tools which are now available. A great deal is going to depend on the extent to which men and women learn to use the opportunities which are now to hand better in the future than they have in the past, especially in the West during the last quarter of the twentieth century.

Notes

Preface

1. *Tackling Britain's False Economy* by John Mills. London: Macmillan, 1997.
2. *Europe's Economic Dilemma* by John Mills. London: Macmillan, 1998.
3. *America's Soluble Problems* by John Mills. London: Macmillan, 1999.

Chapter 1

1. Page 13 in *The Age of Diminished Expectations* by Paul Krugman. Cambridge, Mass: MIT Press, 1990.
2. Table G-3 in *Monitoring the World Economy 1820–1992* by Angus Maddison. Paris: OECD, 1995.
3. *The Limits to Growth.* Club of Rome Report. Potomac Associates, 1972.
4. Pages 26 and 27 in *National Accounts 1960–1992*. Paris: OECD, 1994, supplemented by page 19 in *Main Economic Indicators*. Paris: OECD, 1998, and Table 0101 in *Eurostatistics*. Luxembourg: European Union, 1999.
5. ILO Labour Force Surveys.
6. Table B-35 in *Economic Report of the President*. Washington DC: US Government Printing Office, 1999.
7. Ibid, Tables B-9 and B35.
8. Table 747 in *Statistical Abstract of the United States*, Washington DC: US Department of Commerce, 1998.
9. Table B-42 in *Economic Report of the President*. Washington DC: US Government Printing Office, 1999.
10. All figures taken from Table D-1a in *Monitoring the World Economy 1820–1992* by Angus Maddison. Paris: OECD, 1995.
11. Ibid, Table B-10a.
12. Ibid, Tables D-1a and B-10a.
13. Ibid, Table B-10e.
14. Table 33 in *Trade and Development Report*, 1997. New York and Geneva: United Nations, 1997.
15. All the preceding data in this paragraph is from *Hutchinson's Encyclopedia*, Oxford: Helicon, 1998, page 867.
16. Newspaper reports in April 1999 indicated that Bill Gates of Microsoft had personal assets worth in excess of $100bn.
17. Page 133 in *A History of Europe* by J.M. Roberts. Oxford: Helicon, 1996.
18. Accounts of all these developments are to be found in *The Discoverers* by Daniel J. Boorstin. New York and London: Penguin, 1983.
19. Page 53 in *A History of Economics* by John Kenneth Galbraith. London: Penguin Group, 1987.
20. Table 33, page 108, and accompanying text in *Trade and Development Report, 1997*. New York and Geneva: The United Nations, 1997.

21. See *Butterfly Economics* by Paul Ormerod. London: Faber and Faber, 1998, for a devastating criticism of the ineffectiveness of short-term fiscal changes on controlling the macro-economy.

Chapter 2

1. Table G-2 in *Monitoring the World Economy 1820–1992* by Angus Maddison. Paris: OECD, 1995.
2. Tables 11.13 and 11.14 in *Trends and Statistics in International Trade*. Geneva: World Trade Organisation, 1995.
3. Table US.11 in *Economic Statistics 1900–1983* by Thelma Liesner. London: *The Economist*, 1985.
4. Tables B-13, B-46 and B-100 in *Economic Report of the President*. Washington DC: US Government Printing Office, 1999.
5. Calculated from the figures in Table 2.3.
6. Table US.1 in *Economic Statistics 1900–1983* by Thelma Liesner. London: *The Economist*, 1985.
7. Table D, page 19 in *Historical Statistics 1960–1986*. Paris: OECD, 1998.
8. Ibid.
9. Table 0601 in *Eurostatistics*. Luxembourg: European Union, 1999.
10. Table B-110 in *Economic Report of the President*. Washington DC: Government Printing Office, 1999.
11. Page 182 in *International Financial Statistics Yearbook*. Washington DC: IMF, 1979.
12. Ibid, pages 182 and 183.
13. *The Rise and Decline of Nations* by Mancur Olson. New Haven and London: Yale University Press, 1982.

Chapter 3

1. Table 5.1, page 100 and succeeding pages in *Guns, Germs and Steel* by Jared Diamond. London: Jonathan Cape, 1997.
2. The description of the development of credit and money in this section draws heavily on an as yet unpublished work by Christopher Meakin and Geoffrey Gardiner.
3. Pages 242 and 276 in *Hutchinson's Encyclopedia*. Oxford: Helicon, 1998.
4. Page 54 in *American Economic History* by John O'Sullivan and Edward F. Keuchel. Princeton and New York: Markus Wiener Publishing, 1989.
5. Page 1009 in *Hutchinson's Encyclopedia*, Oxford: Helicon, 1998.
6. Ibid, page 390.
7. Page 29 in *Frozen Desire* by James Buchan. London: Picador, 1997.
8. Page 96 in *Hutchinson's Encyclopedia*. Oxford: Helicon, 1998.
9. Page 96 in *The Wealth and Poverty of Nations* by David Landes. London: Little, Brown, 1998.
10. Pages 283–5 in *Economic History of Europe* by Herbert Heaton. New York and London: Harper Bros, 1935.
11. Page 310 in *A History of Europe* by J.M. Roberts. Oxford: Helicon, 1996.

12. Page 168 in *The Death of Inflation* by Roger Bootle. London: Nicholas Brealey, 1996.
13. Calculation from Shaun Stewart.
14. Table B-10a in *Monitoring the World Economy 1820–1992* by Angus Maddison. Paris: OECD, 1995.
15. Page 673 in *Economic History of Europe* by Herbert Heaton. New York and London: Harper Bros, 1935.
16. Page 390 in *Economic Development in Europe* by Clive Day. New York: Macmillan, 1946.
17. Statistics provided by Shaun Stewart.
18. Figures calculated from Table B-10a in *Monitoring the World Economy 1820–1992* by Angus Maddison. Paris: OECD, 1995.
19. Ibid, Table D-1a.
20. Tables UK.3 and G.2 in *Economic Statistics 1900–1983* by Thelma Liesner. London: *The Economist*, 1985.
21. Ibid, Tables UK.3 and G.2.
22. Table A-2 in *Monitoring the World Economy 1820–1992* by Angus Maddison. Paris: OECD, 1995.
23. Pages 12 and 13 in *American Economic History* by John O'Sullivan and Edward F. Keuchel. Princeton and New York: Markus Wiener Publishing, 1989.
24. Ibid, page 49.
25. Table C88–114 in *Historical Statistics of the United States*. Washington DC: US Department of Commerce, 1960.
26. Table B-16a in *Monitoring the World Economy 1820–1992* by Angus Maddison. Paris: OECD, 1995.
27. Ibid, Tables B-10a and D-1a.
28. Ibid, Table A-3a.
29. Ibid, Table C-16a.
30. Page 116 in *American Economic History* by John O'Sullivan and Edward F. Keuchel. Princeton and New York: Markus Wiener Publishing, 1989.
31. Figure 3.2 page 76 in *Monitoring the World Economy 1820–1992* by Angus Maddison. Paris: OECD, 1995.
32. Ibid, Table D-1a.
33. Ibid, Table C-16a.
34. Various tables in *Historical Statistics of the United States*. Washington DC: US Department of Commerce, 1960.
35. Table K-1 in *Monitoring the World Economy 1820–1992* by Angus Maddison. Paris: OECD, 1995.
36. Ibid, pages 40–2.
37. Table B-46 in *Economic Report of the President*. Washington DC: US Government Printing Office, 1999.
38. Pages 67 and 68 in *American Economic History* by John O'Sullivan and Edward F. Keuchel. Princeton and New York: Markus Wiener Publishing, 1989.
39. Ibid, pages 69 and 70.
40. Page 320 in *A History of the American People* by Paul Johnson. London: Weidenfeld and Nicolson, 1997.
41. Tables E1–12 and E13–24 in *Historical Statistics of the United States*. Washington DC: US Department of Commerce, 1960.

42. Page 57 in *American Economic History* by John O'Sullivan and Edward F. Keuchel. Princeton and New York: Markus Wiener Publishing, 1989.
43. Ibid, page 345.
44. Table U1–14 in *Historical Statistics of the United States*. Washington DC: US Department of Commerce, 1960.
45. Table B-1 in *Economic Report of the President*. Washington DC: US Government Printing Office, 1999.
46. Page 464 in *A History of the American People* by Paul Johnson. London: Weidenfeld and Nicolson, 1997.
47. Table I-2 in *Monitoring the World Economy 1820–1992* by Angus Maddison. Paris: OECD, 1995.
48. Ibid, Table K-1.
49. A series of tables in Part 1 of *The Productivity Race* by S.N. Broadberry. Cambridge: Cambridge University Press, 1997.
50. Table E-2 in *Monitoring the World Economy 1820–1992* by Angus Maddison. Paris: OECD, 1995.

Chapter 4

1. Page 1156 in *Hutchinson's Encyclopedia*. Oxford: Helicon, 1998.
2. Page 331 in *The End of History and the Last Man* by Francis Fukuyama. London: Penguin, 1992.
3. Calculated from figures in Table UK.1 in *Economic Statistics 1900–1983* by Thelma Liesner. London: *The Economist*, 1985.
4. Ibid, Table US.1.
5. Ibid, Tables US.7, UK.7, F.3 and G.3.
6. Page 1155 in *Hutchinson's Encyclopedia*. Oxford: Helicon, 1998.
7. Table F.2 in *Economic Statistics 1900–1983* by Thelma Liesner. London: *The Economist*, 1985.
8. Ibid, Table G.2.
9. Ibid, Table UK.2.
10. For a full account see *The Great Inflation* by William Guttmann and Patricia Meehan. Farnborough: Saxon House, 1975.
11. Table G.3 in *Economic Statistics 1900–1983* by Thelma Liesner. London: *The Economist*, 1985.
12. Ibid, Table F.2.
13. Ibid, Tables G.1 and G.2.
14. Ibid, Tables G.1 and G.2.
15. Ibid, Table G.6.
16. Ibid, Tables UK.1, UK.2 and UK.10.
17. Page 73 in *The European Economy 1914–1990* by Derek H. Aldcroft. London: Croom Helm, 1993.
18. Table G.6 in *Economic Statistics 1900–1983* by Thelma Liesner. London: *The Economist*, 1985.
19. Ibid, Table G.1.
20. Page 85 in *The European Economy 1914–1990* by Derek H. Aldcroft. London: Croom Helm, 1993.

21. Table G.1 in *Economic Statistics 1900–1983* by Thelma Liesner. London: *The Economist*, 1985.
22. Ibid, Table G.3.
23. Ibid, Table G.1.
24. Ibid, Table UK.15.
25. Calculations by Shaun Stewart.
26. Table UK.2 in *Economic Statistics 1900–1983* by Thelma Liesner. London: *The Economist*, 1985.
27. Ibid, Table UK.9.
28. Ibid, Table UK.7.
29. Ibid, Table UK.2.
30. Ibid, Table UK.15.
31. Note from Shaun Stewart.
32. Tables F.1, F.2 and F.6 in *Economic Statistics 1900–1983* by Thelma Liesner. London: *The Economist*, 1985.
33. Ibid, Tables F.2, G.2 and UK.3.
34. Table US.1 in *Economic Statistics 1900–1983* by Thelma Liesner. London: *The Economist*, 1985.
35. Ibid, Tables US.1, US.2 and US.9.
36. Page 163 in *American Economic History* by John O'Sullivan and Edward F. Keuchel. Princeton and New York: Markus Wiener Publishing, 1989.
37. Tables US.1, US.6 and US.7 in *Economic Statistics 1900–1983* by Thelma Liesner. London: *The Economist*, 1985.
38. Page 165 in *American Economic History* by John O'Sullivan and Edward F. Keuchel. Princeton and New York: Markus Wiener Publishing, 1989.
39. Ibid, page 167.
40. Tables US.1, US.2 and US.10 in *Economic Statistics 1900–1983* by Thelma Liesner. London: *The Economist*, 1985.
41. Chapter 10 in *American Economic History* by John O'Sullivan and Edward F. Keuchel. Princeton and New York: Markus Wiener Publishing, 1989.
42. Table US.15 in *Economic Statistics 1900–1983* by Thelma Liesner. London: *The Economist*, 1985.
43. Ibid, Tables US.1, US.2 and US.10.
44. Page 187 in *American Economic History* by John O'Sullivan and Edward F. Keuchel. Princeton and New York: Markus Wiener Publishing, 1989.
45. Table US.7 in *Economic Statistics 1900–1983* by Thelma Liesner. London: *The Economist*, 1985.
46. Page 187 in *American Economic History* by John O'Sullivan and Edward F. Keuchel. Princeton and New York: Markus Wiener Publishing, 1989.
47. Tables US.1 and US. 2 in *Economic Statistics 1900–1983* by Thelma Liesner. London: *The Economist*, 1985.
48. Ibid, Tables US.1, US.2, US.7 and US.9.
49. Table B-10a in *Monitoring the World Economy 1820–1992* by Angus Maddison. Paris: OECD, 1995.
50. Page 169 in *Towards True Monetarism* by Geoffrey Gardiner. London: The Dulwich Press, 1993.
51. Pages 233–5 of *A History of Economics* by John Kenneth Galbraith. London: Penguin, 1987.

52. *The Economic Consequences of Mr Churchill* by John Maynard Keynes. London: Published by Leonard and Virginia Woolf at The Hogarth Press, 1925.
53. House of Lords Record of Debates.
54. Page 239 in *A History of the World Economy* by James Foreman-Peck. Hemel Hempstead: Harvester Wheatsheaf, 1995.
55. Ibid, page 239 *et seq*.
56. Table G-2 in *Monitoring the World Economy 1820–1992* by Angus Maddison. Paris: OECD, 1995.
57. Ibid, Table C-16a.
58. Ibid.
59. Page 157 in *International Financial Statistics Yearbook*. Washington DC: IMF, 1998.

Chapter 5

1. Table G.2 in *Economic Statistics 1900–1983* by Thelma Liesner, London: *The Economist*, 1985.
2. Ibid, Tables UK.2 and F.2.
3. Ibid, Tables G.1, G.2 and G.7.
4. Ibid, Tables F.1, F.2 and F.7.
5. Ibid, Table UK.1.
6. Ibid, Table UK.15.
7. Ibid, Tables UK.1, UK.2, F.1, F2, G.1,G.2, It.1 and It.2.
8. Page 173 in *Treaties establishing the European Communities*. Luxembourg: Office for Official Publications of the European Communities, 1973.
9. Page 23 in *The New European Economy* by Loukas Tsoulakis. Oxford: Oxford University Press, 1993.
10. Table UK.1 in *Economic Statistics 1900–1983* by Thelma Liesner. London: *The Economist*, 1985.
11. EC and UK Tables in *National Accounts 1960–1992*. Paris: OECD, 1994.
12. Page 450 in *National Accounts of OECD Countries 1953–1969*. Paris: OECD, 1960.
13. Table US.1 in *Monitoring the World Economy 1820–1992* by Angus Maddison. Paris: OECD, 1995.
14. Ibid, Tables 16-a and G-2.
15. Table US.14 in *Economic Statistics 1900–1983* by Thelma Liesner. London: *The Economist*, 1985.
16. Ibid, Table US.11.
17. Ibid, Table US.11.
18. Ibid, Table US.9.
19. Table I-2 in *Monitoring the World Economy 1820–1992* by Angus Maddison. Paris: OECD, 1995.
20. Tables B-79 and B-80 in *Economic Report of the President*. Washington DC: US Government Printing Office, 1999.
21. Ibid, Tables B-1 and B-29.
22. Ibid, Table B-79.
23. Ibid, Table B-80.
24. Ibid, Table B-2.

25. Ibid, Table B-5.
26. Ibid, Table B-2.
27. Page 245 in *American Economic History* by John O'Sullivan and Edward F. Keuchel. Princeton and New York: Markus Wiener Publishing, 1989.
28. Table B-63 in *Economic Report of the President*. Washington DC: US Government Printing Office, 1999.
29. Ibid, Table B-103.
30. Table US.11 in *Economic Statistics 1900–1983* by Thelma Liesner. London: *The Economist*, 1985.
31. Table B-63 in *Economic Report of the President*. Washington DC: US Government Printing Office, 1999.
32. Ibid, Table B-35.
33. Ibid, Table B-103.
34. Page 154 in *National Accounts 1960–1992*. Paris: OECD, 1994.
35. Table G-2 in *Monitoring the World Economy 1820–1992* by Angus Maddison. Paris: OECD, 1995.
36. Page 172 in *International Financial Statistics Yearbook*. Washington DC: IMF, 1998.
37. Table B-4 in *Economic Report of the President*. Washington DC: US Government Printing Office, 1999.
38. Ibid, Table B-35.
39. Ibid, Table B-63.
40. Page 52 *et seq* in *Monitoring the World Economy 1820–1992* by Angus Maddison. Paris: OECD, 1995.
41. Ibid, Tables D-1a and D-1e.
42. Page 569, *Hutchinson's Encyclopedia*, Oxford: Helicon, 1998.
43. Chapter 23 in *The Wealth and Poverty of Nations* by David Landes. London: Little Brown, 1998.
44. Page 53 in *Monitoring the World Economy 1820–1992* by Angus Maddison. Paris: OECD, 1995.
45. Ibid, Table C-16a.
46. Page 379 in *The Wealth and Poverty of Nations* by David Landes. London: Little, Brown, 1998.
47. Table C-16a in *Monitoring the World Economy 1820–1992* by Angus Maddison. Paris: OECD, 1995.
48. Ibid, Table B-16a.
49. Page 196 in *A History of the World Economy* by James Foreman-Peck. Hemel Hempstead: Harvester Wheatsheaf, 1995.
50. Table B-16a in *Monitoring the World Economy 1820–1992* by Angus Maddison. Paris: OECD, 1995.
51. Ibid, Table D-1a.
52. Table J.5 in *Economic Statistics 1900–1983*, by Thelma Liesner. London: *The Economist*, 1985.
53. Table D-1a in *Monitoring the World Economy 1820–1992* by Angus Maddison. Paris: OECD, 1995.
54. Page 245 in *A History of the World Economy* by James Foreman-Peck. Hemel Hempstead: Harvester Wheatsheaf, 1995.
55. Table J.2 in *Economic Statistics 1900–1983*, by Thelma Liesner. London: *The Economist*, 1985.

56. Page 569, *Hutchinson's Encyclopedia*, Oxford: Helicon, 1998.
57. Table I-2 in *Monitoring the World Economy 1820–1992* by Angus Maddison. Paris: OECD, 1995.
58. Ibid, Tables I-2 and I-4.
59. Table J.2 in *Economic Statistics 1900–1983*, by Thelma Liesner. London: *The Economist*, 1985.
60. Table C-16a in *Monitoring the World Economy 1820–1992* by Angus Maddison. Paris: OECD, 1995.
61. Ibid, Table A-3a.
62. Ibid, Table D-1a.
63. Page 154 in *National Accounts 1960–1992*. Paris: OECD 1994.
64. Answer to a Parliamentary Question..
65. Table 3.19 in *Monitoring the World Economy 1820–1992* by Angus Maddison. Paris: OECD, 1995.
66. Table 8.15, *Historical Statistics*. Paris: OECD, 1988.
67. Table B-110 in *Economic Report of the President*. Washington DC: US Government Printing Office, 1999.
68. Page 525, *International Financial Statistics Yearbook*. Washington DC: IMF, 1998.
69. Ibid, pages 522 and 523.
70. Ibid, pages 524 and 525.
71. Table C-16c in *Monitoring the World Economy 1820–1992* by Angus Maddison. Paris: OECD, 1995.
72. Ibid, Table 3–4.
73. Ibid, Tables D-1a and D-1c.
74. Ibid, Table B-10c.
75. Page 1088 in *Hutchinson's Encyclopedia*. Oxford: Helicon, 1998.
76. Table C-16c in *Monitoring the World Economy 1820–1992* by Angus Maddison. Paris: OECD, 1995.
77. Page 1088 in *Hutchinson's Encyclopedia*. Oxford: Helicon, 1998.
78. Table C-16c in *Monitoring the World Economy 1820–1992* by Angus Maddison. Paris: OECD, 1995.
79. Ibid.
80. Page 28 in *The End of History and the Last Man* by Francis Fukuyama. London: Penguin, 1992.
81. Table C-16c in *Monitoring the World Economy 1820–1992* by Angus Maddison. Paris: OECD, 1995.
82. Ibid, Table D-1c.
83. Page 1088 in *Hutchinson's Encyclopedia*. Oxford: Helicon, 1998.
84. Page 133 in *Monitoring the World Economy 1820–1992* by Angus Maddison. Paris: OECD, 1995.
85. Ibid, Table B-10c.
86. Table 1–2 in *Monitoring the World Economy 1820–1992* by Angus Maddison. Paris: OECD, 1995.
87. Ibid, Table 1–3.
88. Ibid, Table 3–1.
89. Ibid, Table 1–3.
90. Ibid, Table 3–17.
91. Ibid, Table 1–3.

92. Ibid, Table 3–1.
93. Ibid, Table G-1.
94. Ibid, Table G-3.
95. Pages 220, 534 and 1033 in *Hutchinson's Encyclopedia*. Oxford: Helicon, 1998.
96. Tables D-1b, D-1d, D-1e, I-1 and I-2 in *Monitoring the World Economy 1820–1992* by Angus Maddison. Paris: OECD, 1995.

Chapter 6

1. Pages 174 to 177 in *Main Economic Indicators*. Paris: OECD, 1999.
2. Table 20, pages 128 and 129 in *National Accounts 1960–1992*. Paris: OECD, 1994.
3. Table US.11 in *Economic Statistics 1900–1983* by Thelma Liesner. London: *The Economist*, 1985.
4. Ibid, Tables US.3 and J.2.
5. Table 318 in *Statistical Abstract of the United States*. Washington DC: US Department of Commerce, 1998.
6. Table 5.2, page 228 in *Economic Trends 1996/97 Annual Supplement*. London: Office for National Statistics 1997.
7. Pages 88 and 89 in *International Financial Statistics*. Washington DC: IMF, 1998.
8. Various tables in *National Accounts 1953–1969* and *National Accounts 1960–1992*. Paris: OECD, 1971 and 1994.
9. Table 0601, *Eurostatistics* 03/99. Luxembourg: The European Community, 1999.
10. ILO Labour Force Survey reports.
11. Tables G-2 and C-16a in *Monitoring the World Economy 1820–1992* by Angus Maddison. Paris: OECD, 1995.
12. Page 176 in *International Financial Statistics Yearbook*. Washington DC: IMF, 1998.
13. Pages 20 and 21 in *National Accounts 1960–1992*. Paris: OECD, 1994.
14. Page 122 in *International Financial Statistics Yearbook*. Washington DC: IMF, 1998.
15. Page 272 in *The Economics of Europe* by Edward Nevin. London: Macmillan, 1994.
16. Ibid, pages 273 and 274.
17. Ibid, page 275.
18. Page 122 in *International Financial Statistics Yearbook*. Washington DC: IMF, 1998.
19. Tables 0943 and 0955 in *Eurostatistics* 5/88. Luxembourg: The European Community, 1988.
20. Table C-16a in *Monitoring the World Economy 1820–1992* by Angus Maddison. Paris: OECD, 1994; and Table 0101 in *Eurostatistics* 4/99. Luxembourg: The European Community, 1999.
21. Pages 17 and 33 in *National Accounts 1960–1992*. Paris: OECD, 1994.
22. Table D-1a in *Monitoring the World Economy 1820–1992* by Angus Maddison. Paris: OECD, 1995.
23. Page 123 in *National Accounts 1960–1992*. Paris: OECD, 1994.

24. Page 172 in *International Financial Statistics Yearbook*. Washington DC: IMF, 1998.
25. Table US.11 in *Economic Statistics 1900–1983* by Thelma Liesner. London: *The Economist*, 1985.
26. Table B-103 in *Economic Report of the President*. Washington DC: US Government Printing Office, 1999.
27. Ibid, Table B-73.
28. Ibid, Broad Index in Table B-110.
29. Table D-1a in *Monitoring the World Economy 1820–1992* by Angus Maddison. Paris: OECD, 1995.
30. Table B-12 in *Economic Report of the President*. Washington DC: US Government Printing Office, 1999.
31. Ibid, Table B-46.
32. Ibid, Tables B-1 and B-32.
33. Tables C-16a and D-1a in *Monitoring the World Economy 1820–1992* by Angus Maddison. Paris: OECD, 1995.
34. Table B-47 in *Economic Report of the President*. Washington DC: US Government Printing Office, 1999.
35. Ibid.
36. Table 747 in *Statistical Abstract of the United States*. Washington DC: US Department of Commerce, 1998.
37. Ibid, Table 757.
38. Ibid, Table 764.
39. Ibid, Table 747.
40. Table B-95 in *Economic Report of the President*. Washington DC: US Government Printing Office, 1999.
41. Ibid, Table B-1.
42. Ibid, Table B-96.
43. Table B-79 in *Economic Report of the President*. Washington DC: US Government Printing Office, 1999.
44. Ibid, Table B-20.
45. Table B-21 in *Economic Report of the President*. Washington DC: US Government Printing Office, 1998.
46. Table B-83 in *Economic Report of the President*. Washington DC: US Government Printing Office, 1999.
47. Ibid, Tables B-1 and B-87.
48. Ibid, Table 103.
49. Ibid, Table 104.
50. Table 1295, page 791 in *Statistical Abstract of the United States*. Washington DC: US Department of Commerce, 1997.
51. Table 1305, page 789 in *Statistical Abstract of the United States*. Washington DC: US Department of Commerce, 1998.
52. Tables B-69 and B-1 in *Economic Report of the President*. Washington DC: US Government Printing Office, 1999.
53. Table B-32 in *Economic Report of the President*. Washington DC: US Government Printing Office, 1999.
54. Ibid, Table B-103.
55. Ibid, Table B-2.
56. Ibid, Table B-103.

57. Ibid, Table B-110.
58. Ibid, Table B-43.
59. Ibid, Table B-63.
60. Ibid, Table B-2.
61. Ibid, Table B-35.
62. Table B-63 in *Economic Report of the President*. Washington DC: US Government Printing Office, 1999.
63. Ibid, Table B-42.
64. Ibid, Table B-78.
65. Ibid, Table B-110.
66. Ibid, Table B-103.
67. Ibid.
68. Page 173 in *International Financial Statistics,* Washington DC: IMF, 1998.
69. Based on Table G-2 in *Monitoring the World Economy 1820–1992*, by Angus Maddison. Paris: OECD, 1995.
70. Table 11.13 in *Trends and Statistics – International Trade*. Geneva: World Trade Organisation, 1995.
71. Tables A-3e, F-4 and G-1 in *Monitoring the World Economy 1820–1992*, by Angus Maddison. Paris: OECD, 1995.
72. Ibid, Table I-2.
73. Pages 162/163 in *International Financial Statistics Yearbook*. Washington DC: IMF, 1998.
74. Ibid, pages 542/543.
75. Table 28 in *Trade and Development Report*. Geneva: United Nations, 1997.
76. Table 25, page 200 in *Human Development Report 1997*. New York and Oxford: Oxford University Press for the United Nations Development Programme, 1997.
77. Table 2–9 in *Monitoring the World Economy 1820–1992*, by Angus Maddison. Paris: OECD, 1995.
78. Table 33 in *Trade and Development Report*. Geneva: United Nations, 1997.
79. Various entries in *Hutchinson's Encyclopedia*. Oxford: Helicon, 1998.
80. Page 157 in *International Financial Statistics Yearbook*. Washington DC: IMF, 1998.
81. Table 6.3.
82. Page 849 in *International Financial Statistics Yearbook*. Washington DC: IMF, 1998.
83. Ibid, page 845.
84. Ibid, page 523.
85. Ibid, pages 525, 849, 545, 723 and 601.
86. Ibid, page 599.

Chapter 7

1. Tables 0201 and 0601 in *Eurostatistics*. Luxembourg: European Union, 1999.
2. Table B-35 in *Economic Report of the President*. Washington DC: US Government Printing Office, 1999.
3. Ibid, Tables B-1 and B-35.
4. Tables 0101, 0201 and 2401 in *Eurostatistics*. Luxembourg: European Union, 1999.

5. Page 154 *et seq* in *Trade and Development Report, 1997*. Geneva: The United Nations, 1997.
6. ILO Labour Force Surveys.
7. Ibid.
8. Table B-35 in *Economic Report of the President*. Washington DC: US Government Printing Office, 1999.
9. Various Tables in *Labour Force Statistics 1970–1990*, Paris: OECD, 1992, and Table 0203 in *Eurostatistics*, Luxembourg: European Union, 1999.
10. Table B-34 in *Economic Report of the President*. Washington DC: US Government Printing Office, 1999.
11. Population figures by country in *International Financial Statistics Yearbook*. Washington DC: IMF, 1998.
12. Tables 0202 and 0601 in *Eurostatistics*. Luxembourg: European Union, 1999.
13. ILO Labour Force Surveys.
14. Table C-16 in *Monitoring the World Economy 1820–1992* by Angus Maddison. Paris: OECD, 1995; tables for all EU countries in *International Financial Statistics*. Washington DC: IMF, 1998.
15. Various Tables in *Labour Force Statistics 1970–1990*, Paris: OECD, 1992, and Table 0203 in *Eurostatistics*, Luxembourg: European Union, 1999.
16. Table 2.15 in *Historical Statistics 1960–1986*. Paris: OECD, 1988.
17. Table 0601 in *Eurostatistics*. Luxembourg: European Union, 1999.
18. Table B-35 in *Economic Report of the President*. Washington DC: US Government Printing Office, 1999.
19. Various Tables in *Labour Force Statistics 1970–1990*, Paris: OECD, 1992, and Table 0203 in *Eurostatistics*, Luxembourg: European Union, 1999.
20. Calculated from Tables B-2 and B-35 in *Economic Report of the President*. Washington DC: US Government Printing Office, 1999.
21. ILO Labour Force Surveys.
22. Tables B-44 and B45 in *Economic Report of the President*. Washington DC: US Government Printing Office, 1999.
23. Confirmed on page 16 of *Employment in Europe*. Luxembourg: European Commission, 1997.
24. Successive *Economic Reports to the President*. Washington DC: US Government Printing Office. Various years.
25. *Employment Policy Institute Economic Report* Vol. 9, No. 9, November 1995.
26. The subject of a number of best-selling books, as well as official reports.
27. Page 63 in *International Finance* by Keith Pilbeam. London: Macmillan, 1994, contains a table summarising recent research findings on import and export elasticities over a large number of developed and developing countries.
28. Table 0601 in *Eurostatistics*. Luxembourg: The European Union, December 1998.
29. Broad Real Index from Table B-110 in *Economic Report of the President*. Washington DC: US Government Printing Office, 1999.
30. Ibid.

Chapter 8

1. Pages 159 and 161 in *International Financial Statistics*. Washington DC: IMF, 1998.

2. Pages 58 and 59 in *International Financial Statistics*. Washington DC: IMF, 1979.
3. Page 31 in *Debt and Delusion* by Peter Warburton. London: Allen Lane The Penguin Press, 1999.
4. Country by country tables in *International Financial Statistics Yearbook*. Washington DC: IMF, 1998.
5. Answer to a Parliamentary Question.
6. Pages 122 and 123 in *International Financial Statistics Yearbook*. Washington DC: IMF, 1998.
7. Ibid.
8. Ibid.
9. Ibid.
10. Ibid.
11. Ibid, pages 100 and 101.
12. Tables B-1 and B-69 in *Economic Report of the President*. Washington DC: US Government Printing Office, 1999.
13. Calculation by Shaun Stewart.
14. Tables B-69 and B1 in *Economic Report of the President*. Washington DC: US Government Printing Office, 1999.
15. Table 324 in *Statistical Abstract of the United States*. Washington DC: US Department of Commerce, 1998.
16. Information obtained from the German Embassy in London.
17. Information obtained from the Japanese Embassy in London.
18. Table 5.8 in the *Annual Abstract of Statistics*. London: Central Statistical Office, 1995.
19. ILO Labour Force Surveys.
20. Country by country tables in *National Accounts of OECD Countries 1953–1969*. Paris: OECD, 1970.

Chapter 9

1. Pages 261 and 262 in *Peddling Prosperity* by Paul R. Krugman. New York and London: W.W. Norton & Co., 1994.
2. Table 687 in *Statistical Abstract of the United States*, Washington DC: Department of Commerce, 1998.
3. See *Rethinking International Trade* by Paul R. Krugman, Cambridge, Mass. and London: MIT Press, 1994, for a full discussion of this topic.
4. Page 525 in *International Financial Statistics*. Washington DC: IMF, 1998.
5. Well described in *The State We're In* by Will Hutton. London: Vintage, 1995.

Bibliography

Aldcroft, Derek H. *The European Economy 1914–90*, London: Routledge, 1993.

Aldcroft, Derek H. and Ville, Simon P. *The European Economy 1750–1914*, Manchester: Manchester University Press, 1994.

Ayres, Robert U. *Technological Forecasting and Long Range Planning*, New York etc: McGraw Hill Book Company, 1969.

Bainbridge, Timothy and Teasdale, Anthony *The Penguin Companion to the European Union*, London: Penguin, 1996.

Bairoch, Paul *Economics and World History – Myths and Paradoxes*, Chicago: Chicago University Press, 1993.

Barro, Robert J. *Determinants of Economic Growth*, Boston: Massachusetts Institute of Technology, 1999.

Beckerman, Wilfrid *In Defence of Economic Growth*, London: Jonathan Cape, 1974.

Beckerman, Wilfrid *Small is Stupid: Blowing the Whistle on the Greens*, London: Duckworth, 1995.

Beloff, Lord *Britain and the European Union: Dialogue of the Deaf*, London: Macmillan – now Palgrave Macmillan, 1996.

Bernstein, Peter L. *Against the Gods – The Remarkable Story of Risk*, New York: John Wiley & Sons, 1996.

Blaug, Mark *Economic History and the History of Economics*, New York etc: Harvester Wheatsheaf, 1986.

Blaug, Mark *Economic Theory in Retrospect*, Cambridge: Cambridge University Press, 1996.

Blinder, Alan S. *Hard Hearts Soft Heads*, Reading, Mass: Addison-Wesley, 1987.

Block, Fred L. *The Origins of International Economic Disorder*, Berkeley, Los Angeles and London: University of California Press, 1977.

Boorstin, Daniel J. *The Discoverers*, New York and London: Penguin, 1983.

Booker, Christopher and North, Richard *The Castle of Lies*, London: Duckworth, 1996.

Bootle, Roger *The Death of Inflation*, London: Nicholas Brealey, 1996.

Brandt Commission *North–South Co-operation for World Recovery*, London and Sydney: Pan Books, 1983.

Brittan, Samuel *The Price of Economic Freedom*, London: Macmillan – now Palgrave Macmillan, 1970.

Brittan, Samuel *Is there an Economic Consensus?*, London: Macmillan – now Palgrave Macmillan, 1973.

Brittan, Samuel *A Restatement of Economic Liberalism*, London: Macmillan – now Palgrave Macmillan, 1988.

Brittan, Samuel *Capitalism with a Human Face*, London: Fontana Press, 1995.

Broadberry, S.N. *The Productivity Race*, Cambridge: Cambridge University Press, 1997.

Burkitt, Brian and Baimbridge, Mark *What 1992 Really Means*, London: British Anti-Common Market Campaign, 1989.

Burkitt, Brian, Baimbridge, Mark and Whyman, Philip *There is an Alternative*, London: Campaign for an Independent Britain, 1996.

Buchan, James *Frozen Desire – An Inquiry into the Meaning of Money*, London: Picador, 1997.

Caves, Richard E. *Britain's Economic Prospects*, Washington: The Brookings Institution, 1968.

Coates, Ken and Santer, Jacques *Dear Commissioner – An Exchange of Letters*, Nottingham: Spokesman Books, 1996.

Chafe, William H. *The Unfinished Journey: America Since World War II*, New York and Oxford: Oxford University Press, 1995.

Chowdhury, Anis and Islam, Iyanatul *The Newly Industrialising Economies of East Asia*, London and New York: Routledge, 1995.

Connolly, Bernard *The Rotten Heart of Europe*, London: Faber and Faber, 1995.

Crosland, C.A.R. *The Future of Socialism*, London: Jonathan Cape, 1956.

Davies, Norman *Europe – A History*, Oxford: Oxford University Press, 1996.

Denison, Edward F. *Why Growth Rates Differ*, Washington DC: The Brookings Institution, 1969.

Denison, Edward F. *Accounting for United States Growth 1929–1969*, Washington DC: The Brookings Institution, 1974.

Denison, Edward F. *Accounting for Slower Economic Growth*, Washington DC: The Brookings Institution, 1979.

Denman, Roy *Missed Chances: Britain and Europe in the Twentieth Century*, London: Cassell, 1996.

de Soto, Hernando *The Mystery of Capital*, London: Bantam Press, 2000.

Diamond, Jared *Guns, Germs and Steel*, London: Jonathan Cape, 1997.

Eichengreen, Barry *Globalizing Capital – A History of the International Monetary System*, Princeton, N.J.: Princeton University Press, 1996.

Einzig, Paul *The Case Against Joining the Common Market*, London: Macmillan, 1971.

Elliott, Larry and Atkinson, Dan *The Age of Insecurity*, London: Verso, 1998.

Eltis, Walter *Growth and Distribution*, London: Macmillan – now Palgrave Macmillan, 1973.

Feldstein, Martin *The Risk of Economic Crisis*, Chicago and London: The University of Chicago Press, 1991.

Ferris, Paul *Men and Money: Financial Europe Today*, London: Hutchinson, 1968.

Foreman-Peck, James *A History of the World Economy since 1850*, New York etc: Harvester Wheatsheaf, 1995.

Friedman, Irving S. *Inflation: A World-wide Disaster*, London: Hamish Hamilton, 1973.

Fukuyama, Francis *The End of History and the Last Man*, London: Penguin, 1992.

Galbraith, J.K. *The Affluent Society*, London: Hamish Hamilton, 1960.

Galbraith, J.K. *American Capitalism*, London: Hamish Hamilton, 1961.

Galbraith, J.K. *The New Industrial State*, London: Hamish Hamilton, 1968.

Galbraith, J.K. *Economics and the Public Purpose*, London: André Deutsch, 1974.

Galbraith, J.K. *Money – Whence It Came, Where It Went*, London: André Deutsch, 1975.

Galbraith, J.K. *A History of Economics*, London: Penguin, 1987.

Galbraith, J.K. *The Culture of Contentment*, London: Sinclair-Stevenson Ltd, 1992.

Galbraith, J.K. *The Good Society: The Humane Agenda*, Sinclair-Stevenson Ltd, 1996.

Gardiner, Geoffrey *Towards True Monetarism*, London: The Dulwich Press, 1993.

Goldsmith, James *The Trap*, London: Macmillan – now Palgrave Macmillan, 1994.

Gordon, David and Townsend, Peter *Breadline Europe: The Measurement of Poverty*, Bristol: The Policy Press, 2000.

Grieve Smith, John *Full Employment: A Pledge Betrayed*, London: Macmillan – now Palgrave Macmillan, 1997.

Gunther, John *Inside Europe Today*, London: Hamish Hamilton, 1961.

Guttmann, William and Meehan, Patricia *The Great Inflation*, Farnborough: Saxon House, 1975.

Hallett, Graham *The Social Economy of West Germany*, London: Macmillan – now Palgrave Macmillan, 1973.

Hama, Noriko *Disintegrating Europe*, London: Adamantine Press, 1996.

Harvey-Jones, John *Getting it Together*, London: Heinemann, 1991.

Hayek, F.A. *The Road to Serfdom*, London and Henley: Routledge & Kegan Paul, 1944.

Henderson, Callum *Asia Falling*, New York: McGraw-Hill, 1998.

Henig, Stanley *Political Parties in the European Community*, London: George Allen & Unwin, 1979.

Herman, Valentine and Lodge, Juliet *The European Parliament and the European Community*, London: Macmillan – now Palgrave Macmillan, 1978.

Hicks, John *Capital and Growth*, Oxford: Clarendon Press, 1965.

Hicks, John *A Theory of Economic History*, Oxford: Clarendon Press, 1969.

Hirsch, Fred *Money International*, London: Allen Lane, 1967.

Hirsch, Fred *Social Limits to Growth*, Cambridge, Mass: Harvard University Press, 1976.

Holland, Stuart *Out of Crisis: A Project for European Recovery*, Nottingham: Spokesman Books, 1983.

Holt, Stephen *Six European States*, London: Hamish Hamilton, 1970.

Howarth, Catherine *et al. Monitoring Poverty and Social Exclusion 1999*, York: The Rowntree Trust, 1999.

Hutchinson's Encyclopedia, Oxford: Helicon, 1998.

Hutton, Will *The State We're In*, London: Jonathan Cape, 1995.

Giddens, Anthony *The Third Way*, Cambridge: Polity Press, 1998.

Gray, John *False Dawn*, London: Granta Books, 1998.

Ito, Takatoshi *The Japanese Economy*, Cambridge, Mass. and London: The MIT Press, 1996.

Isard, Peter *Exchange Rate Economics*, Cambridge: Cambridge University Press, 1995.

Jamieson, Bill *Britain beyond Europe*, London: Duckworth, 1994.

Jay, Douglas *Sterling: A Plea for Moderation*, London: Sidgwick & Jackson, 1985.

Jay, Peter *Employment, Regions and Currencies*, London: Eurofacts, 1996.

Jay, Peter *Road to Riches or the Wealth of Man*, London: Weidenfeld and Nicolson, 2000.

Johnson, Christopher *In with the Euro, Out with the Pound*, London: Penguin, 1996.

Johnson, Paul *A History of the American People*, London: Weidenfeld and Nicolson, 1997.

Jones, E.L. *The European Miracle*, Cambridge: Cambridge University Press, 1993.

Keen, Steve *Debunking Economics*, London and New York: Zed Books, 2001.

Kemp, Tom *Industrialization in Nineteenth Century Europe*, London: Longman, 1994.

Kenny, Anthony *A Brief History of Western Philosophy*, Oxford: Blackwell, 1998.

Keynes, John Maynard *The Economic Consequences of Mr Churchill*, London: Hogarth Press, 1925.

Keynes, John Maynard *The General Theory of Employment, Interest and Money*, London: Macmillan, 1957 edition. First published 1936.

Kindleberger, Charles P. *World Economic Primacy 1500 to 1990*, New York and Oxford: Oxford University Press, 1996.

Krugman, Paul R. *The Age of Diminished Expectations*, Cambridge, Mass. and London: The MIT Press, 1990.

Krugman, Paul R. *Peddling Prosperity*, New York and London: Norton, 1994.

Krugman, Paul R. *Rethinking International Trade*, Cambridge, Mass. and London: The MIT Press, 1994.

Krugman, Paul R. *Strategic Trade Policy and the New International Economics*, Cambridge, Mass. and London: The MIT Press, 1995.

Krugman, Paul R. *The Self-Organizing Economy*, Malden, Mass. and Oxford: Blackwell, 1996.

Krugman, Paul R. *Pop Internationalism*, Cambridge, Mass. and London: The MIT Press, 1997.

Krugman, Paul R. *The Return of Depression Economics*, London: Allen Lane The Penguin Press, 1999.

Kuznets, Simon *Modern Economic Growth*, London: Yale University Press, 1965.

Lamont, Norman *Sovereign Britain*, London: Duckworth, 1995.

Landes, David *The Wealth and Poverty of Nations*, London: Little, Brown, 1998.

Lang, Tim and Hines, Colin *The New Protectionism*, London, Earthscan, 1993.

Layard, Richard *How to Beat Unemployment*, Oxford: Oxford University Press, 1986.

Leach, Rodney *Monetary Union – A Perilous Gamble*, London: Eurofacts, 1996.

Lingle, Christopher *The Rise & Decline of the Asian Century*, Hong Kong: Asia 2000, 1997.

Lipton, Michael *Assessing Economic Performance*, London: Staples Press, 1968.

Little, I.M.D. *A Critique of Welfare Economics*, Oxford: Oxford University Press, 1957.

Lomborg, Bjørn *The Skeptical Environmentalist*, Cambridge: Cambridge University Press, 2001.

Maddox, John *What Remains to be Discovered*, London: Macmillan – now Palgrave Macmillan, 1998.

Maynard, Geoffrey and van Ryckeghem, W. *A World of Inflation*, London: Batsford, 1976.

Maddison, Angus *Economic Growth in the West*, London: George Allen & Unwin, 1964.

Maddison, Angus *Economic Growth in Japan and the USSR*, London: George Allen & Unwin Ltd, 1969.

Maddison, Angus *Dynamic Forces in Capitalist Development*, Oxford: Oxford University Press, 1991.

Maddison, Angus *Monitoring the World Economy 1820–1992*, Paris: OECD, 1995.

Marris, Robin *How to Save the Underclass*, London: Macmillan – now Palgrave Macmillan, 1996.

Marsh, David *Reculer pour mieux sauter*, London: Prospect, 1997.

Mayhew, Nicholas *Sterling – the History of a Currency*, London: Penguin, 1999.

Mayne, Richard *The Recovery of Europe*, London: Weidenfeld & Nicolson, 1970.

Meade, James E. *The Intelligent Radical's Guide to Economic Policy*, London: George Allen & Unwin Ltd, 1975.

Michie, Jonathan and Grieve Smith, John *Unemployment in Europe*, London: Harcourt Brace, 1994.

Minford, Patrick *Markets not Stakes*, London: Orion Business Books, 1998.

Mishan, E.J. *21 Popular Economic Fallacies*, London: Allen Lane, 1969.

Mishel, Lawrence, Bernstein, Jared and Schmitt, John *The State of Working America 2000/2001*. New York: Cornell University Press, 2001.

Moggridge, D.E. *Maynard Keynes – An Economist's Biography*, London: Routledge, 1995.

Monti, Mario *The Single Market and Tomorrow's Europe*, London: Kogan Page, 1996.

Nevin, Edward *The Economics of Europe*, London: Macmillan – now Palgrave Macmillan, 1994.

North, Douglass C. *The Economic Growth of the United States 1790–1860*, New York and London: W.W. Norton & Co., 1966.

Nove, Alec *The Soviet Economy* London: George Allen & Unwin, 1961.

OECD *The Residual Factor and Economic Growth*, Paris: OECD, 1971.

Okita, Saburo *The Developing Economies and Japan*, Tokyo: University of Tokyo Press, 1980.

O'Leary, James J. *Stagnation or Healthy Growth? The Economic Challenge to the United States in the Nineties*, Lanham, New York, London: University Press of America, 1992.

Olson, Mancur *The Rise and Decline of Nations*, New Haven and London: Yale University Press, 1982.

Ormerod, Paul *The Death of Economics*, London: Faber and Faber, 1995.

Ormerod, Paul *Butterfly Economics*, London: Faber and Faber, 1998.

O'Sullivan, John and Keuchel, Edward F. *American Economic History: From Abundance to Constraint*, Princeton, N.J.: Markus Wiener Publishing Inc., 1989.

Patten, Chris *East and West*, London: Macmillan – now Palgrave Macmillan, 1998.

P.E.P. *Economic Planning and Policies in Britain, France and Germany*, London: George Allen & Unwin, 1968.

Pilbeam, Keith *International Finance*, London: Macmillan – now Palgrave Macmillan, 1994.

Pinder, John *The Economics of Europe*, London: Charles Knight, 1971.

Pinker, Stephen *How the Mind Works*, London: Allen Lane The Penguin Press, 1997.

Porter, Michael E. *et al. Can Japan Compete?* London: Macmillan – now Palgrave Macmillan, 2000.

Postan, M.M. *An Economic History of Western Europe 1945–1964*, London: Methuen, 1967.

Reader, John *Africa: A Biography of the Continent*, London: Penguin, 1998.

Robbins, Lord *Money, Trade and International Relations*, London: Macmillan – now Palgrave Macmillan, 1971.

Roberts, J.M. *The Hutchinson History of the World*, London: Hutchinson, 1976.

Roberts, J.M. *A History of Europe*, Oxford: Helicon, 1996.

Rohwer, Jim *Asia Arising*, London: Nicholas Brealey Publishing, 1996.

Roll, Eric *A History of Economic Thought*, London: Faber and Faber, 1973.

Rome, Club of *The Limits to Growth*, London: Potomac Associates, 1972.

Roney, Alex *EC/EU Fact Book*, London: Chamber of Commerce and Industry/Kogan Page, 1995.

Rostow, W.W. *Why the Poor Get Richer and the Rich Slow Down*, London: Macmillan – now Palgrave Macmillan, 1980.

Rostow, W.W. *The Stages of Economic Growth*, Cambridge: Cambridge University Press, 1960.

Salter, W.E.G. *Productivity and Technical Change*, Cambridge: Cambridge University Press, 1969.

Sampson, Anthony *The New Europeans*, London: Hodder and Stoughton, 1968.

Schonfield, Andrew *In Defence of the Mixed Economy*, Oxford: Oxford University Press, 1984.

Schumpeter, Joseph A. *Capital, Socialism and Democracy*, London: George Allen & Unwin, 1943.

Schumpeter, Joseph A. *History of Economic Analysis*, London: Routledge, 1997 reprint.

Sen, Amartya *On Ethics & Economics* Oxford: Blackwell, 1995.

Sen, Amartya *Development as Freedom*, Oxford: Oxford University Press, 1999.

Shonfield, Andrew *In Defence of the Mixed Economy* Oxford: Oxford University Press, 1984.

Singh, Jyoti Shankar *A New International Economic Order*, New York and London: Praeger Publishers, 1935.

Skousen, Mark *The Making of Modern Economics*, Armonk, New York and London: M.E. Sharpe, 2001.

Slichter, Sumner H. *Economic Growth in the United States*, Westport, Connecticut: Greenwood Press, 1961.

Smith, Adam *The Wealth of Nations Books I–III*, London: Penguin Books, 1997 edition. First published 1776.

Soros, George *The Crisis of Global Capitalism* London: Little, Brown and Company, 1998.

Spence, Jonathan *The Chan's Great Continent*, London: Allen Lane The Penguin Press, 1998.

Spiegel, Henry William *The Growth of Economic Thought*, Durham and London: Duke University Press, 1996.

Stein, Herbert *The Fiscal Revolution in America*, Chicago and London: University of Chicago Press, 1969.

Stewart, Michael *Keynes in the 1990s: A Return to Economic Sanity*, London: Penguin, 1993.

Stone, P.B. *Japan Surges Ahead*, London: Weidenfeld & Nicolson, 1969.

Thurow, Lester C. *The Zero-Sum Society*, New York: Basic Books, 1980.

Tsoukalis, Loukas *The New European Economy*, Oxford: Oxford University Press, 1993.

US Council of Economic Advisers *Economic Report of the President*, Washington, DC: US Government Printing Office, 1999.

van Doren, Charles *A History of Knowledge*, New York: Ballantine Books, 1991.

Warburton, Peter *Debt and Delusion*, London: Allen Lane The Penguin Press, 1999.

Wheen, Francis *Karl Marx*, London: Fourth Estate, 1999.

Wilson, Edward O, *Consilience: The Unity of Knowledge*, London: Little Brown and Company, 1998.

Wray, L. Randall *Understanding Modern Money*, Northampton, Mass: Edward Elgar, 1998.

Index

The subjects listed in the index do not include references to Britain, Europe, France, Germany, Japan, the United States and World Wars I and II, because references to them occur so frequently in the text.

Galbraith, John Kenneth, 1, 17, 225,
Gardiner, Geoffrey, ix
General Agreement on Tariffs and
    Trade, 94
Genghis Khan, 15
George, Henry, 18
German Democratic Republic, 121
Glass Manufacturing, 60
Global Warning, 15
Gold Standard, The, 66, 67, 75, 78,
    93, 95, 202, 215
Gorhachev, Mikhail, 226
Gould, Bryan, ix
Great Exhibition, 67
Great Society Program, 110, 204
Greece, 59, 60, 62, 65, 134,
Greek Learning, 59
Greenhouse Gases, 15
Gunpowder, 16, 60

Hargreave, James, 59
Hayek, Friedrich Auguste von, 17, 132
Hero of Alexandria, 59
Hiroshima, 115
Hitler, Adolf, 81, 85
Hong Kong, 150, 151, 170
Hoover, Herbert, 90

Ice Age, 57
Immigration, 71
Import Duties, 33
Import Led Stagnation, 53
Income Tax, 171
India, 15, 60, 62, 113, 123, 124, 125,
    158
Indonesia, 113,123, 155
Industrial Revolution, 2, 3, 6, 11, 27,
    54, 56, 59, 60, 61, 62, 63, 64, 68,
    76, 168, 230, 232
Industrialisation, 62
Inflation, 48, 49, 59, 81, 83, 87, 112,
    115, 133, 139
Inflation Rates, 104
Inflationary Pressures, 47
Inner-City areas, 8
Interest Rates, 54,136, 137, 161
International Labour Organisation,
    161
International Monetarism, 48

International Monetary Fund, 94, 55,
    191
Investment Rates, 36
Ireland, 105
Islamic Countries, 60, 62
Israel, 112,
Italy, 28, 60, 61, 65, 84, 85, 98, 99,
    102, 142, 181

J Curve Effect, 51
Jackson, Andrew, 74
Jay, Douglas (Lord), ix
Jenkins, Roy (now Lord), 141
Jevons, William Stanley, 79
Johnson, Lyndon, 109, 110

Kay, John, 59
Kazakhstan, 120
Kennedy, John F, 109
Keynes, John Maynard, 16, 17, 18, 20,
    78, 81, 82, 92, 93, 94, 95, 96, 106,
    112, 127, 132, 140
Keynesian Policies, 21
Khruschchev, Nikita, 120
Kohl, Helmut, 121
Korean War, 99, 105, 203, 207
Kreditanstalt, 85
Krugman, Paul, 2, 17, 229
Kuznets, Simon, 17

Labour Force in the European Union,
    159
Labour Government, 48, 99, 204,
Labour Party, 22
Labour Theory of Value, 18
Laffer Curve, 146
Lateen Sails, 60
Latin America, 122, 123
Law of One Price, 48
Lenin, 119
Leonardo Fibonnacci, 60
Leonardo of Pisa, 60
Liesner, Thelma, ix
List, Friedrich, 70
Locke, John, 65
London, 80
Lump of Labour Fallacy, 168
Luxembourg, 181
Lydia, Kingdom of, 58